Dynamic Utopia

Dynamic Utopia

Establishing Intentional Communities
as a
New Social Movement

Robert C. Schehr

BERGIN & GARVEY
Westport, Connecticut • London

Library of Congress Cataloging-in-Publication Data

Schehr, Robert C.
    Dynamic utopia : establishing intentional communities as a new
social movement / Robert C. Schehr.
        p.   cm.
    Includes bibliographical references and index.
    ISBN 0–89789–450–2 (alk. paper)
    1. Social movements. 2. Collective settlements. 3. Communal
living. 4. Civil society. I. Title.
HM281.S343   1997
303.48′4—dc20   96–41450

British Library Cataloguing in Publication Data is available.

Library of Congress Catalog Card Number: 96–41450
ISBN: 0–89789–450–2

First published in 1997

Bergin & Garvey, 88 Post Road West, Westport, CT 06881
An imprint of Greenwood Publishing Group, Inc.

Printed in the United States of America

The paper used in this book complies with the
Permanent Paper Standard issued by the National
Information Standards Organization (Z39.48–1984).

10 9 8 7 6 5 4 3 2 1

This book is dedicated to James and Jean Schehr, and to my wife Lynn, and my daughter Hanna.

CONTENTS

Acknowledgments   ix

1.   Social Movements and the Decolonization of the Lifeworld   1

2.   Reflecting on Community   25

3.   Reconstructing the Multiple: Social Movement Theory and
     Civil Society   53

4.   Chaos Theory, Metaphor, and Social Movements   105

5.   The Utopian Imaginary: Critical Memory and the
     Persistence of Resistance   133

6.   Conclusion: Embracing Heterogeneity   173

Selected Bibliography   193

Index   207

ACKNOWLEDGMENTS

I would like to recognize the following for their many valuable insights and support throughout the research and writing of this book. For his knowledge of intentional comunity building, his ongoing efforts to realize sustainable agriculture, and his friendship, I would like to formally acknowledge Winston Gordon. Similarly, I would like to offer thanks to Dean Mogelard. His sincere pursuit of economic, political, and cultural justice continues to be an inspiration for me. Members of the Common Place Land Trust, Birdsfoot Farm, and Common Ground intentional communities receive recognition for their kind responses to numerous inquires into their daily activities. I would like to recognize representatives of the Fellowship of Intentional Communities for their willingness to provide me with information and dialogue. I wish to recognize Gail Doering and the Oneida Community in Oneida, New York, Skip Reed, Matthew Potteger, Howie Hawkins, Paul Glover, Barbara and Bruce Kantner of Gaia Education Outreach Institute, and Mike Cummings. I also wish to express my thanks to Barbara Herbek for her help in producing the final copy of this manuscript. Carol and James Spence deserve recognition for their patience, generosity, and that inspirational summer spent enjoying the white sands and warm breezes graciously offered by the Gulf of Mexico. Finally, my deepest gratitude and heartfelt support goes to all the intentional communitarians who are brave enough and have vision enough to serve as a beacon for political, economic, and cultural change.

1

SOCIAL MOVEMENTS AND THE DECOLONIZATION OF THE LIFEWORLD

When into the womb of time everything is again withdrawn chaos will
be restored and chaos is the score upon which reality is written.
                                        Henry Miller, *Tropic of Cancer*

What you have before you is a cultural artifact. Like all cultural products,
it emerges from a vast and complex milieu comprising numerous political,
economic, and cultural experiences that shape my comprehension of our
culture and the challenges we currently face. What this means is that the
work you are about to interpret is situated in its own historicity, its own
theoretical, ideological, and phenomenological context. For ours, it will be
argued, is at once a reflexive and positional relationship to culture, identity,
and transpraxis[1] (Milovanovic, 1993b). We each inhabit and are constituted
by a tangled web of intersecting lines of influence, each producing a
fractured state of consciousness that makes it possible for us to carry out
our numerous cultural responsibilities (work, family, education, civic) while
virtually assuring multiple possible interpretations of "the real" and "the
good.

I clearly must acknowledge the source of my interpretation of contemporary cultural events to be the product of my experiences with cultural
capital, including years of arduous study as, first, an undergraduate student
of labor and later as a graduate student studying political economy and
social movements. While a student at both the graduate and undergraduate

levels, I, like many around me, participated in myriad political and social justice activities comprising grassroots organizing campaigns around such issues as environmental degradation, war prevention (Persian Gulf) and related demilitarization, domestic violence, and graduate student unionization. More recently I have participated in the development of an intentional community to serve the poor, in facilitating the adoption of a service-credit (alternative money) system, and the creation of a food circle system to diversify agricultural production and rotate needed foodstuffs to participating land trusts.[2]

I relay these remarks to signify a dilemma posed from within the social movement literature. Conventional occidental readings of social movements largely originate from within a discourse inspired by Enlightenment beliefs in the linear progression of history, anthropology, and social change. Accompanied by emerging capitalist social relations, the firm belief in the predictive capacity of modern scientific methodology and technology provided the context for believing in the anthropomorphic mastery of the natural world. Application of the scientific method to questions of predictability and causality meant that replication and validity became firmly ensconced in the academic pursuit of the known. Inspiration emerged from, among others, Sir Francis Bacon (considered the father of Western science), Charles Darwin and his theory of evolution, Sir Isaac Newton, Herbert Spencer, Auguste Compte, Emile Durkheim, and Vilfredo Pareto. Even Marx, who considered dedicating the first volume of *Capital* to Darwin, articulated an evolutionary theory of social movements and change. Establishing sociology as a social science suggested a predictive capacity similar to that celebrated in the natural sciences. But as Roger Penrose argues in an interesting review of the predictive capacity of many theories, even "Einstein's General Theory is [only] accurate to about one part in 10" (Young, 1990: 1). Penrose's conclusions prompted T. R. Young to conclude that "by these standards, social sciences are next to useless. Marx, Durkheim, Spencer, Weber, Mead, Cooley, Blumer, Goffman, and Garfinkle are seen as casual, intuitive, armchair amateurs" (1). Moreover, Young asserts that in terms of their predictive capacity, sociological theories of alienation, anomie, and happiness are at best artful speculations, adroit poetry. Nonlinear dynamics, originally emerging during the nineteenth century, has re-emerged to challenge claims of linearity and predictability emanating from Newtonian mechanics. As we will see later and in Chapter 4, chaos theory suggests that rather than operating at near-equilibrium conditions, natural and possibly social systems are far more unstable, often exhibiting non-linear and ambulant movement.

Returning for a moment to my brief biographical indulgence, it was clear to me upon completing my graduate studies that existing social scientific theorizing on social movements fell far short of being able to fully express the dynamism occuring within civil society. My own experiences with numerous political campaigns and social justice projects had assured me, and friends and colleagues with whom I interacted, that there was a rich caldron of cultural expression perpetually hovering at the level of the lifeworld where creativity, anxiety, anger, rage, love, compassion, confusion, mistrust, allegiance, dedication, violence, peace, awareness, and ignorance each comprised a complicated composition of cultural actors. Phenomenologically, I was aware of the distinctions actors drew between official political expressions of their reality. While a student, for example, I was able to monitor and participate to a minor degree in negotiations between representatives of labor and management working for the Cincinnati Metro bus company who had gathered to discuss the implementation of a quality circles program. Conversations with workers during break periods and at lunch confirmed in that environment the vast gulf separating employee perceptions of this "management" initiative ("we've heard all this before," "it won't change anything"), from those expressed by both labor and management during the formal proceedings. These anecdotal remarks have, of course, been confirmed by numerous studies, some of which are considered in Chapter 5. They point to, among other things, the complicated interplay of external economic conditions, power imbalances, struggles for control at the point of production, and identity. More recent sociological research on intentional communities (ICs), the exemplar for my particular effort, added to the dissonance I had experienced in attempting to determine the potential meaning signified by actors such as those living in ICs. As I will discuss in detail below, both classical and contemporary sociological theorizing on social movements has disregarded ICs by either dismissing them as "utopian" or "communal," that is, as non-movements, even the antithesis of a movement. Or they incorrectly identify them as a social movement in the classical collective behavior traditon. The problem, I contend, is both epistemological and methodological. Our best sociological theorizing on social movements, especially those pertaining to the working class or ICs, has been unable to capture the full dynamism of subaltern modes of resistance. This has occurred, despite a rich and continually growing database, which ethnographically documents the various modes of resistance carried out by the poor, minorities, women, production and service workers, peace and justice organizations, environmentalists, and anti-nuclear activists.

Contemporary Social Movement Theory:
A Brief Introduction

While it is the purpose of this book to analyze this phenomenon in detail, this introductory chapter will seek to locate my interpretation of contemporary social movements within the growing postmodern and chaos theoretic literatures. A recurring theme will be the theoretical and conceptual inability of conventional social movement literatures to deconstruct the rapid transformation of postindustrial America, and with it, to identify the dynamic range of resistance modes perpetually operating within civil society. And to the extent that conventional theory continues its search for this or that movement as the singular representatives ordained to reign in the new, the revolutionary agents for change, I argue that contemporary social movement theory is too severely hampered by entrenched conceptual articulations to offer insight into what now portends to be a new period of transpraxis, a dynamic interplay of agentic activism with a specific emphasis on identity, spirituality, time and space relations, non-violent conflict resolution, sexual experimentation, renewed conceptions of leisure and expressions of desire, and a redefinition of work roles and childcaring. Furthermore, this component of contemporary resistance efforts signifies attempts by the subaltern to appropriate civil society and lifeworld by invoking each with dynamic meaning. That is, occuring within civil society at the level of the lifeworld is a sempiternal construction and reconstruction of intra and interpersonal relations. This aspect of social movement has largely been overlooked in sociological theorizing and, I argue, must be rectified to provide a more thorough explication of cultural angst, fear, conflict, and stakes involved in political, economic, and cultural confrontations.

In America, two predominant paradigms constitute much of contemporary theoretical analyses of social movements, although variations permeate each. They either stress the instability constitutive of collective behavior and the subsequent collapse of consensus, or they prioritize the mobilization of organizational, symbolic, and capital resources in the struggle for state-based political representation and acknowledgment. Neither, I will argue, is able to effectively elucidate the complex interrelation between contemporary movement actors seeking wholistic transformations in their relationship to each other, society, the environment, and themselves. Unlike their American colleagues, European authors, particularly those writing in the aftermath of the "May Movement" in France, and similar student and worker uprisings in Germany and Italy during the middle and late 1960s, did seek articulation of social movement organizations and actors that

contextualized movement activities as a component of postindustrial transformations largely characteristic of Western industrialized nations. According to authors rendering evaluations of these new social movements (NSM),
structural malaise had produced a crisis in meaning for an entire generation
of young people who, in rejecting the value structures of their parents,
openly repudiated what they perceived to be the alienating components of
capitalist production and consumption. Writers addressing NSMs have
established a sophisticated and lucid alternative to American social movement theory. They will be discussed in Chapter 3 as offering an advance
over both the classical and resource mobilization theories of social movements. However, there are conceptual shortcomings that inhibit NSM theory
from recognizing the perpetual nature of subaltern resistance. For now, let
us consider the structural conditions giving rise to a needed rearticulation
of social movement theory. I will follow this discussion with recognition of
what I perceive to be a seminal flaw in contemporary social movement
theory, including NSM theory, which will serve to initiate our introduction
to postmodern and chaos theoretic insights.

Postindustrialism and New Social Movements

Discourse surrounding postmodernism and postindustrialism has rue-
fully lamented the incipience of a new era, one that replaces the political,
economic, philosophical, and even cultural precepts of modernism. While
debates abound concerning the relative merit of these theoretical propositions, it is clear that contemporary global crises signal certain need for
theoretical clarity and a genuine haste with regard to sociological leadership. Examples of global decay are numerous: international monetary
instability, environmental degradation, political instability with concomitant nuclear proliferation, international intensification of labor discipline,
transformations in industrial production and cybernetics including the
continued deskilling of the traditional manufacturing base in the West, plant
closings, and the internal colonization of communities by multinationals
through the vehicle of enterprise zones (foreign and domestic), the North
American Free Trade Agreement (NAFTA), the General Agreement on
Tariffs and Trade (GATT), and increasing penetration of state and federal
welfare agencies at the individual, instrumental, symbolic, and institutional
levels to serve as steering mechanisms for an increasingly irregular postindustrial capitalist accumulation. Moreover, contemporary global social
relations and political maneuvering are increasingly characterized by cultural animus over reproductive freedom for women, acknowledgment of the

civil rights of gays and lesbians, the continued deterioration of relations between members of historically antagonistic race or ethnic groups, and the growing pool of underemployed and unemployed, whose sinking standard of living continues to be associated with increasing levels of street crime, domestic violence, and a general fatalism expressed by youth and adults alike.

The considerable urgency with which sociologists must confront the issues indicated above concerns the struggle over the ability of academics, politicians, political think tanks, and the media complex to frame issues and people in such a way that humanistic or progressive solutions are marginalized in the public discourse. This point will be taken up in greater detail in Chapter 3, but for now it is important to keep in mind that sociologists play a role (of debated significance) in the struggle to liberate the voices of the dispossessed. Failure to adequately recognize the multiple layers of resistance within civil society leaves us with the grand narrative of dominant culture. That is, and Paulo Freire has written extensively on this, without a "conscientization" (Freire) of identity that seeks to reconcile agentic struggles over signification with material conditions and ideology (Milovanovic, 1995: 39), all we are left with is the message of the status quo. Marginalization of localized voices occurs within sociological theorizing on social movements when efforts are made at composing grand theories of social movements, what historians have referred to as "covering law" theory. Operating at macrostructural levels of abstraction requires by fiat the prioritization of a linear cognitive framework for viewing social change. That is, social change must be determined as having moved from one point on the chess board of history to another. The assumption is that if we have information on a specific starting point, we can predict with relative accuracy future manifestations. This assumption is not only at odds with the predictive capacity of social scientific methods, but it also tends to gloss over the richness of resistance, which is seldom articulated in grandiose ways, a point more fully explored in Chapter 5. If sociologists allow the language of resistance to be appropriated by dominant cultural interests, indeed, if we ourselves play into that dominant discourse, we risk opportunities to eliminate or at least soften the burden of contemporary social problems. For an example of the appropriation of the rhetoric of opposition for political purposes, consider the debates during 1995 and 1996 to determine the Republican presidential nominee, especially those relating to economic matters. The shrinking American manufacturing base and concomitant multinationalization of the global economy, coupled with devastating attacks on domestic and international unionization, and an increasing income gap between the nation's wealthiest and those drawing median income (adjusted for inflation to be roughly $38,782 in 1994 dollars; U. S. Census Bureau) generated a "populist" rhetoric from among the least likely of Republican presidential candidates, Patrick Buchanan. Buchanan succeeded in appropriating the language of class conflict, traditionally a left-wing rhetorical message, by chiding unethical and unsympathetic multinational corporations for their unwillingness to manufacture products in the United States, opting instead to boost profits by exploiting low wage workers in international markets. Buchanan's message, like that of left-wing activists and scholars, finds support in federal data on the domestic distribution of income and wealth. Average weekly earnings for the 80 percent of working Americans who constitute production and non-supervisory worker categories, adjusted for inflation, fell by 18 percent between 1973 and 1995, from $315 per week to $258 per week. By contrast, during the period between 1979 and 1989, the real annual pay of corporate chief executives increased by 19 percent—66 percent after taxes (Bureau of Labor Statistics (BLS), January 29, 1996, in Head, 1996). Moreover, unlike periods of economic expansion prior to the 1970s, which tied pay and benefit increases to productivity growth, the period between 1973 and 1995, which realized a productivity increase of 25 percent per worker for non-farm laborers, saw a real hourly earnings decrease of 12 percent (BLS, January 1996). Further indication of the inherent danger of a mounting wealth and income chasm between production and non-farm laborers, and those in supervisory positions comes from Federal Reserve Chair Alan Greenspan. According to Simon Head, Greenspan, while not suggesting the Federal Reserve had any pivotal role to play in resolving the problem, "warned Congress in July 1995 that the growing inequality of income in the United States could become a 'major threat to our society' "(47). In a similar vein, Robert Sutlow, an MIT professor awarded the Nobel Prize for economics, "warned of a society 'which might turn mean, limited in what it can do, worried about the future' "(47).

While the "broadening" of the negative effects of capitalist rationalization, domination, and state regulation (Offe, 1985) persists on an international scale, it is also true that global actors have initiated many attempts to (re)appropriate lifeworld activities in order to recapture for themselves a social space that allows for the rearticulation of self-identity and community autonomy. The task confronting sociologists, and I share this conviction with others (e.g., Touraine, 1988; Melucci, 1980), is to successfully identify those actors, issues, conflicts, and stakes involved in the preservation and perpetuation of civil society.

With that in mind, it is worth taking a moment to briefly distinguish the ideas presented here with those currently in vogue in political, sociological, and philosophical circles and referred to as "communitarian." What is at stake in the current political, economic and cultural arena is nothing less than our ability to construct meaningful, healthy, satisfying lives for ourselves, our families, and our global neighbors. This, of course, includes remaining cognizant of our responsibility as stewards in the preservation of the ecosystem. In joining social theorists in the recognition of actors, issues, conflicts, and stakes, we must closely scrutinize the multiple voices clamoring for attention (including my own!). This requires a perceptive ability and stern commitment to wade through rhetorical expressions of "Truth," while noting differences and commonalities within existing theoretical and philosophical work. Consider, for example, the widely publicized round of philosophical, then political, invective emerging during the early 1980s and continuing to present, reflecting the perception and concern over an international expression of anomie characteristically noted in the works of French and American postmodernists and postindustrialists. Unlike their postmodern and postindustrial counterparts, however, this literature, loosely identified as communitarian, took as its point of departure not the celebration of heterogeneity and abstraction characteristic of a postmodern rendering, but rather its opposite, the decline of community. Philosophers writing in this vein selected as their point of attack the 1971 publication of John Rawls's *A Theory of Justice*. While Rawls argued for the preservation of the rights bearing individual, philosophers like Charles Taylor, Alisdair MacIntyre, Michael Walzer, and Michael Sandel countered with a moratorium on new rights,[3] arguing instead that it has been preservation of a neo-Kantian individualism that has shattered any hope for realizing truly meaningful interpersonal relations. While it is not my endeavor here to deconstruct this debate,[4] I mention it because it parallels much of the discussion in the coming chapters, but with considerable theoretical and philosophical differences. It is my contention that what lies ahead for sociologists studying social movements is the urgent need to conceptualize the perceived postmodern or postindustrial cultural malaise, disintegration, and fragmentation so much a part of our everyday rhetoric and experience, within a context capable of addressing humanist claims to eliminate hunger, poverty, economic degradation, gender oppression, and the like, while celebrating the heterogeneous composition of American society as well as international expressions of subaltern autonomy. I am neither seeking solace in a "return to tradition" nor am I arguing that components of tradition or historical memory are completely without merit in subaltern expressions of resistance and identity. But where I perceive the communitarian literature to be proselytizing for a nationalist ethic based on cultivation of a consensus through socialization carried out by the usual bearers of this responsibility (family, school, media, religion), I privilege heterogeneity, difference, and the multiple expressions of values and beliefs to be more typical of complex postindustrialized societies. I will argue that what is needed is a new conceptualization of social movements, one capable of recognizing and accentuating subaltern expressions of resistance operating within civil society at the level of the lifeworld. To make this point more succinctly and to provide some foundation for the theoretical work to begin below, I want to establish: 1) the relevance of ICs as an expression of subaltern resistance; and 2) my perception of the differences between contemporary sociological theories of social movements and the perspective I will adopt in this book, which prioritizes postmodernism and chaos theory.

Intentional Communities as a Social Movement

I have selected ICs as my unit of analysis because I believe, for numerous reasons discussed in Chapter 2, they have played and will continue to play a significant role in rearticulating meaning that is in many ways contrary to our current postindustrial malaise. In doing so, I will attempt to conflate the persistence and relevance of contemporary ICs with the familiar torch-bearers of the NSM literature, the women's, environmental, peace, urban, and student movements. My purpose is to draw attention to the stakes of a "new class conflict," one in which the dominant class, for steering purposes, legitimacy, and conflict homogenization, engages in the proliferation of sign values[5] intensifying the colonization of the lifeworld. To counter this tendency, sociologists have problematized or "sociologized" (Melucci, 1980) lifeworld concerns over identity, sexuality, time, and space primarily within the confines of NSM theory and research. I will attempt to show that at the symbolic level ICs represent what is perhaps the most all-inclusive affront to dominant efforts at intensifying rationalization. But more important, beyond the level of symbolism, I will argue that contemporary ICs be recognized by sociologists as a social movement complete with their own domestic and international modes of communication (books, newsletters, lectures, and conferences), research, education, production, distribution, and interpersonal non-violent conflict-management techniques, each of which represents alternatives to the proliferation of dominant cultural capital, and, while primarily directed at the lifeworld, the possibility of broader system-level change.

Students of ICs, or communes, as earlier writers referred to them,[6] will not perceive word of their designation here as a social movement as peculiar or in any way inaugural. It is my belief, however, that earlier references to communes as "social movements" mystified their content and purpose by inadequately distinguishing their uniqueness as movement entities. For example, in his extensive work on communes, Zablocki (1980) refers to American communitarianism as a social movement. His definition of social movement follows Heberle's (1951) differentiation between social movements as social collectives (following Tonnies) and social movements as processes. Heberle argues for the former, associating the latter with social trends (1951: 8, 9). But Zablocki's appropriation of Heberle's social movement definition is incomplete. While Zablocki does accurately identify Heberle's distinction between collectivity and process, he overlooks the component of Heberle's definition that places Heberle squarely in the classical social movement literature. That is, what Zablocki ignored was Heberle's insistence that "the main criterion of a social movement is that it aims to bring about fundamental changes in the social order, especially in the basic institutions of property and labor relationships" (1951: 6). Heberle proclaims what has been a foundational prerequisite for sociologists studying social movements for most of this century—that in order for collective behavior to be perceived as a social movement, it must direct its antipathy toward structural transformations at the level of the state. I will refer to this component of social movement theory throughout this book because it lies at the center of the distinction I will draw between current sociological theorizing and a postmodern and chaos-inspired analysis. Consider for yourself whether, in order to qualify as a social movement, collective actors need to direct their energies toward state-based social change or cultivation of political parties. NSM literature emerged in the early 1980s to critique this "foundational" view of social movements and allow for a more abstract and differentiated conceptualization. Let us return now to Zablocki's conceptualization of the "communal movement," based as it is on Heberle's articulation of what qualifies as a social movement, to illuminate the way in which he comes to determine the efficacy of commune members as change agents.

Like most who are afflicted with what Melucci has termed the "myopia of the visible," Zablocki's attention is directed not at the relevant levels, aspects, and elements of action (Melucci, 1988), but rather at the decline of the "communal movement" as he and his colleagues identified it. Such a "myopia" leads Zablocki to view communes through a conceptual frame guilty of "ingenuous historicism" (Melucci's phrase), one that assumes historical continuity—a perpetual state of birth, growth, and decay—and inevitably what leads him to the conclusion that "by 1976, more people saw communal living as a viable *temporary* alternative life-style, whereas the number of those committed to lifetime communitarianism continued to decrease" (1980: 56, emphasis added).

This observation, which has not to my knowledge been re-evaluated, begs a critical response. The perception that "there's nothing new under the sun" is at odds with the activities of contemporary ICs, which range from small-scale agricultural work to federally funded experiments on the promise of fuel-alcohol production and commercial greenhouse construction, with a full panoply of activities to complement the continuum.[7] This suggests that communal experiments existing prior to the 1970s differ, at times markedly, from those emerging between the late 1960s and the 1970s, and that both of these epochs, while sharing some commonalities, are noticeably different from ICs that were initiated in the 1980s and continuing to the present. Most significant for my purposes is that the differentiation among and between ICs—that is the multiple ways in which they identify their communal mission—is also what demands their recognition as social movement actors.

In my estimation, it was Zablocki's conceptualization of social movement that led him to prognosticate the death knell of communal living. In doing so he inadvertently directed sociological attention to the "biography" of the communal phenomenon comprising a specific historical period (1960s–70s). He was not alone, however, in this regard. In a similar way Kanter (1973) is equally culpable when she equates the "success" of communities persisting throughout the nineteenth century with their longevity. Here, the question is whether a protracted institutional life is a valuable indicator of success. In my experience, most who live in contemporary intentional communities would consider longevity but one of several factors indicating success, along with self-improvement, fulfilling social relationships, and community activism.

In the end it was Zablocki's foundational articulation of social movement that prevented him from prioritizing a mode of resistance that, while not visibly conforming to theoretical prescriptions due to its often unceremonious cultivation of the lifeworld, persisted in its affront to dominant cultural captital. Where contemporary ICs differ from those existing prior to the 1980s, these differences appear to be precisely those addressed by the NSM research; there appears to be a conscious and thorough articulation by members of ICs to engage levels of historicity.[8] But even within the NSM tradition, significant theoretical confusion continues to pervade efforts to precisely operationalize social movements as a collective phenomenon. Specifically, NSM theory reiterated the one-dimension characteristic of all previous conceptual efforts—that in order to qualify as a social movement, actors and organizations must express overt, typically state-directed conflict.

Italian theorist Alberto Melucci (1980, 1985, 1985, 1990), who, along with French sociologist Alain Touraine (1988), was largely responsible for propelling NSM theory to disciplinary prominence, has persistently emphasized the necessity of conflict as a requisite condition of social movement status. Melucci identifies the three most significant dimensions of social movements as: 1) solidarity; 2) conflict; and 3) breaking the limits of compatibility of a system (1990: 29). Conflict is defined as struggling against an opponent to secure the same goods or values (29). Similarly, in his earliest attempt to distinguish social movements from other forms of collective behavior, Melucci argues that collective action must "go beyond the rules of the political system and/or attack the structure of a society's class relations" (1980: 202). Melucci's closest empirical reference to ICs is his disapproving reference to "regressive utopia." In his identification of the qualifying characteristics of NSM phenomena, Melucci celebrates the "end of the separation between public and private spheres," but simultaneously cautions against movement actors slipping into a "regressive utopia," articulated as group identification with traditional values, often having a religious component. Regressive utopias consist of "communal integralism, politico-religious integralism, and mystico-aesthetic integralism" (1980: 222). His critique of regressive utopias clearly signifies his allegiance to overt forms of conflict as a significant dimension of effective social movements that in fact break the limits of compatibility of the system. According to Melucci, regressive utopias direct the preponderance of their activities toward the "reappropriation of identity" and as a result are rendered politically impotent. To be fair, in his most recent evaluations of cultural expressions of social movement identity, Melucci has been showing signs of moving away from the traditional theoretical emphasis on overt conflict (cf. 1994, 1995).

Alain Touraine (1988) has further disaggregated societal conflict to include collective behavior, struggles, and social movements. Collective behavior is typically defensive in nature and primarily seen as an effort to preserve or adapt "sick" elements of social structure. Struggles seek direct access to decision-making power within the confines of political parties. But social movements are viewed as a special category of collective phenomena in which actors are engaged in conflictual actions seeking "to transform the relations of social domination that are applied to the principal cultural resources (production, knowledge, ethical rules)" (Touraine, 1988: 64). In a manner analogous to Melucci's conceptualization of "regressive utopia," Touraine also identifies the political and cultural ramifications of slipping into "anti-movements." For Touraine, anti-movements consist of collective actions appealing to the community in defense of some external enemy. They impede the expansion of group interests, prohibiting its blossoming into a social movement, leaving the door open for further domination and exploitation.

Each of these typological articulations of social movement, if taken literally, precludes the inclusion of ICs. While it is true that one of the defining components of contemporary ICs is their commitment to the cultivation of a "planetary consciousness" (e.g., localized community activism), with few exceptions (e.g., The Farm, The Movement for a New Society), overt conflict as expressed in the establishment of, say, an Intentional Community Party, or direct pleas to state agencies, is not characteristic of the movement *in toto*. What then should we make of ICs?

The writings of Melucci and Touraine, while setting limitations on the adaptation of social movement status relative to ICs, have also provided us with ample theoretical latitude. More specifically, one can find in the works of both authors conceptual space for the inclusion of ICs. It's almost as if each is unwilling to foreclose his theoretical models to the possibility—indeed, the inevitability—of actor-oriented innovation originating at the level of the lifeworld. The conceptual ambiguity surrounding inclusion of ICs as NSMs is apparent when, for example, Melucci suggests that the self-limiting, self-conscious, disaggregated components of contemporary collective behavior be viewed not as "folkloristic phenomena," but rather as "the seeds of qualitative change in contemporary collective action" (1985: 810). Rather than arguing for inclusion within dominant culture, NSMs are struggling for recognition and acceptance of difference. Here Melucci seems willing to expand his conceptualization of social movement; at one point in this essay he argues (following Mcluhan): "Medium is the message, and action sends back to the system its own paradoxes" (812). This is a component of a revised social movement theory that I will return to throughout the chapters to follow,that by their very presence, ICs constitute a radical juxtaposition to contemporary dominant cultural capital, offering a visible living example of difference as alternative.

Similarly, Touraine acknowledges the uniqueness of NSMs and their emphasis on cultural values. He contextualizes their overt challenge to contemporary concerns over resource depletion, media penetration, sexuality, domination, and the like by recognizing both the symbolic and literal significance of their autonomy from dominant political parties and the state. In that way, members of NSMs appear as a rhizomatic alternative to rationalized modes of living. So it is possible, in my estimation, to identify within the work of both Melucci and Touraine theoretical fissure substantial enough to conceptualize and incorporate ICs. There is in their work an empathy for the mode of expression exemplified by them. However, for both, ICs represent social movement potential, not a movement entity in and of itself. Herein lies the primary difference. While NSM theory initiated efforts to conceptualize contemporary movement actors within the broader context of a postindustrial West, and to articulate sensitivity to modes of resistance that link movement expressions to lifeworld concerns, it nonetheless continues to cling to the conflict-centered litmus test inherited from classical social movement research. In my estimation, NSM theory cannot carry us far enough in being able to successfully identify actors, like members of ICs, who have channeled their energies toward the reconstitution of localized space. For this we must move to a growing body of theoretical and philosophical insight that traces its origins to Neitzsche and Heidegger. Following Thomas Kuhn, we in the social sciences have been exposed to a paradigmatic alternative that challenges the very legitimacy of Enlightenment rationality. It is to a brief discussion of this history and the differences between modern and postmodern conceptualizations that I now turn.

Enter Chaos

The prevailing theme in this introductory statement, as well as in Chapter 4, is that sociological theorizing of social movements has been confounded by an Enlightenment-inspired dedication to linear theoretical models, models that attempt to identify a clear organic or evolutionary movement from some initial point to another. Modernism emerged from the creative energy of the Enlightenment, with its characteristic emphasis on an individuated rational thought, scientific reasoning, mastery over nature, and capitalist political, economic, and cultural relations. As if drawing directly from the modern scientific model, the collective behavior tradition within sociology adopted the notion of stability to explain the functioning of institutions within the social organism. In doing so, these theorists reasoned that collective behavior, representing as it did a deviation from the normative functioning of the social system, was an inherently negative social force. Alternatively, a chaos theory recognizes the normalcy of instability over stability and therefore views flux and social disorganization as the expected manifestation of any complex system of interacting agents. Ultimately, the gift of a chaos and postmodern approach to social change is its emphasis on variation and unpredictability. Initiating analyses of complex sociological phenomena from the vantage of chaos facilitates opportunities to identify crucial moments of institutional intervention. Unique historical moments, locations, and policies can each be exposed to the critical analysis of chaos theory, enabling sociologists to intervene with alternate policy recommendations. This is conceivable due to recent innovations emerging from nonlinear mathematics.

Perhaps the most significant finding was by Mitchell Feigenbaum, who discovered that natural systems tended toward stability as long as the number of bifurcations remained below three.[9] Once natural systems moved beyond three bifurcations, their behavior became progressively more erratic to the point of producing a dissipative structure. The precise number calculated by Feigenbaum to indicate the initiation of a dissipative structure was 4.669 (now commonly known as the Feigenbaum Number). In general, there is no way to predict what the outcome will be once a system moves to the point of dissipating. Feigenbaum's number can be applied to the social sciences, as discussed later, to offer guidance in the prediction and identification of possible points of structural fissure or instability.

There are numerous axes on which to juxtapose modernism with postmodern analyses of cultural phenomena. To expedite this discussion I will briefly present five of the eight recently submitted by Milovanovic (1995) in his attempt to clarify on these distinctions. Milovanovic suggests that the seminal concerns addressed by each paradigm are: society and social structure, social roles, subjectivity/agency, discourse, knowledge, space/time, causality, and social change. While there is considerable merit in pursuing each parameter identified by Milovanovic, I will be introducing only society and social structure, knowledge, space/time, causality, and social change. Moreover, chaos theory will be offered as a component of a postmodern social critique as it has emerged to extend both theoretical and empirical support to the presence of non-linear systems and the perpetual nature of systemic flux.

A modernist rendering of society and social structure emphasizes the characteristics of stasis, order, homogeneity, consensus, and, perhaps most important, as it pertains to our interests in social movement research, in totalizing, or all-encompassing grand theory. This is what Derrida referred to as a metaphysic, an effort by theoreticians and philosophers to produce a singular explanation for political, economic, and cultural processes.

Within sociological theory the chief proponents of a modernist consensus-based model of systemic composition are Spencer, Durkheim, Parsons, Luhmann, and those affiliated with structural-functionalism. For them, systems operate through an integrated network of shared norms and values, an orderly consensus around what is considered to be appropriate system-reproducing behavior.

In contrast, a postmodernist and chaos analysis will contend that the defining characteristics of society and social structure are flux, heterogeneity, diversity, orderly disorder, chance and spontaneity. The work of chaos theorists (the mathematical explication of non-linearity) and quantum mechanics, among others, has introduced scientific evidence into our social scientific thinking about order and disorder in social systems. Following the insights of Godel's theorum (1962), and Lyotard's (1984) conceptualization of paralogism, we witness the celebration of heterogeneity, instability (Lyotard), and a related expression of the impossibility of structural closure (Godel) and order, posing a direct challenge to structural-functionalism and most sociological theory. Milovanovic suggests that it is the privileging of far-from-equilibrium conditions that enables postmodern theorists to articulate a model of social change that is much more dynamic and capable of capturing the volatile nature of real social systems. Here he bases some of his insight on the work of Baker (1993) and his conceptualization of dissipative structures. According to Baker, dissipative structures are the antithesis of functionalist theorizing since they are only relatively stable and always interacting with their environment, producing perpetual change. Complementing Baker are numerous efforts to construct a reflexive or constitutive analysis of actors and their interaction with social structure. Here the emphasis is on recognition of local, subaltern voices typically drowned out by dominant rhetorical positions and grand theory. Milovanovic argues, and I concur, that what postmodern theory encourages of us is the advocacy of the "marginalized, disenfranchised, disempowered, and otherwise exluded voices" (23). This works nicely to complement theories of social change when one introduces the innovations of chaos theory. Here, small changes in initial conditions (i.e., the local community, the city) may have profound consequences at the macrostructural level. Linear scientific models are typically unable to capture the relevance of the local due to their avoidance of micrological perturbations. The same can be said, of course, for sociological theorizing on social movements. Moreover, a postmodern and chaos theory is able to conceptualize both structure and process. As with contemporary sociological accounts, prefiguring structure or process is largely a factor of emphasis. When considering cultural events in the present, the emphasis is on process and fluidity. Floating above the immediate to consider the entirety of a phase space[10] will indicate structure.

The second conceptual difference lies in the explication of knowledge. The Enlightenment initiated the scientific search for the Truth. The deductive reasoning emanating from master theoretical narratives would produce "facts" readily recognizable to all learned enough to perceive their correlation. One component of the master narrative of science that is crucial to our interests here is the tendency for deductive reasoning to replace narrative knowledge and expression as the language of the sophisticated, the enlightened. As a host of authors have recognized (e.g., Benjamin, 1969; Freire, 1985; Scott, 1991; and Welch, 1985 [each is discussed in detail in Chapter 5]), the narrative knowledge articulated through myth, folklore, tales, and legends served as the predominant mode of cultural identity prior to the ascendance of science. Milovanovic rightly emphasizes the juxtaposition between the modernist pursuit of closure as a component of scientific explanation, and narrative knowledge, which was and continues to be constituted by the free play of cultural imagery. This distinction is not without significant merit in our interpretation of social movements. Ernst Bloch (discussed in Chapter 5), for example, will go so far as to contend that a society dispossessed of the narrative skill to envision alternative political, economic, and cultural constructions is dead. But in the language of the master narrative, that is, modern science, expressions of this sort are little more than flirtations with fancy, regressive utopia. However, as we will see in the coming chapters, it has been the character of ICs to envision alternative communal associations largely through narrative references to mythistory, legend, and folklore, which enliven the creative potential leading to cultural change. Students of social movements have been exposed to a master narrative, firmly ensconced in the logic of science, that prioritizes the knowledge of the academy over that of indigenous populations. What emerges is a simultaneous bifurcation and privileging of the knowledge of the academy over that of the subaltern. This has been most clearly articulated by Derrida (1976) and later by Ryan (1982). What emerges in the discourse of the master narrative is a vision of society that is closed and centered. As is most apparent in the systemic logic propounded by structural-functionalism and even some variants of Marxism, all institutions, actors, and activities must serve the reproduction of the whole. Systemic needs and normative values are cloaked in the language of ideology and emerge to define what is counterhegemonic as negative, dysfunctional, abnormal, and so on. What emerges, according to Derrida, is an artificial bifurcation of interests framed as opposites in which one, the master narrative, is superior to the other. Ryan (1982) concedes that the master narrative comes to be viewed as "society's ideal image of itself, an image reinforced by the negative image of the marginals who are excluded from it" (127). A society guided by the scientific pursuit of Truth privileges linearity, methodologically seeking to establish "facts" based on deductive logic. In this sense, the narrative logic of the subaltern has been marginalized by the established methodological and explanatory weight granted to science. It is little wonder that conceptualizations of movement actors that privilege the local have typically been underemphasized in most sociological theorizing on social movements.

Postmodernists vehemently stand in opposition to metatheoretic and globalized explications of cultural activities. Privileged are the voices of the dispossessed, the subaltern. Unlike modernist theorists, postmodernists view knowledge as "fragmented, partial, and contingent" (Ryan, 1982: 31). By recognizing and accentuating localized knowledge, we become more aware of the multiple sites of knowledge production, perceptual differences, and competing truth claims. There is, in this schema, no all-encompassing Truth, no master plan, no singularly correct way to arrange cultural, political, or economic institutions and their consequent social relations. Here the language of the possible is free to circulate in narrative creativity through the vehicle of folklore, critical memory, nostalgia, tales, and myth. Rather than anticipating closure, accentuation of the local recognizes the instability of life; the unanticipated emerges as the norm. Grand theorizing and master narratives subsume local knowledge to dominant cultural expressions of normativity largely through the vehicle of cultural capital experienced by all children as a product of their education.

Following Pierre Bourdieu (1984), children experience symbolic violence when, in the course of their educational training, they are not exposed to their histories, to the histories of working people, unions, the poor, racial and ethnic minorities, women, and gays and lesbians. Considered normative are the values, tastes, habits, dress, wit, and language styles of the dominant cultural elite. All others are marginalized, perceived in the best case scenario as less significant, in the worst, as culturally, morally, and ethically deficient and inferior. But it is not true that the marginalized uncritically accept the dominant portrait of them. Henry Giroux (1988, 1989) and Paulo Freire, among others, confirm a sempiternal interplay between cognitive understanding and ideology which, when infused with narrative knowledge, evokes instability in the rhetoric of dominant culture.

The third dimension I wish to speak of concerns space and time. For modernists, space and time configurations are based on Newtonian mechanics (Milovanovic: 33). By Newton's articulation, the laws of physics projected an absolute time and space. This is relevant to our purposes because acceptance of absolute points in time and space imply systemic order. One need only have information on point "a" to determine outcome at point "b". This is what Deleuze and Guattari refer to as striated space, complete with channels, stripes, or contiguous lines. In short: predictability and order. The metaphor for striated space is the board game chess[11] where each chess piece is imbued with a predetermined role designating mobility. The positivistic tradition in sociology, and the social sciences more generally, is framed upon the terrain of striated space. More importantly for us, research on ICs and social movements within sociology are based on the assumptions of striated space. That is, our best models of social movements prioritize morphological accounts, documenting their origins, growth, maturity, and decay. The models are linear, striated. This is clearly the analysis of ICs, which has prevailed to present.

Postmodernists and chaos theorists view space and time in dramatically different ways. For chaos theorists, a subject thoroughly discussed in Chapter 4, Newtonian mechanics is flawed in its explanatory power. The contribution of chaos theorists to our understandings of space and time are exemplified in the conceptualization of fractals. In opposition to striated space, chaos and postmodern theorists view natural and social space as smooth. It entertains and indeed cultivates ambulant and often unpredictable behavior. Mobility is not bound by predescribed paths or patterns but rather is free to adventure into multiple paths within a particular outcome basin.[12] Fractals emerge in phase-space as degrees of irregularity in objects (Young, 1990). In that way it is easy to see that social interaction is inherently fractal; that is, each of us in carrying out our day-to-day responsibilities assumes multiple roles. We never repeat in precisely the same way our movements over weeks, months or years (Young, 1990: 6). And so it is that working with fractals or multiple degrees of freedom amplifies systemic complexity, making meta-narratives virtually impossible to support. There is simply too much diversity within natural and social systems to accurately predict outcomes unless there is an artifically designated order, an ideal type, with which to compare natural and social systems. This is the conclusion of a recent article by Justin Rosenberg (1996), whose compelling analysis of international relations is framed on smooth space. Rosenberg's conclusion, much like Nietzsche's, is that what often happens in the social sciences is explanation after the fact. This occurs from our need to impose order due to our fear of multiplicity. This theme was addressed during the mid-nineteenth century by American philosopher C. S. Peirce (1957) in his essay "The Fixation of Belief." In this essay Peirce laments over the ways people, when confronted with flux, return to the familiar confines of tradition. When facing the cultural anxiety that seems to stream from heterogeneity, Peirce suggests that we turn to the scientific method since it is our most rational means for discerning Truth. By way of contrast, Rosenberg contends that "we cannot begin with a logical model of homogenous states: the variety of political forms is simply too great. We would have to begin instead with a historical analysis which reconstructs the uneven and combined international development of capitalism which has produced such a variegated world of states" (8). And in critiquing the linear theoretical exposition comprising "balance-of-power" theory, a master narrative, Rosenberg goes on to add: "In this role it [balance-of-power theory] becomes, and has in fact always been, not the masterpiece of the discipline but its jailer, imprisoning it within an impoverished conception of reality" (14). Similar commentary can and will be directed at traditional theoretical models of social movements, as their rise to disciplinary prominence has marginalized alternate perceptions of subaltern resistance.

The final two dimensions, causality and social change, will be discussed simultaneously. Causality for modernists, following as it does the theoretical insight of Newtonian physics and striated space, is linear, deterministic, predictable. Mathematical models developed in the positivist tradition predict that unit changes in variable "a" will produce unit changes in variable "b". Postmodernists and chaos theorists, not surprisingly, argue the opposite. They make no assumption that a unit change in variable "a" will produce a linear unit change in variable "b". On the contrary, uncertainty and unpredictability are prioritized as explanatory prerequisites because causality is inherently fractal. Here, small perturbations at the micro level, say at the level of the lifeworld, can produce large-scale unpredictable changes at the level of social structure. That being the case, chaos and postmodern theorists will show greater restraint with respect to interpretations of their findings since what is considered a "fact" or the "Truth" is colored by the designated levels of analysis researchers use to confirm their findings.

In a practical way, it would be impossible to predict with any accuracy the conceivable outcomes people may experience over their lifecourse relative to work, school, family, religion, and politics. What can be determined is that when bifurcations in any of these areas increase beyond the ratio of 1:3 (recall the Feigenbaum number), plausible conditions exist for political, economic, and cultural tumult. For example, T. R. Young (1990) contends that:

In terms of wealth, when land holdings bifurcate such that the average holdings of one group are doubled four times, i. e. , are 16 or more times as large as land holdings of a second group, one can expect chaos. Or, in the case of demographics, if one group has an infant mortality rate two, then four, then eight, then 16 times as high as a second, more privileged group, unstable chaotic systems can be expected (17).

Young's assessment can, of course, be extended to many issues facing contemporary postindustrial societies (for example, crime, wealth and income, health care coverage, education).

Social change, the crux of our concern in this book, again presents us with austere philosophical and theoretical juxtapositions. For modernists, social change is evolutionary, linear, based on the Darwinian logic of systemic (natural and social) adaptations to environmental stimuli. Post-modernists, on the other hand, see social change through the lens of transpraxis; it is unpredictable, contigent, spontaneous, and marginal (Milovanovic, 1995: 39). Transpraxis elucidates the interplay among cognition, ideology, cultural capital, and agency. Perhaps the most interesting component of the postmodern look at social change is its emphasis on contingency. Among social movement theorists, those working in the NSM literature have taken the lead in this regard, challenging classical and resource mobilization theories by noting the unique ways contemporary social movement actors join ranks with organizations sharing similar, typically issue-specific concerns, often despite numerous differences between them on other issues. It is this contingency, so celebrated by postmodernists and chaos theorists, that makes predictability of outcomes virtually impossible.

It should be clear that what follows is a perception of social movements at times vastly at odds with those most familiar to sociologists. I contend throughout, however, that what is gained from a reconceptualization of social movements from within the postmodern and chaos theory paradigms is a theory of social movements capable of expanding its perceptual and explanatory powers by recognizing modes of resistance hovering within the lifeworld. While they may not express their interests and desires in overtly conflictual confrontations with the statutory or regulatory agencies of the state, they, nevertheless, engage in modes of communication with other, more localized groups sharing similar concerns. What I hope to show in subsequent chapters is that ICs qualify as a social movement when one considers most of the criteria registered by NSM theory.

I initiate discussion of ICs in Chapter 2 by reviewing the continuity of their historical emergence throughout Europe and America. I spend a considerable amount of time discussing those variants of utopian life and philosophy that seem to echo most closely the philosophical components of communal efforts up to the 1960s. I then attempt to distinguish contemporary communitarians from their pre-1980s counterparts. This is significant since it indicates a level of sophistication atypical of communal living in totem prior to this time.

Chapter 3 comprises two sections. In the first, I will review contemporary social movement theory, endeavoring to denote relevant characteristics by comparing American and European versions. In the second part of this chapter, I will attempt an initial movement away from more commonly accepted theories of social movements by entertaining the insights of Laclau and Mouffe's (1985) articulation of radical democracy. Radical democracy is a conceptualization of social movements closely related to the one I suggest here, with some significant differences. Most striking is Laclau and Mouffe's neglect of civil society and lifeworld, a crucial cultural space necessary for the cultivation and proliferation of subaltern identities.

Chapter 4 takes us beyond conventional social movement theory with a more exhaustive appraisal of postmodern and chaos theory. Here I will denote the multiple differences separating conventional social movement theory with references to the destabilizing power of resistance modes hovering within the lifeworld. Members of ICs will be viewed as movement actors who are both, of yet, not of dominant culture. This kind of frame is conceivable only within the confines of a revitalized and reconceptualized theory of social movements.

The last of the substantive chapters, Chapter 5, will address the primary criticism of ICs—their "utopian" qualities. This discussion is crucial to contextualization of a reconceptualized social movement theory because it privileges local knowledge and the skill with which the subaltern appropriate, interpret, and manifest their folkloric, mythic, and symbolic histories, what Touraine refers to as engaging levels of historicity. ICs do appropriate components of utopian traditions and experiments. What they do, I will argue, should be viewed not as an indication of the futility of their becoming a social movement, but rather, assuming a renewed conceptualization of social movement, that they offer a radical juxtaposition to contemporary social conditions, making them "always already" a significant beacon for alternative living. Let us move now to initiate our journey into the historical evolution of communal living.

Notes

1. The concept of transpraxis has been used to promote a nonlinear and often quite unpredictable perception of social change actors that endeavors to distinguish analyses of social change emerging in Hegel and, later, Marx from those of Nietzsche. Rather than conceptualizing and privileging either instrumental or structural relationships between capitalists (the means of production and the social relations of production), a transpraxis argues for recognition of an agency-centered revolutionary discourse that simultaneously cultivates images of alternate visions of reality while internally augmenting cultural criticism. Emphasis is placed on a perpetual interplay between the language of dominant culture and the interpretation and reinterpretation of that language, that reality, by subalterns with regard to their interests and concerns.

2. Establishing an intentional community for the poor and the cultivation of food circles characterize an ongoing effort to create alternative living arrangements for interested residents of upstate New York. Actions taken to establish a service-credit system were pursued in a separate effort in the small village where I resided in upstate New York. It is conceivable that all of these efforts become parts of a larger whole as they complement the goals of autonomy and "right living" sought by participants. This is particularly the case given the impressive success of Ithaca, New York's alternative money economy. More will be said about each of these projects as I continue.

3. For a thorough review of the communitarian manifesto, see Amitai Etzioni (ed.), *Rights and the Common Good: The Communitarian Perspective*. New York: St. Martin's Press, 1995.

4. I will more thoroughly address the communitarian literature from within the theoretical paradigm initiated by chaos theory in my "Chaos and New Social Movements," in D. Milovanovic (ed.) *Chaos, Criminology and Social Justice: The New (Dis)order* (Westport, Conn.: Greenwood Press, 1997).

5. The concept of sign values refers in the work of Baudrillard (1981) to the relationship between commodities and their perceived meaning within a specific culture at a particular historical moment. It is the linguistic and interpretive correlation between signifier (a word) and signified (that which the word expresses).

6. Many attempts have been made to conceptually differentiate communes, collectives, coops, and intentional communities. Zablocki (1980) defines commune as "any group of five or more adult individuals (plus children if any), the majority of whose dyads are not cemented by blood or marriage, who decided to live together, without compulsion, for an indefinite period of time, primarily for the sake of an ideological goal, focused on the achievement of community, for which a collective household is deemed essential" (7).

Patrick Conover (1978) distinguishes among communes, intentional communities, and collectives. A commune is defined as "a group of five or more adults who have pooled their resources and labor and who make the vast majority of important expenditures from a common purse. Intentional communities share some but not all resources and make only some important expenditures from a common purse. They have formed their community by a mutual choice rather than because of family relationships, to affirm common aspect of ideology or lifestyles. A collective is a cooperative living arrangement between people who share some living expenses" (5).

McLaughlin and Davidson (1990) suggest that the differentiation is primarily a semantic one. Most contemporary groups prefer use of the term "community" over "commune" to differentiate themselves from the mid-1960s "crash pads." Even greater richness of definition can be found in Kanter's (1972) *Commitment and Community* (esp. pp. 2, 3).

7. A somewhat more detailed analysis of Zablocki's predominant theme is forthcoming. What significantly separates my analysis from his and should be recognized from the outset are his obvious Smelserian influences. The model he articulates in *Alienation and Charisma* (as the title suggests) is predicated on a theoretical belief not unlike that of classical social movement theorists who argued that social movement actors were driven by interests in defending invaded turf from outside sources, be they industrialization or threatening groups. While I do not wish to completely discard the merit of this argument, for there is certainly an element of truth in it, to remain at this rather undifferentiated level of analysis obscures those "offensive" or positive community efforts—the "intentional" in intentional community designations.

8. Alain Touraine conceptualizes historicity to mean the ways in which society "acts upon itself," the management of cultural resources and models (Touraine, 1988: 8).

9. Bifurcations refer to moments or points within systems at which "the previous, simpler organization can no longer support the intensity or frequency of its own fluctuations, and either disintegrates or jumps to a new level of order and integration" (Porush, 1991: 68).

10. A phase space refers to a three-dimensional topographical map that is composed of multiple combinations of time-series data. Analysis of phase space comes closest to a structural interpretation of naturally existing phenomena found within chaos theory.

11. For a thorough articulation of the distinction between striated and smooth space, see Deleuze and Guattari, *A Thousand Plateaus: Capitalism and Schizophrenia* (Minneapolis: University of Minnesota Press, 1987).

12. "Basin" refers to a specific region within a larger outcome field that holds within it the possibility of numerous nonlinear fractal dimensions. Initial conditions give rise to movement of a specific type within the basin. Patterns emerging within the basin are refered to as attractors. There are endless possible concatenations of basins and attractors, each operating within an outcome field. Outcome fields represent all of the possible outcomes of myriad bifurcations. Recall, that once the number of bifurcations surpasses three, instability and thus unpredictability of outcomes are the norm.

2

REFLECTING ON COMMUNITY

Let the beauty we love be what we do.

Rumi, *The Essential Rumi*

The initial step on our journey to establish contemporary ICs as a social movement will be to locate them within a long history of global and domestic communal efforts. Doing so satisfies sociological concerns with recognizing in contemporary social phenomena their historical lineage, enabling us to better understand their motivations which are compounded by specific political, economic, and cultural catalysts compelling them toward community. This chapter, then, will begin with an historical overview beginning roughly 2,000 years ago and moving swiftly over the course of Western experimentation to account for periods of particularly American communal growth. I will spend the remainder of this chapter discussing communal efforts leading to the 1960s and will initiate my comparison of these efforts with the most recent ones beginning in the late 1970s and early 1980s.

What should become clear as we proceed is that while one can identify numerous components of classical efforts at community within contemporary ICs, contemporary ICs differ, in some ways dramatically, from not only their pre-twentieth-century predecessors but also from efforts emerging as recently as the 1960s.

The Communal Movement in History

Zablocki (1980) locates the earliest known period of communitarianism within the Roman Empire between the years 100 B.C. to around A.D. 100. These early communitarians were sectarians from Roman Palestine who, having experienced the Hellenization of Judaic culture, withdrew to community. Additionally, Christians living in the first century A.D. sought the cultural and political freedom of community. Evidence for communal living can be found in Paul's letters and in Acts. Indeed, it was St. Paul who initiated the Christian communitarian movement throughout Asia Minor.

The next wave of communitarianism occurred during the twelfth and thirteenth centuries and included Christian monasteries as well as the emergence of communes analogous to those characteristic of the 1960s. Bennett argues that, "the mountain paths and town ghettos all over Europe were overrun from time to time by wandering fanatics, militants, flower people, most of whom preached brotherhood and poverty and were a thorn in the side of Church" (in Zablocki, 1980: 27). Drawing historical parallels with the communitarian impulse of the 1960s and early 1970s, Zablocki, following Cohn (1957), argues that the motivation for this wave of communitarianism was the emergence of new wealth in Western Europe, producing rapid economic and social change.

The sixteenth and seventeenth centuries produced what sociologists have referred to as a "commune belt" (Zablocki, 1980: 29), which thrived between the Protestant and Catholic regions of central Europe and the British Isles.[1] It is argued that ideological confusion produced a vibrant lifeworld replete with cultural and political opportunities (Bestor, 1950). Zablocki further contends that the "the absence of consensus on meanings and values brought about by ideological fragmentation creates pockets of longing for communities of belief"(1980: 29). During the seventeenth century, migration from Europe to the Americas produced a renewed energy around communitarian efforts in the New World.

The Communitarian Movement in America

North Americans have sempiternally lived in community. It is an experience that for more than 300 years has represented a significant dialectical counterweight to the American political, economic, and cultural mosaic. Historian Robert Fogerty concurs, suggesting that "collective settlements grew organically from a utopian tradition that was deeply rooted in American history" (1990: 8). The remainder of this chapter will focus exclusively on the development of collective settlements in North America, thus providing us with the necessary historical context within which to locate our discussion of contemporary intentional communities.

Early communitarian efforts in America can be identified with the Plymouth Pilgrims who established the first commune in 1620. Early settlers at the Massachusetts Bay Colony have been characterized as "conservative, Christian, and Utopian" (Lockridge in Fogerty, 1990: 8). Most communities and townships of the seventeenth and eighteenth centuries were philosophically inspired by the theological and millennialist teachings exemplified in John Winthrop's articulation of the *City Upon a Hill*. Winthrop, while traveling aboard the ship Arbella in 1630, proclaimed, "We must consider that we shall be a City Upon a Hill, the eyes of all people are upon us" (Fogarty, 1990: 8). In 1663, Plockhoy's Commonwealth was established only to be destroyed by the English one year later. Perhaps the most successful of the seventeenth century communal efforts was the Labadie community, which lasted forty-two years (Zablocki, 1980: 33). Bender argues that each new community initiated in America was, in effect, a communal effort since, in many cases, each new member was required to sign a covenant to join (in McLaughlin and Davidson, 1990: 86). Moreover, each town typically shared ideological beliefs, made decisions by consensus, and shared skills, knowledge, and resources to ensure their survival. While Durkheim and Tonnies wrote critically of the demise of *Gemeinschaft*, Tocqueville pointed to eighteenth-century townships emerging throughout America as a conscious effort to establish a social space between communitarianism and utilitarian individualism. In America, particularly during the post-Civil War period, the township manifested itself as a return to tradition, the ideal of perfected community, articulated as shared symbols, common rituals, and common goals.

The eighteenth and nineteenth centuries witnessed a fulmination of communitarian efforts, some of which persist to the present. In the eighteenth century there was the arrival of the Amish in 1727, the Morovian colony in Bethlehem, Pennsylvania in 1741 (complete with communal economy in 1744), and the arrival in 1774 of Ann Lee and the Shakers (Zablocki, 1980: 33). Among the more notorious of these communities were the Harmony Society (1804–1904), Oneida (1848–1881), Zoar (1818–1898), Amana (1843–1933), Brook Farm (1841–1947), and the Hutterian Brethren (1873–present) (McLaughlin and Davidson, 1990: 87).

The Utopian Socialist movement from 1824 to 1848, produced what was up to that time the most rapid proliferation of communes in American history. Largely viewed as a response to the inhumanity of industrialization, the socialist communities of the mid-nineteenth century were inspired by the ideas expressed in the work of Robert Owen, Charles Fourier, and Etienne Cabet in Europe, and Horace Greeley and Albert Brisbane in America (McLaughlin and Davidson, 1990: 87). Indicative of the spirit of the time, Holloway (1966) cites correspondence between Ralph Waldo Emerson and Carlyle as evidence of the communal spirit: "We are all a little wild here with numberless projects of social reform. Not a reading man but has a draft of a new community in his waistcoat pocket" (19). McLaughlin and Davidson add that, while lesser known than the popular socialist communities of the mid-nineteenth century, there were other, more spiritually oriented communities that contributed to scientific and cultural innovation in America. Among them are Point Loma (1897), Halcyon (1903), and Krotona (1912 to present), each of the theosophical communities was located in California. Halcyon was the site of the first X-ray machine, and Point Loma had the first Greek theater in America. Innovations like these were not atypical within communities. McLaughlin and Dividson, among others, have noted the numerous innovations cultivated within the New Harmony community including the first kindergarten, infant school, free public school, the first free library, and the first geological survey in America. The Shaker communities produced furniture still in high demand today.

The birth of the utopian movement was apparent by the conclusion of the nineteenth century. Notable inspiration came from political economists Edward Bellamy, Henry Demarest Lloyd, and Henry George, who "attempted to present a vision of a new America based on a redefined social and political economy and [who] hoped to create an adversary culture able to combat the growing power of trusts" (Fogerty, 1990: 9). It was during this period, from 1860–1914, that utopian writers and practical communists combined their efforts. Three common interests served to ideologically and philosophically augment this relationship. The first was an immanent critique of American culture coupled with an evolutionary belief in the inevitability of a cooperative state. The second shared belief was based on the perceived availability of seemingly limitless expanses of land. The West, metaphorically and literally, offered communitarians the space for creating community. Finally, following in the path of Owen and Fourier, communitarians believed that they would come to symbolize for all the world what was possible, the true fulfillment of human nature; they would indeed become laboratories for experimentation.

Fogerty (1990) proposes three categories of communal society founded during the post-Civil War period: the cooperative colonizers, the charismatic perfectionists, and the political pragmatists. Following Robert Owen, Horace Greeley, and George Jacob Holyoake, cooperative colonizers "believed that secular salvation could be attained by establishing groups in new settlements and that, by collectively assuming responsibility for the financial future of the communities, the colonists would improve both their moral and their economic conditions" (Fogerty: 16). Cooperative colonies were viewed as structural alternatives to economic insecurity, moral disintegration, and family preservation. Charismatic communities, according to Fogerty, represented both the largest number of groups emerging during this period and those that survived the longest. They were considered "charismatic" because of the "personal sanctity of the membership as a whole or special gifts, or powers of a forceful leader"(Fogerty: 17). Their perfectionism was based on the belief that "the perfected life could be attained within the confines of community" (Fogerty: 17). Charismatic perfectionists cared less for social problems and more for the sanctity of the spirit and efforts to attain holiness within the community.

The third category of communitarians was overtly political. Inspired by economic and political repression, and the depression of the late 1800s, these socialists, anarchists, and Christian socialists attempted to create an economic alternative to capitalism. Frustrated with the seemingly ineffective efforts of unions, and the reformist and ideologically mystifying suffrage, activists articulated cooperative community as a viable alternative to economic instability and political and cultural oppression. Challenging the prevailing Marxist belief in the imminence of class warfare, socialists like Albert Kimsey Owen, the founder of Topolobampo colony on the west coast of Mexico, offered an alternative vision:

The mission of the Socialists is to force upon the consideration of our people of every class the vital issues underlying the second great problem of civilization (wages, transportation) and to urge by organizing cooperative industries and exchanges the application of equity in the affairs of mankind, at the same time that our home industries are protected. (in Fogerty, 1990: 18)

In the end, internally divided and with poor admission policies, the political cooperatives proved to be too volatile to persevere, and most were short-lived.

While there continue to exist many contemporary intentional communities closely approximating the charismatic perfectionist model of the nineteenth century, this chapter, and more broadly speaking, this book, will focus on the contemporary articulation of community and its antecedents in the cooperative community espoused by, among others, Robert Owen, and the political pragmatism practiced by socialists. It is my belief that contemporary intentional communities share a common *Zeitgeist* with their nineteenth century predecessors. They do not, however, share the same experiences (historical, political, economic, cultural) as those early communitarians and it is this very significant distinction that separates them. It is a crucial designation mediated along a temporal-spatial continuum. In the section to follow I will discuss the proliferation of political communes in the nineteenth century. By doing so I hope to establish both their similarities to and their differences from contemporary intentional communities. Moreover, and this addresses the more significant concerns of this book, I will attempt to distinguish the nineteenth century political communes from both the communal efforts of the 1960s and those persisting into the 1990s as a new social movement.

Marxism and Utopia

The record of the post-Civil War period on the establishment of political communes is clear. Socialists pursued cooperative community as an alternative to the continued inhumanity, degradation, and class oppression characteristic of late nineteenth-century capitalist social relations. Prominent socialists, including Henry D. Lloyd, Frank Parsons, Eugene V. Debs, Henry R. Legate, C. F. Taylor, Hiram Vrooman, Stephen Maybell, Thadeus Wakeman, James G. Clark, Charlotte Perkins Stetson, F. M. Sprague, William H. Muller, W.D.P. Bliss, Clarence Powderly, Henry Sharpe, and Alice Rhine, articulated their commitment to cooperative community efforts through their written work and their organizing activities. While division among socialists did emerge around the issue of cooperative community efforts, this was not until the 1890s, when many socialist experiments were already well under way. What is most anachronistic in the socialist experiment with community is its apparent divergence from Marx. Marx remained throughout his life an open critic of utopian socialism. However, it can also be argued that many of the ideas incorporated into both the *German Ideology* and the *Communist Manifesto* were heavily inspired by, among others, Saint-Simon and Charles Fourier. Engels, very familiar with the work of Robert Owen, expressed considerable admiration for the man and his ideas.

Marx and Engels were heavily influenced by the left-wing ideals of French communism. Hobsbawm (1982: 6) identifies a direct link from "Babeuf's Conspiracy of Equals through Buonarroti with Blanqui's revolutionary societies of the 1830s through the 'League of the Just'. " The organization later came to be known as the Communist League for which Marx was commissioned to write the *Communist Manifesto*. Marx reserved his most ardent enthusiasm for babouvist and neo-babouvist activists like Laponneraye, Lahautiere, Dezamy, Pillot, and Blanqui who, while lacking theoretical sophistication, nevertheless engaged in revolutionary praxis. Moreover, Marx and Engels were impressed by the ability of these French activists to enjoin the efforts of workers, establishing a truly proletarian revolutionary body. This they contrasted with the largely middle-class constituency comprising the utopian socialists.

But it was in the articulation of the programmatic component of socialism that the influence of utopian socialists on the theoretical and political development of Marx and Engels can be seen. Hobsbawm (1982) argues that the nineteenth-century conceptualization of socialism was varied and complex. At the most superficial level, it comprised both critical and programmatic components, with each bearing further division into two subcomponents. It is only the programmatic which concerns us here. The first subcomponent, and the one with which I am most interested in, consisted of "a variety of proposals to create a new economy on the basis of cooperation, in extreme cases by the foundation of communist communities"(8). Marx and Engels were emphatically opposed to efforts to create utopian communities, arguing that they were "politically negligible."[2] They viewed these communities as, at best, simulations of communal living under communism. Perhaps most important, however, they had little knowledge of or experience with accomplished utopian communities since this was an almost exclusively American phenomenon. But even those attempts to organize skilled artisans into worker cooperatives, as were initiated by Robert Owen in England, either passed unnoticed or, as Hobsbawm contends, were viewed with great skepticism.

Robert Owen (1771–1857), Saint-Simon (1760–1825), and Charles Fourier (1772–1837) were acknowledged by Marx and Engels as intellectually and philosophically lucid or as politically pragmatic. Each of these utopian social theorists influenced the philosophical evolution of Marx and Engels.

Among Robert Owen's numerous efforts at social reform, three are emblematic of his lifelong struggle to secure happiness for the working poor: New Lanark, the Parallelograms, and the labor exchanges. In his publication *The Book of the New Moral World*, Owen argues, consistent with liberalism, that universal happiness would signify the zenith of human evolution. He contends:

The primary and necessary object of all existence is to be happy. But happiness cannot be obtained individually; it is useless to expect isolated happiness; all must partake of it, or the few will never enjoy it; man can, therefore, have but one real and genuine interest, which is to make all of his race as peaceful in character and happy in feeling as the original organization of nature of each will admit.[3]

Inspired by his friend and colleague Jeremy Bentham, Owen pursued a rationalist course to address those cultural, political, and economic constraints impeding the full realization of human character and potential. Character flaws and unhappiness were the product of culture, not indices of genetic imperfection.

Robert Owen was a businessman, a clothier. Having successfully apprenticed for a well-known Manchester mill where he later became superintendent, Owen orchestrated the purchase of New Lanark Mill in 1799 for $300,000. Owen started work at New Lanark in January 1800. Prior to his arrival, the town of New Lanark was characterized by extreme poverty, drunkenness, theft, fighting, and excessive child labor. There were between 1,300 to 1,400 hundred families in residence, most living in one-room shacks (Laidler, 1968: 87). In response to the social problems in the mill town Owen initiated the first of his efforts at "social engineering." In subsequent years he established prohibitions on drinking, created strict sanitary rules, constructed new housing, established company-owned stores that sold goods at cost, and provided for the education of each child in the town. It was his efforts at New Lanark that provided Owen with his greatest success. In a matter of years he transformed the mill town into one of the most respected and most profitable mill communities in the country.

While his work at New Lanark was significant, it was not utopian. It was not until 1817 that Owen placed himself squarely within the utopian tradition. It was during this time when England passed through its first crisis of overproduction and underconsumption. Owen, by that time a well known proponent of full employment, argued that with the increased commodification of daily life we had become individuals "standing upon the narrow causeway of a narrow abyss." The overproduction of goods, initiated by increasing investments in constant capital, culminated in the displacement of workers who had become too productive. The consequent inability of existing markets to absorb the excess product had led to a crisis of overproduction, the solution to which, Owen argued, was communism. The way to communism would be paved with an incremental transformation of society starting with the composition of small villages or cooperative communities of unemployed workers. The Parallelograms as they were later to be known, would consist of

about one thousand to fifteen hundred acres of land and accommodate between five hundred and two thousand persons, who were to engage both in agriculture and manufacturing. They were to live in large buildings (quadrangles) built in the form of a square, situated in the center of each community and containing common dormitories, dining rooms, libraries, reading rooms and schools (Laidler, 1968: 92).

Furthermore, the architectural design provided space in the center of each quadrangle and beyond it for gardens and playgrounds, while laundry, factories, and farm buildings were placed beyond the outside gardens. All children were to be raised by and live with their parents until the age of three, when the community assumed responsibility for their education. They would return to their parents for meals and other social events. Despite his popularity and the economic crisis within England, working men voted against his proposal, feeling it was too paternalistic and restricted individual freedom (Laidler, 1968: 95). Owen's only attempt to establish a cooperative community came in 1824, when he purchased 30,000 acres of land in Harmony, Indiana, from the German Rappist community. His *New Harmony* lasted for only three years.

Following the collapse of New Harmony, Owen returned to England, where he established a system of labor exchanges, based on the principle of a service-credit system, whereby skilled and semi-skilled workers would deposit their goods at the exchange and receive in return a labor note. The value of labor notes was determined by the amount of the labor time necessary for the completion of the product. Workers would then be able to use the notes to procure items of like or less value.[4]

While Owen's practical efforts to procure the happiness of workers languished, his ideas and his steadfast perseverance inspired not only nineteenth-century communtarians (e.g., Carlyle), but also many of the contemporary communal efforts to be discussed later. His influence on Marx and Engels, however, was mixed.

Robert Owen was known only superficially by Marx but very well by Engels, who respected him as a conscientious and practical businessman and critic of the bourgeois society emerging with the Industrial Revolution. Engels once referred to Owen as "one of the few born leaders of men" (Laidler, 1968: 86). But perhaps most important, Engels found the practical and businesslike manner with which Owen approached the design and application of his utopian communities as exemplary, saying: "from an expert's standpoint, there is little to be said against the actual detailed arrangements" (Hobsbawm, 1982: 10). It is also true, however, that Engels seemed to overlook the extensive working-class support of Owen's ideas, particularly those surrounding labor exchanges and the prohibition of child labor. Marx seemed content to ignore the more praxis-oriented insights of Owen, perceiving Owen's theoretical sophistication to be deficient relative to the French.

Unlike Owen, Saint-Simon and later the Saint-Simon "school" had a profound impact on the development of socialism and the philosophical, political, and economic thought of Marx and Engels. Saint-Simon articulated a model of French class struggle dating to the conquest of the Gauls by the Franks. His evolutionary model of historical development was informed by the belief that "social systems are determined by the mode of organization of property, historic evolution of the development of the productive system, and the power of the bourgeoisie on its possession of the means of production" (Hobsbawm, 1982: 11). Saint-Simon opposed the principles of liberty and equality as espoused during the French Revolution, convinced they would only propel France toward individualism and economic utilitarianism. For him, the time was right for a new social system characterized by universal association, established through the unity of knowledge, science, and industry. It was his belief that in securing universal association, provisions would be made for the employment of all workers in which remuneration would be based on merit. Later, followers of Saint-Simon insisted that each shall labor according to their capacity and receive a reward according to services rendered. These sentiments are repeated in the *Communist Manifesto* where Marx, addressing the distributive phase of communism, reworks the Saint-Simonian phrase "From each according to his abilities, to each ability according to his work." Until his death in 1825, Saint-Simon firmly believed that "the golden age of humanity is not behind us; it is to come, and will be found in the perfection of the social order" (Laidler, 1968: 50–51). On his death bed, Saint-Simon pleaded with his followers to continue his struggle "to guarantee to all men the freest development of their faculties" (Laidler, 1968: 51), a statement later appropriated by Marx in *The German Ideology*.

Three pivotal principles articulated by Saint-Simonians influenced Marx and Engels: Industry should move from private to public ownership, inheritance should be abolished, and women should be the equal of men in all social arrangements. Saint-Simonians crafted a production plan characterized by a hierarchically structured bureaucracy of gradually diminishing rank and authority. Those dominating decision-making would determine which goods to produce and how. While never articulating precisely how positions within the bureaucracy would be filled, it seemed that there was some belief in the "natural" abilities of workers to propel themselves into positions within bureaucracies in which they might fully utilize their respective skills. There could be no inheritance since it would impede the natural flow of skilled workers to positions within the bureaucracy, and it violated their belief in reward based on merit. The aim of Saint-Simonians was to establish "a cooperative commonwealth ruled bureaucratically by an aristocracy of science" (Laidler, 1968: 53). Their emphasis on centralized planning and reward according to merit inspired many twentieth-century socialists. Engels, for example, drawing upon the insights of Saint-Simon, anticipated the eventual subsumption of politics to economics, and the abolition of the state, and argued for the liberation of women, particularly in marriage. It is clear that while they were not communists, Saint-Simon and his followers had a significant impact on the intellectual development of Marx and Engels.

Although contemporaries, Charles Fourier and Saint-Simon represented philosophically divergent views on the path toward reconstruction of the social system. While Saint-Simon favored centralized planning and the adoption of a new social system *en masse*, Fourier articulated the need to seek human emancipation through small-scale community development. Three significant ideas emerge in Fourier's work which later appear in both the work of Marx and Engels, and communitarians. First is the principle of attraction. Fourier believed that there existed in the world an ever-present power of attraction that, if uninhibited, would lead humanity to coalescence, or community. Mortal obstacles to community have, however, led humanity to anti-social activities. Overcoming these obstacles would produce a state of universal harmony. Fourier identified twelve passions that, in the proper communal environment, would lead toward harmony: 1) the five senses; 2) the four "group passions" of friendship, love, the family feeling (familism), and ambition; and 3) the three distributive passions for planning, for change, and for unity. All twelve passions combine into one supreme passion of love for others, united in society (Laidler, 1968: 58). To facilitate the cultivation of the twelve passions Fourier proposed the construction of the phalanx.[5] Drawing heavily from the insights of Robert Owen, the phalanx was Fourier's alternative to disharmony, it was to be a community of between 400 and 2,000 members living in a centralized phalanstery resembling contemporary hotels. Industry would be primarily agricultural. The organization of work was designated by a complex system of groups and series. Groups were organized to facilitate the completion of chores. Within groups, there were numerous series which amounted to components of each chore. Community members could choose to work in any group, and select any series within that group. Rotation between groups and series was frequent, thereby avoiding boredom.

There would be no construction of individual living units. Members would occupy apartments in the phalanstery where they would all gather to eat in a centralized dining hall meals prepared in one immense kitchen. Fourier also instituted a system of labor credits that divided labor into three categories—necessary, useful, and agreeable—with the necessary receiving the highest reward and the agreeable the least. Fourier's unique distribution of surplus led him to appropriate Saint-Simon's motto while adding his own twist: "from each according to his capacity, and to each according to his labor, capital, and talent" (Laidler, 1968: 59). Fourier was certain that while vestiges of family ties would remain, in time the family would disappear. He argued that a communal life of shared love, affection, and friendship would replace the rather narrowly focused attention of two partners.

The influence of Fourierism on American communitarians emerged during the 1840s and attracted the attention of Horace Greeley, Albert Brisbane, and Charles A. Dana, among others. Brook Farm remains the best known of the Fourierest efforts.

Among the three utopian socialists discussed, Marx and Engels were most influenced by the work of Fourier and his acerbic critique of bourgeois behavior, his views on the liberation of women, and his essentially dialectical view of history (Hobsbawm, 1982: 12). Engels found Fourier's individualized conceptualization of labor, in which people can choose work most suitable to their skills and interests, and the notion that labor and enjoyment are identical, to be of supreme importance. Moreover, relative to other utopian writers, Fourier was considered to be among the most prolific advocates of feminist socialist ideals. He argued not only for the political emancipation of women but also, as a logical consequence, for their sexual liberation.

Marx, unlike Engels, clearly rejected Fourier's analogy between work and play. Although there are obvious affirmative Fourierist influences throughout the *German Ideology* ("to hunt in the morning, to fish in the afternoon, to rear cattle in the evening, and criticize after dinner"), the mature Marx rearticulates, and in doing so, transcends Fourier's assessment of labor and human activity. But, as Hobsbawm contends, the fact that Marx deconstructs Fourier's theory to articulate his own is recognition of the significance of Fourier's ideas for him.

In the end, the utopian socialists were viewed by Marx and Engels as peculiar and often ridiculous. While they offered much in the way of a

critique of bourgeois society, historical analysis, and perhaps most important an enthusiastic embrace of the possibility of socialism, utopian socialists suffered two significant weaknesses. First, the eccentricity of many of
the communitarians made the likelihood of their leading a socialist transformation of society improbable. But perhaps most important, and this is
the most significant critique for our purposes, they were essentially apolitical. The efforts of utopian socialists, with the exception of the Saint-Simonians who coddled capitalist entrepreneurs, were not directed at cultivating
alliances with any particular class. Even, as in the case of the Owenites,
where workers were the primary focus of ideological and political propa-
ganda, there was never any effort toward a proletarian revolution.

Post-Civil War America proved to be the experimental laboratory for
cooperative, charismatic, and political communities. Despite the architec-
tonic criticism from Marx, the influence of socialism on the evolution of
communitarian efforts in the United States was considerable. In the next
section I will center my attention on American communal efforts recognizably influenced by socialist philosophy. My interest in these communal
efforts, as with the influence of Marx and Engels, is to establish the closest
historical approximation to contemporary intentional communities. To most
adequately establish the uniqueness of contemporary intentional communities I must offer a brief summation of their nineteenth-century predecessors. I will begin by acknowledging those characteristics of the American
labor movement that placed it in a historically unique position relative to
its European counterpart on the construction and proliferation of class
consciousness. Doing so may suggest possible answers to questions concerning why, despite the numerous efforts to establish socialist or worker-
based communities, most were considered unsuccessful.[6] I will conclude
this section with a discussion of specific socialist-inspired communes.

Socialism and Community in the United States

During the nineteenth century there existed in America and in Europe a
widely held belief that despite numerous efforts to establish working-class
communities in the United States, the historical constitution of the American working class had produced a vacuous class consciousness, making
cooperation illusory. Henry Villard, a member of the American Association
for the Promotion of Social Sciences, noted in an 1872 report evaluating the
state of the cooperative movement in America three characteristics prohibiting cooperation: higher wages (than in Europe), cheap land, and a concomitant individualism.

Numerous books and articles have established the unique constitution and evolution of the American working class. I wish here to provide a cursory glance at the most significant aspects affecting American working-class consciousness as gleaned from these earlier works.

Perhaps the most exhaustive treatise on the question of "American exceptionalism" was Mike Davis's (1986) publication of *Prisoners of the American Dream*. For Davis, as for others preceding him, the United States presented a historically unique politico-juridical composite of three attributes: the absence of a pre-capitalist estate structure imbued with consequent institutions and social relations, the elimination of property qualifications for suffrage (restricted to white males), and the bourgeois character of the American ruling body (Davis, 1986: 11). The historical significance of the absence of feudal political, economic, and cultural relations for the development of American consciousness cannot be understated. Davis, concurring with the Hartzian school,[7] argues that "the Northern colonies were a transplanted "fragment" of the most advanced production relations and ideological superstructures of the seventeenth century: British merchant and agrarian capitalism, Puritan religion, and Lockean philosophy." He suggests that by "no later than 1750 from one-half to three-quarters of the adult white males in New England, including much of the artisanal population, were already exercising a local franchise" (Davis, 1986: 11). The proliferation of a class of petty bourgeois craft workers and farmers had two vital consequences. First, it inaugurated an alliance between petty bourgeois capitalists and the ruling bourgeoisie, thereby augmenting elite power. Next, it established the ideological significance of the prospect of class mobility, again leading toward the unification of the Lockean-liberalist-inspired preoccupations of petty bourgeois capitalists with the governing interests of the ruling elite. Coupled with the decision to eliminate property qualifications for suffrage, which perpetuated a view of the state as an entity of democratic reform, America had embarked upon a course toward bourgeois ideological, political, and economic hegemony unlike that in Europe.

However, by the 1830s American workers had begun to "contrast their political liberty with their economic exploitation" (Davis, 1986: 14) resulting in the initiation of the American labor movement. While I do not wish to elaborate on the numerous labor upheavals of the nineteenth century, it should be recognized that the early 1830s to the 1860s, and the post-Civil War years of 1877, 1884–1887, and 1892–1896 represent significant transformational episodes in the constitution of the American labor movement. From the Workingmen's Parties of the late 1820s, the Knights of Labor, the American Railroad Union led by Eugene Debs, and countless other fleeting organizing efforts, American workers coalesced to address their political, economic, and cultural concerns. But the experience of nineteenth-century labor organizations suggests a perpetual effort to command greater control over the labor process, improve working conditions, increase wages, eliminate child labor, restrict immigration (Locofocos), and, in some cases, liberate women (particularly true of the Knights of Labor, which pushed for the elimination of both gender and race discrimination). Conspicuously missing from either their rhetoric or their praxis was any indication that organized labor in America could or should consider the way of Robert Owen. While predominant labor organizations refrained from articulating a move toward cooperative communities, there were, however, numerous socialist-inspired efforts to do just that.

Despite American exceptionalism, the inspiration for communal efforts persisted. Much like Robert Owen before him, Henry Villard promoted the transition to collective life as perhaps the only viable alternative to the vagaries of fluctuating markets and urban blight. Most of the post-Civil War experiments with community were similar to the experiences of the Philadelphia community initiated by Haupt in Virginia in 1872. Haupt's primary appeal was to recent immigrants and native artisans unable to secure the necessary finances to purchase a home. In an effort to counter anticipated concerns over paternalism, Haupt assured prospective participants of absolute individual freedom. Workers would not be classified by trades or marital status. Additionally, Haupt provided life insurance to members of the community so that, in the event of the death of one or both of the parents, surviving children would continue to find care and support within the community. Fogarty (1990) contends that despite these provisions and numerous efforts to procure the support of skilled urban mechanics, the project seems to have gone nowhere.

Despite numerous failures, socialist-inspired efforts to establish cooperative communities during the post-Civil War period symbolize a persistent faith in their ameliorative qualities. Here, I will be drawing from Fogarty, particularly his 1990 work *All Things New*, in which he clearly articulates the resolute commitment of socialists and radical Christians to establish safe havens for working people. While it is true that the decade of the 1870s, perhaps stimulated by the panic of 1873, produced roughly thirty cooperative community efforts, there was only one coordinated effort to organize working people into community. In 1879, with "poor relief" as their vision, R. Heber Newton, Felix Adler, and O. B. Frothingham secured needed funds for the purchase of land and created the Cooperative Colonization Aid Society. Their stated purpose was to "relieve the unemployed working man at the same time by stimulating and guiding a return to that agricultural life which is the natural life of man" (Fogarty, 1990: 102). Workers were encouraged to establish colonies of associated labor in which family life was to be respected. Free education was offered by organizers. All production and domestic responsibilities were to be organized collectively, cooperatively. The largest land settlement was procured in Salina, Kansas, and from German socialists in Lynchburg, Virginia where some colonists had already settled.

Alcander Longley founded the "colony of communists" or Esperanza Community in 1877. Its philosophy was liberal communism and it had the enthusiastic support of the Socialist Labor Party. Esperanza clearly articulated positions on many of the social problems facing the decade of the 1870s, including: "a demand for the eight-hour day, and the direct popular recall of elected officials. Their fifteen-point platform called for liberal legislation regulating sanitary conditions, child labor, accident insurance, a graduated income tax, a national bank system, and the equalization of wages for men and women" (Fogerty, 1990: 104).

While Esperanza is believed to have lasted less than a year, it has been credited with initiating the transition in the composition of cooperative communities toward those espousing socialist or communist philosophies. By the end of the decade of the 1870s communitarians believed that communism was the alternative to poverty, unemployment, and crime. The 1880s produced roughly twenty-four community efforts, the most notable being the Topolombapo community established in 1886 by Albert Kimsey Owen. But it was the 1890s—inspired by increased labor activism, the publication in 1888 of Edward Bellamy's *Looking Backward*, and the depression of 1893—that produced the most prolific period of communal expansion in the century.

It was during the 1890s that socialists initiated internal dialogue on the "colonization question" with colonization articulated as the only viable alternative to the vagaries of capitalism. Two prominent figures symbolize the theoretical tenor of socialist-inspired participation in the development of cooperative communities: Cyrus Willard and Norman W. Lermond. Willard was a member of the Virginia chapter of the Knights of Labor, a socialist reporter of labor issues, and a passionate advocate of cooperative colonization. Willard's belief in trade unionism and his unswerving support of a socialist transformation of America were manifested in the proposed colonization of Washington state. Socialists, he argued, could move to Washington, elect political representatives, and live without fear of retribution and political oppression.

Following his belief that socialism had to be practiced, Norman Lermond made a similar plea. Writing in 1896, Lermond found the construction of a "people's trust" the only way to combat economic and political exploitation and oppression. Lermond's vision of cooperative colonies required each participant to pay $100. Pooling those resources, Lermond felt, would establish an economic counterweight to the prevailing trusts. His vision included the construction of factories, which would increase employment and lead to greater investments, additional colonies, factories, and so forth. With a diversified composition of colonies and their consequent productive facilities, it was Lermond's belief that these colonies could relinquish their dependence on currency and thereby enhance their autonomy. Like Willard, Lermond believed that socialists should seek to colonize a particular state or region of the country. His example was found at the Hiawatha Colony in Michigan. Founded by Abraham Beyers in 1893, the Hiawatha Colony was organized on the model espoused by Lermond with the addition of a labor-credit system. At its peak, the Hiawatha Colony claimed 225 members, and over twenty structures. Economic difficulties led to its collapse in 1896 (Fogarty, 1990: 140–141).

The stimulating articulation of colonization by Willard and Lermond during the 1890s provided the context for socialist-inspired colonization efforts persisting well into the early twentieth century. In 1901, publication of J. Herbert Rowell's "Everybody's Opportunity, or Quick Socialism" was published and distributed by the Free Socialist Union of Chicago. Consistent with earlier explications of colonization, Rowell's plan was directed at socialists interested in the transformation of American society. He called for establishing an initial base of 500 socialists who would form a "colony school" or "working group" on free government land. Fogarty (1990) claims that Rowell's philosophy comprised two principles: equal liberty and voluntary and reciprocal cooperation. There is no evidence that Rowell's plan was ever initiated.

The Knights of Labor produced some the of the most prolific advocates of colonization, among them Terence Powderly and Henry Sharpe. Powderly, then the Grand Master workman, "advised the General Assembly to pursue cooperation as a means to colonization" (Fogarty, 1990: 145). Among the five men appointed to the "cooperative board" was Henry Sharpe. Following in the tradition of Willard, Sharpe advocated, along with the establishment of cooperative efforts, the establishment of state-based colonization to offer working people "insurance, education, and profit sharing." As an experimental effort, and following the philosophical insights of Sharpe, the Knights established the Eglinton community in Missouri in 1882. However, internal disputes involving Sharpe and his involvement with Eglinton led to his eventual expulsion from the Knights and the disintegration of the community. Sharpe continued his travels throughout the country soliciting support for his colonization efforts from, among others, Debsian socialists. But the Knights withdrew their support for the Missouri colony, arguing that it "had too few resources to carry out a successful plan." Sharpe's influence cannot be underestimated. His articulation of cooperation and colonization, directed as it was toward labor and emanating from one of America's premier labor organizations, contributed mightily to the persistent resonance of the communal option.

Other notable colonization efforts initiated by members of the Knights and other labor-based organizations included Peter McGaughey's work in establishing the Pioneer Association, a community of coopers and printers in Minnesota, and George Holyoake and Burnette Haskell's establishment of the Kaweah colony. Haskell was an activist in the Knights of Labor and founder of the Marxist International Workingmen's Association. Until the establishment of the Coming Nation, the Kaweah colony was the most successful of the worker-based colonies.

Perhaps the most significant attempt at socialism on the model of colonization took place in Ruskin, Tennessee. Following his conversion to socialism, former newspaper editor and real estate magnate Julius A. Wayland founded the Coming Nation in 1894. Members were required to "invest" $500 upon entry to the community, an amount they would receive upon leaving. Appeals for members were primarily directed at garment and mill workers from the upper New England and New York regions. Despite numerous efforts at, among other things, diversified agriculture, publication of Wayland's newspaper, manufacture of chewing gum and wood cabinets, and the operation of a tailoring and laundry shop, the Coming Nation could not secure the needed revenue to keep the colony solvent. In 1899, the Coming Nation disbanded, having hosted more than 200 members during its five-year existence.

The final chapter in the early twentieth-century push for cooperative communities came with the establishment of the American Cooperative Union in 1896. The American Cooperative Union emerged as part of the National Cooperative Congress in St. Louis. Its mission was to "act as a clearinghouse and catalyst for cooperators," as well as "to educate Americans about socialism" (Fogarty, 1990: 163). Most notable perhaps is the enthusiastic participation of Eugene Debs. Debs, for a time the national organizer, found in colonization a way to shelter black-listed unionists. When viewed as a component of the larger vision articulated by people like

Imogene Fales, the head of the American Cooperative Union, socialist-based colonization had returned to its roots in Cyrus Willard and Henry Lermond.

Similar to contemporary intentional communities, proponents of colonization during the late nineteenth and early twentieth centuries refrained from contextualizing their efforts in ideological terms. Their motives appear to have been driven by pragmatic efforts to ameliorate the suffering of the urban poor and working class. To that end, colonization offered a form of social security to the poor, the aged, the sick, the widowed, orphaned, and homeless. While never relinquishing the possibility that their efforts would be seen as laboratories of alternative cultural and economic reconfiguration, colonists were primarily concerned with actively engaging civil society in the construction of a new reality. However (and this significantly separates earlier colonization efforts from their contemporary counterparts), it is clear that reformers, through a combination of voluminous and impassioned explications of the dire state of industrializing America, and through the elaboration of their conception of colonization, experienced their most significant influence as rhetorical. This is not to suggest that their efforts were insignificant, for they surely aroused debate (as, for example, within the Socialist Labor Party, the Knights of Labor, and the American Cooperative Union), and made some modest efforts at colonization. But unlike their contemporary counterparts, as we shall see below, these protagonists were not as engaged in the practice of "creating community" as they were in the rhetorical struggle to advance colonization as an alternative reality.

Comparing the Pre-Twentieth Century Communes with Contemporary Communities

While there are many recognizable similarities between early communal efforts and those of the late twentieth century (e. g., non-violence, cooperation, living close to the land, and so forth), their differences are stark. In their work on communes and collectives, Corrinne McLaughlin and Gordon Davidson (1990) have provided what is perhaps the most comprehensive comparison to date. Among the many differences, they have identified the following as most significant:

- Most communities today are not as communal or as restrictive.
- Most communities today do not require members to give all their possessions, pool all their resources, or raise their children communally.
- Most communities today are much smaller than in the past.

- Most contemporary communities apply psychological methods of conflict resolution and problem solving.

- Views on sex have changed dramatically from celibacy in the 1800s (with the exception of the Oneida), to "free love" in the 1960s, to a balance between these in the late 1980s and 1990s.

- Internal governance has evolved from hierarchical, authoritarian leadership often surrounding charismatic personalities in the 1800s to a more egalitarian, feminist-inspired interest in consensus.

- Increased communication with the surrounding community.

- Networking between communities.

- A philosophical articulation of "planetary consciousness," which prevents communities from isolating themselves and directs their efforts toward community outreach (89–90).

The necessity for distinguishing between these earlier communal efforts, including those of the 1960s, and those persisting into the 1990s is to firmly establish my contention that contemporary intentional communities differ in significant ways in their philosophical orientation, their manipulation of symbol systems, and practical applications of productive and social activity from their nineteenth-century predecessors. This is significant since it is my contention that contemporary cultural, political, and economic circumstances are constituted by a post-industrial shift in particularly Western political-economic relations. The result is the cultivation of interests and needs that are expressed in terms of renewed identity construction and a rearticulated reappropriated lifeworld (discussed in Chapter 3), consciously engaged to transform interpersonal and intrapersonal relations. The practices directed to these transformations by members in ICs are indicative of participants in NSMs generally, but ICs go even further in that they attempt, as a social movement, to engage the entirety of human social existence. This commitment they share, in a general way, with their pre-twentieth-century predecessors.

Distinguishing the 1960s and the 1990s

While it is relatively easy to draw distinctions between the pre-twentieth-century communal efforts and contemporary models, a similar activity directed toward the communes of the 1960s requires cognizance of NSM qualities that will theoretically and practically differentiate these historically significant moments. Issues and lifeworld concerns that a century before had initiated the utopian movement were recognizable in communal actors in the 1960s. The decade of the 1960s produced the most expansive wave of communal activity in American history, with conservative estimates of over 2,000 communes in thirty-four states. Actors experimenting with alternative community lifestyles were searching for simplicity, reconnection with nature, pursuit of meaningful existence, and spirituality, often with the aid of mind-expanding drugs, to counter the prevalence of greed, alienation, violence, and war. Writers like Ram Das (1971), Leary (1968), Watts (1962), Weil (1972), and Ginsberg (1971) provided "a philosophy focused on the here-and-now, on hedonism, on warm interpersonal relations, on non-competition and non-exploitation" (Conover, 1975: 454). The exhilaration produced by the hippie movement is expressed in the following passage by two activists and commune members:

All who experienced the tremendous exhilaration and freedom of the hippie movement have never been the same. We knew the power that comes from being totally unpredictable and flexible. We all had a strong sense of moral integrity that obliged action against injustice (McLaughlin and Davidson, 1990: 93).

This passage is interesting not only its free play with structural boundlessness, simplicity, and relative freedom, but also its emphasis on praxis. While the vast majority of communes persisting throughout the 1960s were not of an overtly political nature, some were, intentionally or not, considered political communes. I draw attention to this communal type here to suggest its affiliation with the active component of contemporary communes. Rather than the exception, contemporary ICs have as a defining characteristic a "planetary consciousness" framing not only their overt, typically regionally directed political activities but also serving as a significant symbolic affront to dominant cultural capital. However, there are compelling differences. Political communes of the 1960s were defined by their ideological commitments and activist participation directed toward institutional changes at the state and federal levels. They smoked lots of dope, dropped acid, and listened to rock and roll searching for answers to unparalleled social problems, but they lacked the sophistication necessary for maintaining community.[8] Contemporary ICs have come a long way in terms of conflict resolution and sophistication in articulating their political, cultural, and economic concerns.

Other examples of innovation in IC include the Farm in Tennessee, which has established satellite communities in New York City and in Latin America to serve the poor, and the Movement for a New Society in Philadelphia, which still has a strong focus on demonstrations, civil disobedience, and the like, but which has pioneered efforts at community conflict resolution and the management of social relations (Gowan et al., 1983).

While vestiges of the communal experience of the 1960s appear in contemporary intentional communities, their differences enable us to distinguish them as a current force for social change. I will briefly identify some of the more significant distinctions between the communal efforts of the 1960s and their 1990s counterparts by drawing on the insights of McLaughlin and Davidson, themselves community members for most of their lives. McLaughlin and Davidson have published their experiences with intentional community in their 1990 *Builders of the Dawn*.

A number of factors distinguish contemporary ICs from their predecessors, and while there are equally numerous lines of intersection with previous generations of communitarians relative to values, goals, and methods, it is the differences noted below that designate contemporary members as constituting a NSM. There are eight significant characteristics which distinguish contemporary ICs:

- They exhibit an aggressive pursuit of innovative modes of enhanced human cohabitation through the application of numerous spiritual, philosophical, psychological, and sociological insights, that is, members are not regressing as they move "back to the land."

- They are typically non-hierarchical, often selecting feminist-inspired consensus decision-making models.

- They are both innovators and practitioners of psychologically sophisticated methods for non-violent conflict resolution and personal growth (e.g., Creative Conflict, Clear Mind Training based on Zen philosophy, Gestalt).

- They utilize appropriate technology where it is not ecologically intrusive (e.g., tractors, solar-powered computers).

- There is a strong philosophical dedication to community outreach,[9] often pursued through slide shows, book publications, newsletters, and conferences.

- There is an effort to maintain balance in the pursuit of cultural, economic, and personal liberation and awareness leading to inspired and ostensibly more humane experiences of love, sex, play, work, child caring, self-identity, relationships to time, space, and the like.

- There is a firm belief in economic self-sufficiency that is experienced in many ways, including innovative efforts at alternative farming cooperatives (concentrating on organic whole foods), food circles (organization of multiple community land trusts within a specific region to produce diversified food for circulation among the communities), production, and circulation of alternative money, and experimentation, production, and marketing of alternative energy devices.

- There is a firm commitment among communitarians to non-violence, race and gender harmony, and peace. In general, it is when viewing contemporary ICs in totem that their levels of sophistication in all aspects of human experience reveal their differences relative to their predecessors.

Examples abound. While most intentional communities have centered their political activism around the decolonization of their specific life-worlds, participation in local and regional activities has been impressive. For example, the Twin Oaks community in Virginia manufactures and distributes hammocks, has successfully organized the surrounding community in opposition to a proposed hazardous waste site, and offers seminars on the incorporation of energy-efficient solar designs into building construction. The Sirius community in Massachusetts and Alpha Farm in Oregon have established workshops on various topics from bookkeeping to organic farming to worker-owned and worker-managed firms. Additionally, the Sirius Community donates 10 percent of its profits from the Rainbow Construction Company to non-profit organizations working to benefit society. The Bear Tribe in Washington offers regional seminars on food storage. The Farm in Tennessee provides instruction in soybean production, started *PLENTY*, an organization dedicated to Latin American outreach, publishes books, operates an alternative school, and has established a victim offender mediation center in Nashville, Tennessee. The Farralones Community has pioneered efforts at solar greenhouse design and construction. Similarly, the Stelle Community in Illinois has been at the forefront of research on greenhouse construction and design, and ethanol use for fuel alcohol production. The Stelle Community was awarded a $50,000 federal grant to develop a "1,000 gallon per day fuel-alcohol facility," and a $52,000 federal grant to develop a commercial greenhouse. A brief description of the greenhouse construction will provide an instructive look at the sophisticated levels of research, design, and construction now taking place in some intentional communities.

The frame for the greenhouse uses what is called a tetrahedral space truss in barrel-arch configuration. The greenhouse has fiber-glass insulation one foot thick, two layers of polyethylene film are stretched out and inflated with a small air blower, making it like an air pillow. At night it becomes a "foam home," a generator fills up the cavity between the two layers of film with soap suds (McGlaughlin and Davidson, 1990: 246–247).

In addition to its innovations in energy use and greenhouse design, the Stelle community maintains a holistic health center staffed by a doctor, a psychologist, and an alternative health practitioner.

What is most significant in identifying the activities of these ICs is their commitment to a more holistic vision of community. That is, actors in contemporary ICs view their alternative lifestyle choices as laboratories for what is possible within civil society, conscious of their role as actors in (re)creating meaning. For example, the Federation of Egalitarian Communities, which includes Sandhill (Missouri), East Wind (Missouri), Twin Oaks (Virginia), Ganas (New York), and Community Evolving (California), suggests in its informational material a dedication to "Sharing Lives, Changing The World." The organization identifies as its core values "land held in common, equality (distribution of goods according to need), non-violence, participatory government, non-discrimination, environmental responsibility, and healthy interpersonal relationships." The active component of its mission is clearly articulated in its self-described "outward looking" praxis. It stresses its commitment "to be models of a cooperative, non-violent, egalitarian lifestyle" (Federation of Egalitarian Communities, California, 1993). The Community Catalyst Project, in San Francisco, offers international networking and information sharing on issues of immediate concern to members of the intentional community. Research conducted by the CCP includes: worker-owned businesses, consumer cooperatives, neighborhood organizations, grass-roots action groups, world peace, human rights and social justice, resource stewardship, and so on. The *Community Bookshelf*, operated by the East Wind Community in Missouri, is a mail-order service offering a full range of books on topics ranging from intentional community to feminism to child rearing and ecology. Alpha Farm in Oregon established a restaurant and bookstore to initiate community outreach and dialogue on issues of concern to the lifeworld equally shared with their neighbors. Finally, the Rainbow Construction Company of the Sirius Community has based its organizational structure on the Mondragon of the Basque region of Northern Spain. As such, they have attempted to reappropriate for workers what Braverman (1976) referred to as the separation of conception from execution. All employees have a say in finances, design, remuneration, and employee relations, and there is greater flexibility in hours worked and in pay scales.

Methodological, philosophical, and spiritual innovations in interpersonal and intrapersonal growth percolating during the 1970s emerged in the 1980s as sophisticated techniques for dispute resolution and organization of community power structures. For example, to effectively realize their often lofty mission statements, members of ICs are frequently encouraged to pay closer attention to matters of personal growth. A recent column by Geoph Kozeny (1995), a twenty-year veteran of community life, contends that little community growth can take place without special attention being given to a "personal and/or a collective awareness" of old patterns of interaction. Focusing on four primary modes of interactional feedback—physical, interpersonal, paranormal, and personal—Kozeny describes practical efforts made by board members of the Fellowship of Intentional Community to address such issues. In his closing paragraph Kozeny remarks, "Ultimately, constructive criticism is an art, and we need to learn the philosophy and the tools if we are to use it to our universal benefit, to make the world a better place" (7). It is this persistent attention to the pursuit of profound intrapersonal and interpersonal development, coupled with an outward-looking philosophy, an expression of planetary consciousness, that suggest a clear separation with past communal efforts.

Kat Kinkade, one of the principal founders of the Twin Oaks community, recently initiated a debate over community decision-making models with Mildred Gordon of Ganas.[10] While the text of these debates is interesting, raising as it does issues of authority, hierarchy, and consensus decision-making, what I find most relevant is the fact that this kind of discussion is taking place at all. It seems clear to me that ICs, with little or no fanfare, have engaged some of the most pressing issues of our day and with real insight. That they are not always responsible for the kinds of outcomes anticipated by their members is a rather insignificant point (except for those immediately involved, of course) since the lessons learned from their experimentation propel human cognition and experience.

Finally, and perhaps most important, contemporary members of ICs perceive themselves as the progenitors of cultural changes. This is significant since, as Gusfield (1994) has remarked, when actors perceive themselves as agents in a social movement, a social movement actually exists. Furthermore, the self-conscious recognition of a shared vision, organizational participation (e.g., Fellowship of Intentional Communities), and group participation among members of ICs in numerous regional and national IC events satisfy prerequisites for the existence of a social movement. In their research on contemporary ICs, McLaughlin and Davidson (1990: 37) recall the proclamation of one member of the Twin Oaks community: "My life has political meaning, just by living here and doing what I'm doing. It's a message, an example to people, something they can look at, come to visit, and talk to us and get inspired to change their own life."

My interviews and visits with members of ICs in central New York offer similar conclusions. Members of ICs are sometimes excruciatingly aware of their status as innovators, something which is confirmed with each new request from a "seeker" to visit their homes. My interviews with Hank Strunk, co-founder of the Common Place community in Truxton, New York during the year and a half prior to his death are instructive on this account. For years Strunk had been a community activist in central New York. He produced and distributed cassette tapes calling for a nationalized single-payer heath care system. He was a seemingly tireless campaigner for the poor and underprivileged who saw in community an alternative to the alienating experiences of day-to-day life. His vision and identity were fused in the dual purpose of living lightly on the earth while actively engaging cultural issues. Common Place was his strength.

In general, communitarians have recognized a surge in community activity and interest. For example, in the 1995 publication of the *Communities Directory*, itself a manifestation of conscious efforts to "name and frame" the IC movement, Kozeny writes of a "new wave" of IC differentiated from the 1960s, where at least 160 communities have survived ten years or more, and 80 have lasted more than two decades (24). The directory lists over 500 ICs operating in North America alone. Conversations with numerous members of ICs at the annual Conference on Intentional Communities held in Oneida, New York, confirmed what secondary literature, and my own work with communitarians were saying: There appears to be an emerging interest among community members in the proliferation and cultivation of social movement status.

It should be clear that ICs emerging in the 1970s, 1980s, and 1990s differ, in some ways dramatically, from their predecessors. What remains for discussion is whether and to what extent contemporary intentional communities represent a significant force for social change. Do they command the same attention as NSM actors as has traditionally been directed toward the peace, women's, ecology, and youth movements of the past two decades? Do they fulfill the requisite sociological criteria determining social movement status? To answer these questions, and entertain additional ones, we must turn to the theoretical literature on NSMs.

Notes

1. Generally speaking, the commune belt stretched from London in the west to Berlin in the north, east to Prague, and south to Zurich, with a broad northerly loop around Paris returning to London.

2. It is interesting to note here that Hobsbawm adds his support to Marx and Engels's contention that communist communities were "politically negligible," saying, "Utopian community building they rightly regarded as politically negligible, as indeed it was," (1982: 9, emphasis added). I will argue below that socialists, both American and English, who actively pursued cooperative community saw their efforts as overtly political. But more important, for Hobsbawm to concur with Marx and Engels suggests the current chasm persisting between traditional definitions of social movements and the NSM literature. As we will see below, it is the presence of overt conflict that marks the status of social movement in the traditional sociological literature.

3. Cf., R. Owen, *The Book of the New Moral World*, Part 4, 1836: 54.

4. Contemporary service-credit systems operate in a similar way. In the typical case, small communities survey residents for their interest in the "philosophy" informing service-credit and then secure information relative to the skills each resident has to offer the community. Skills range from computer analysts and music instructors to lawn mowing and painting or hair-cutting. The next step is to advertise the available skills to match those in need with those who have skills. Service-credit differs from bartering since there need not be a direct one-to-one transfer of goods or services. Once the data base has been constructed, an auditor or record-keeper tabulates the flow of goods and services. For example, if I cut grass for my neighbor, my neighbor accrues a debit which he or she must translate into a good or service for me or for someone else. I am owed a good or service equal in amount to that which I provided (I determine the value of my own labor) by someone in the data base, not necessarily the person I cut grass for. The success of service-credit systems derives from their ability to assimilate the community's unemployed and underemployed into the local economy. Since most people can offer at a minimum home-based service skills, they can be rewarded within the community with other goods or services. Moving from service-credit to an alternative money supply and the manufacture of script is the logical end to this process. Here skills are traded, much like Owen's labor exchanges, for a labor note equal to the value of the labor time necessary for the completion of a particular project, skill, or good. Many communities in the United States have established alternative money systems: among the most prolific is the Ithaca Hours system created by Paul Glover in Ithaca, New York.

5. The Greek origin of the word "phalanx" signifies a heavily armed infantry. Combined with the word "phalanstery," the housing for the members, we have an image of community that, while apparently decentralized, is nonetheless, organized for the struggle to redefine political, economic, and social space.

6. This is a significant point since the core of my argument throughout this book will be what is to my mind an inaccurate assessment of the "success" and "failure" of communal living made by sociologists and historians. That the eighteenth-century and nineteenth-century efforts to establish communal living were relatively shortlived says little about their success in raising significant issues of

critique concerning the cultural, political and economic configurations of the time. It is clear that while contemporary ICs differ from their pre-20th-century predecessors, there exists a common ancestry through Eastern and Western history representing a perpetual mode of resistance to perceived inhumane living conditions. By their presence, I will argue, communitarians expose alternatives to normative behavioral prescriptions and in that way produce what Deleuze and Guattari (1983) refer to as "after-images," cultural residue persisting indefinitely and representing a storehouse of possible living alternatives. True measures of this kind of "success" are difficult at best, impossible if one's method is cross-sectional, since they exist on a temporal continuum that may linger far into the future as communitarians return to the past to progress.

7. Cf. Louis Hartz, *The Liberal Tradition in America*. New York, 1955.

8. For a contrary view see Patrick W. Conover (1975). "An Analysis of Communes and Intentional Communities with Particular Attention to Sexual and Genderal Relations." *The Family Coordinator*, 24 (4): 453–464. Conover identifies the many ways that communes and intentional communities had begun expressing their praxis orientation beginning in the early 1970s. While I would not dispute this, it must be recognized that what is missing from this historical period is an identifiable *Zeitgeist* that sets the tone for intentional community, generally speaking.

9. Laird Sandhill, a founding member of the Fellowship of Intentional Communities, wrote in the spring 1995 edition of *Communities* about the relative autonomy of the communitarian movement and the perceived need for a loosely orchestrated organization. The fellowship has initiated efforts to organize ICs nationally by publishing newsletters, establishing electronic mail, sounding boards, and offering advice to seekers and veterans on communal issues. In his words, "We're rather like midwives who barnstorm the continent, hopeful of birthing healthy regional networks" (23).

10. See the fall 1995 issue of *Communities*, pages 28–30.

3

RECONSTRUCTING THE MULTIPLE: SOCIAL MOVEMENT THEORY AND CIVIL SOCIETY

Envisaged from an antiessentialist theoretical perspective, pluralism is not merely a fact, something that we must bear grudgingly or try to reduce, but an axiological principle.

Chantal Mouffe, "Democracy, Power, and The Political"

That ICs differ in various ways from their predecessors, while interesting, takes us only a short distance in establishing their presence as social movement actors. For that we must attempt to locate them along the vast spectrum established by sociologists for identifying social movement organizations, actors, and issues. This chapter and the one to follow address this effort directly. Since it is my contention that sociological theories of social movements must be expanded to include a broader array of resistance potential, I will offer a brief articulation of new social movement theory (NSM), its precepts and insights, followed by a discussion of civil society. In the first part I will review recent attempts to identify those qualities possessed by new social movements that have required researchers to designate their uniqueness relative to social movements prior to the mid-1970s. Research published during the 1990s suggests continued interest in pursuing those specifically cultural innovations initiated by NSMs in pursuit of distinctive modes of social change (Johnston and Klandermans, 1995; Larana et al., 1994). This is a particularly salient feature of ICs as their primary impact is on issues related to the lifeworld. This particular aspect of NSM theorizing, one with a specific interest in cultural innovation, emerges alongside a more general multidisciplinary theoretical thrust challenging traditional structuralist interpretations of social movements (Taylor and Whittier, 1995: 163). I will attempt in this chapter not so much a thorough review of this debate (there are numerous references for those seeking a disciplinary overview), but rather a brief introduction to some of the major tenets of sociological theorizing followed by the potential insights emerging from NSM theory. To accomplish this I will first compare NSMs to the classical social movement research of the collective-behavior tradition, and follow up with a discussion of the more contemporary resource mobilization and action-oriented paradigms. There is one cautionary note: Research proliferating through the 1980s and early 1990s on NSMs has unfortunately led to what Melucci has referred to as an epistemological degeneration associated with the ontologization of the concept "new social movement."[1] To avoid the obvious pitfalls associated with such an activity, Chapters 4 and 5 speak directly to the uniqueness of ICs as NSMs.

Having then established the foundational characteristics of NSM theory, the second part of this chapter is dedicated to the theoretical evaluation of civil society. This is especially cogent since NSM theory requires a social space enabling the cultivation of alternate identities, work roles, conflict resolution strategies, and the like. In this section I will initiate a more expanded conceptualization of social movements with a brief discussion of Ernesto Laclau and Chantal Mouffe's (1985) articulation of radical democracy. This line of inquiry will establish the foundation for Chapter 4. This section will conceptually and symbolically prepare for our final two chapters in which the actual work of cultivating a social movement can begin. Let us begin now with our comparative look at social movement theory.

Collective Behavior

Attempts to distinguish social movement research traditions have called attention to the distinctive analytical priorities of American and European authors. America's classical theoretical paradigm, collective-behavior, was influenced by the research of Herbert Blumer (1955) and symbolic interaction, and the structural-functional model of Talcott Parsons (1971) with its roots in Weber and Durkheim, Neil Smelser (1962), and Turner and Killian (1957). Europe, on the other hand, produced its own philosophically inspired analyses of social movements articulated as movement as institution (Jamison and Eyerman 1991). European social movement research was inspired by Max Weber and Karl Marx, and later Roberto Michels (1959) writing in the Weberian tradition and Manuel Castells (1983) in the Marxist tradition.

The collective-behavior tradition combines two seemingly disparate levels of analysis and theoretical paradigms—the symbolic interactionist and structural-functional. Herbert Blumer's, and later Turner and Killian's (1972) individual level, social-psychological analysis focused on the ways in which negotiation within collective settings served to produce new meanings, emergent norms, and creativity for participants. In the early work of Blumer, and later that of Turner and Killian, crowd behavior, or as Blumer referred to it "adaptive behavior," focused on the coalesence of positive and negative products resulting from collective encounters. The concern for each was identifying the "emergence and construction of new norms of social relationships and new meanings of social life" (Gusfield, 1994: 60). Social movements were the products of interaction processes that engaged people in discourse over issues. Here Blumer confronted the contemporary wisdom of the early twentieth century, which had, especially among American social scientists, written contemptuously of the unscrupulous crowd. Like his colleagues, Blumer could not deny what history had exposed about the negative potential of crowd behavior, but unlike his colleagues, he also recognized the positive, creative possibilities forged in intense social intercourse. Individuals acting collectively frequently broke with the routinized mundanity of daily behavior, vigorously confronting that semi-permeable membrane comprising normatively accepted prescriptions for axiological behavior. In doing so they created a social space necessary for innovative thought and action. Later it will be argued that civil society offers the opportunity for actors to engage historicity, a point Blumer never addressed. Blumer's conceptualization of the origins of social movements was problematic but not without merit. According to Ralph Turner (1994: 79), Blumer viewed social movements as emerging within a specific historical and cultural context and guided by a few prevailing themes. Despite numerous specific differences within each movement, there was a certain congruence with these cultural themes. Moreover, for Blumer social movements were either general, "rather formless in organization and inarticulate in expression," or specific, with "a well defined goal [and] recognized and accepted leadership and a definite membership characterized by a 'we-consciousness' "(79). Application of Blumer's insights to analysis and comprehension of NSMs is instructive. As we will see in our discussion of NSMs that follows, it is possible to discern a general cultural, political, and economic transformation taking place, which has within theoretical circles been referred to as a transition to a postindustrial society, while plunging more deeply into civil society to the lifeworld to view the numerous expressions of resistance emerging and persisting there. The value of Blumer's topology is its effort to bridge macro and micro levels of analysis.

In contradistinction, the structural-functional model first articulated in the mature writings of Talcott Parsons[2] sought to identify the systemic causes for collective action. Structural-functionalists argued that the "strains" caused by various action systems, indicative of modern developed, highly differentiated societies, differentially "moved" people to act in certain ways typically to defend what Parsons referred to as their "societal community."[3] In opposition to the symbolic interaction paradigm, structural-functionalists argued that once arranged as a collective, to speak of "individual" identity was meaningless since a distinctive new collective identity emerged to supersede it.

Following Parsons was Neil Smelser, whose publication in 1962, *Theory of Collective Behavior*, catapulted the structural-functional model of social movements to sociological prominence well into the late 1960s and early 1970s. While staying true to Parsons's initial conceptualization of collective action, Smelser's classifactory contribution was to articulate six conditions under which collective action would be most likely to emerge:

structural conduciveness, the peculiarities of a particular society create different opportunities and avenues for protest; *structural strains*, the actual underlying causes of complaint; *generalized beliefs*, the role of ideologies and ideologists in shaping the way protest and complaint is understood by actors; *precipitating factors*, the specific sparks that ignite protest; *leadership and communication*, to direct and coordinate; and, finally, *the operation of social control*, the way established authorities react (Jamison and Eyerman, 1991: 14).

While the classical paradigms differ in many respects, particularly in the level of analysis and political interests, they do share some common assumptions. In her work on social movement paradigms, Jean Cohen (1985: 671-672) has identified the following characteristics shared by the classical theoretical paradigm:

(1) There are two distinct kinds of action: institutional-conventional and non-institutional collective behavior. (2) Non-institutional collective behavior is action that is not guided by existing social norms but is formed to meet undefined or unstructured situations. (3) These situations are understood in terms of a breakdown either in the organs of social control or in the adequacy of integration, due to structural changes. (4) The resulting strains, discontent, frustration, and aggression lead the

individual to participate in collective behavior. (5) Noninstitutional-collective behavior follows a "life cycle," open to causal analysis, which moves from spontaneous crowd action to the formation of public and social movements. (6) The emergence and growth of movements within this cycle occurs through crude processes of communication: contagion, rumor, circular reaction, diffusion, etc.

However, the most significant critique of the classical paradigm, particularly in its Smelserian form, is its implicit assumption that collective action is inherently irrational. As Jean Cohen suggests, "All collective-behavior theorists stress psychological reactions to breakdown, crude modes of communication, and volatile goals" (1985: 672). In doing so, collective-behavior theorists are unable to capture what is unique or innovative in collective action. Moreover, they are unable to see that collective action need not be, as Kanter (1973) suggests, solely a flight from, but also a seeking for. As we have seen, this is a particularly seminal characteristic of ICs. And finally, as Gusfield (1994) has recently reiterated, rather than being an anomalous deviation from normative activity, collective behavior and conflict are coterminous with normative activity.

This is precisely the theoretical mix that occupied earlier efforts to locate ICs within the social movement literature. Returning for a moment to Zablocki's formulation of "commune as social movement," it is clear that it has its origins in the highly influential collective-behavior theoretical paradigm. Zablocki contends that communitarian social movements are "expressed as ideological confusion and manifested at the individual level as the inability to make choices among a plethora of attractive action alternatives" (1980: 25). Further, and here he is much closer to the collective behavior paradigm, Zablocki contends that "communitarianism has always functioned as a deviant, radical, or otherworldly fringe, drawing off idealists, social malcontents, and dreamers rather than finding a place for itself within the structure of societal institutions" (1980: 31). As these passages suggest, Zablocki's frame, like the collective behavior paradigm generally speaking, can be scrutinized using Cohen's identification of common theoretical assumptions, particularly points three through six.

The theoretical inadequacy of the collectivist tradition became apparent during the 1960s and 1970s, when massive social protest emerged in Europe and the United States. Actors in these movements typically were not the "fragmented, anomic, underprivileged, and irrational deviants" hypothesized by the structural-functional paradigm. Neither did the Smelserian model prove sufficient to predict the "timing, cognitive character, conduct, or goals of movement actors" (Cohen, 1985: 673). In direct contrast to the

Smelserian thesis, the movements of the 1960s and 1970s "were not responses to economic crises or breakdown. They involved concrete goals, clearly articulated general values and interests, and rational calculations of strategies." That collective behavior theorists viewed actors in social movements as "irrational" is clear (LeBon 1960; Smelser 1962; Blumer 1955). But as Taylor and Whittier contend, there need not have been a strict separation between reasoned rational thought and the expression of emotions. Indeed, following Turner and Killian (1972), they argue the dichotomy is artificial since "social movement participants, like all other social actors, are not only thinking but also feeling actors" (1995: 180). While initially relating their insights to feminist rituals, Taylor and Whittier stress a commonality shared by most NSMs, the relevance or perhaps even the necessity of an open expression of emotion and empathy resulting in new cultural codes for the expression of feelings. Strict adherence to collective behavior's emphasis on rationality overlooks this dimension, an "emotion culture of protest" (180), inhibiting a multiplicitous postindustrial comprehension of social movement actors and issues. It had become clear that the decade of the 1960s impelled a reinvigorated sociology of social movements to respond to the vacuity of the structural-functional paradigm with theoretical acuity. In America the product was "resource-mobilization," and in Europe, the "identity" or "action-oriented" paradigm.

Resource Mobilization

Both the resource mobilization and identity-oriented paradigms confront the classical model of collective action on a number of fronts. First, each identifies conflictual collective action as a normative component of societal intercourse, not an aberration, as the classical theorists would have it. Each sees collective action as the manifest behavior of rational actors articulating state, federal, and lifeworld concerns by participating to varying degrees in the perpetual (re)constitution of civil society, typically as members of voluntary associations. This is significant since it confirms the sempiternal presence of organizations and associations persisting over the past three centuries, although with differing historical significance and function, at the level of the lifeworld. These organizations and associations are the sustenance of emerging social movements, often determining their constitution and effectiveness.

In America, perhaps the most influential sociological effort to transcend the classical social movement paradigm has been resource mobilization. Initially inspired by the utilitarian economic models of Mancur Olson

(1965), resource mobilization theorists have characterized social movement phenomena based on "the variety of resources that must be mobilized, the linkages of social movements to other groups, the dependence of movements upon external support for success and the tactics used by authorities to control or incorporate movements" (McCarthy and Zald, 1977: 1213). Resource mobilization theorists center their attention on the rational calculations of movement actors and the interaction between conflictual groups rather than on the social movement per se. Here, there is no interest in the phenomenology of movement ideology or individual identity formation. Olson's influence can be seen early in the development of the resource mobilization perspective when he raised concern over what he called the "free rider" problem. Olson was interested in understanding why anyone would participate in the often messy and sometimes dangerous business of collective action when, as a rational actor who calculates the costs and benefits of her actions, it may serve her direct interests to merely stand by and allow others to take up the drudgery of mobilization. This was and continues to be a significant question for social movement theorists since it goes to the heart of individual and group identity construction and its eventual expression in collective action. But due to the utilitarian and organizational emphases of resource mobilization, adequately addressing these concerns has proven difficult. Efforts to modify the strict utilitarian assertions of Olson have come from within the resource mobilization "camp" (e.g., Tilly, 1975, 1985; Jenkins, 1989; Jenson, 1995) and, as sociologists will recall, from the relentless critique of the utilitarians by Durkheim and, later, Parsons, each arguing that a strict utilitarian analysis cannot explain group solidarity. Tilly (1985), for his part, seems to suggest that there is a certain gravitational field of mobilization activities luring prospective actors. But it is clear that without comprehension of the phenomenological and hermeneutic rationales of individual actors perpetually (re)constituted at the level of the lifeworld, a conceptual shortcoming Tilly confesses to,[4] we find ourselves maneuvering without the theoretical tools necessary to respond to Olson's concern.

Moreover, as I believe Touraine (1988) correctly suggests, to conceptualize social movements using a rational actor model is inherently elitist since all but the most powerful are placed automatically in defensive positions. It is also conceivable that Taylor and Whittier's (1995) critique of collective behavior's reliance on rational behavior could be applied to the resource mobilization paradigm as well. For it is clear that while there has been a paucity of attention directed to the phenomenological composition of social movements, rational calculation of movement resources, strategies, and the like have taken precedence.

Perhaps the most significant critique of the resource mobilization paradigm, relative to NSMs, is its articulation of social movement as a "political campaign." This is particularly evident in the conflict-oriented work of Tilly and Tilly (1975), Tilly (1978), Jenson (1995), and Gampson (1975). Social movements are, for example, viewed by Tilly as originating in the nineteenth century and "consisting in a series of demands or challenges to power-holders in the name of a social category that lacks an established political position" (1985: 735–36). Further, Tilly explicitly rejects the notion that there is anything new in the NSMs, arguing instead that contemporary collective mobilizations and techniques can locate their origins in past movements. For him, mobilizations are of one of three types: competitive, proactive, or reactive, with only the latter two serving as conceptual guides for contemporary action. In both the proactive and reactive conceptualizations, collective action assumes a taking from (as in the case of striking workers who take over a plant), or a reaction to efforts to appropriate resources, seen here as a defensive action (e.g., tax rebellions).

Among recent theorists imaginatively folding components of resource mobilization into cultural politics is Jane Jenson (1995). Her latest effort in this regard pursues political struggles over "naming." Jenson argues that within "imagined communities" (Anderson, 1991) a perpetual struggle exists over the ownership of issues, beliefs, values, and ultimately, organizational names. This is particularly cogent for movements seeking national attention, as they "write and rewrite history in order to justify contemporary definitions of interests and strategies" (1995: 108) and most important resist being "named" by interests outside the group. It is this compelling and important contribution that makes Jenson's work so attractive to social movement theorists, for it initiates an effort to bridge the divide between resource mobilization and strategy, and phenomenological articulations of movement identity. Application of Jenson's work to ICs, however, is difficult. While it is true that there are ICs that select community names consistent with their particular political or spiritual world view (e.g., Sonoran Eco-village, Aquarian Concepts, Mondanock Geocommons Village, Ganas), from my experience many more adopt names identifying their immediate geographic surroundings (e.g., Chester Creek House, Deep Woods Farm, Deer Rock, Griffin Gorge Commons, Green Pastures Estate, Red Mountain, Sunflower House, Shannon Farm, Twin Oaks). Reflected in these names is much less a dialogical struggle over symbolic possession of certain ideals, beliefs, and values than a reminder of the non-combative constitution of ICs as movement actors. This is an important distinction since Jenson, like others in the resource mobilization tradition, privileges movement "frames" (Snow and Benford, 1992; Snow et al., 1986), and collective action. Moreover, and this is my primary critique of her hypothesis, Jenson argues that the process of engaging in the struggle over naming creates "winners" and "losers" (1995: 115), that to maximize political efficacy, social movements "must mobilize a collective identity within the movement [and] seek to compel recognition of that identity by public institutions" (115). While it is clear that ICs have engaged in the cultivation of ritualistic behavior coincident with the constitution of a collective identity, a prerequisite of any social movement, they have not sought (and because they are a movement of a different type, will not seek) to "compel recognition" of their collective identities at the national level. This will be explored more fully below with regard to NSMs, and in detail in Chapter 4. Furthermore, the dualism of "winners" and "losers" is, to my mind, conceptually and experientially flawed. While a more thorough treatment of this issue will follow in Chapters 4 and 5, it is clear that resistance movements around the globe persist in a perpetual struggle to reclaim civil society, accentuating a vast spectrum separating what is articulated here as "winning" and "losing." Indeed, how does one measure victory? For ICs, as with most NSMs, the impact of their brand of social movement is extremely difficult to calibrate since they attempt transformations in identity construction, love, sexuality, play, conflict resolution, and so on. By their efforts, have ICs "lost" if "outside" encounters with their ways of living serve to transform the lives of only ten or twenty?

What makes NSMs unique relative to Tilly's and Jenson's social movement conceptualization is that what they defend is the lifeworld, civil society, the societal space required for the constitution of identity, creativity, vitality, and, in the case of social movements, solidarity. It is what Cornel West (1993) means when he asks "intellectuals" to use their epistemological and analytical foresight to "ameliorate the plight of the wretched of the earth." He argues that the societal space suited for this activity "is the space wherein everyday affairs of ordinary people intersect with possible political mobilization and existential empowerment, for example, in churches, schools, trade unions, and movements" (105). But again it must be emphasized that NSM actors are proactively confronting adversaries at the level of society over the management of social, not solely political, space. While recognizing a seminal inceptionary wave of action, West does not go far enough in his penetration of civil society. NSM actors are not specifically (and some cases not at all) interested in directing their efforts at state-based policy changes or party-based politics.[5] Contemporary actors must, as Touraine suggests, operate with a "limited rationality" where "social agents seek to maximize their interests, but they do so in an environment they control, or even know, only partially" (1988: 37).

The identity-oriented paradigm has emerged to address issues of identity construction and solidarity within social movements: let us now move to a discussion of this theoretical paradigm.

New Social Movements: The Identity Paradigm

European theorists of NSMs have centered their analyses on the integrative dimension of collective action without, as Cohen (1985) observes, reproducing the earlier antinomies of the collective behavior paradigm. And, while inspired by Marx, they do not accept Marxist prescriptions of social movements, which tend to focus on economic segmentation (e.g., Gordon, Edwards and Reich, 1982), structural contradiction (e.g., legitimation crisis), or class conflict. Moreover, these post-Marxists contend that we cannot explain collective behavior by adopting the rational-actor model since contemporary collective actors refrain from, and in some cases never pursue, state-legitimated political recognition, or negotiation among adversaries. Indeed, it is the apparent non-negotiability of NSM axiology, one partly grounded in identity or authenticity-based politics, that has evoked the most fervent response from critics. Environmentalists, feminists, gay and lesbian activists, peace activists, activists for urban social change, and the cultural revolts identified with student rebellion are each recognized as the "torch bearers" of NSM activism. Each has, at times, been criticized for its alleged unwillingness to negotiate on issues of axiological significance since, while there is considerable overlap between organizations, there is also considerable factioning. I would like to raise the most serious allegations brought by detractors of identity-based politics and offer a response from within the NSM paradigm.

Perhaps the most compelling component of NSMs, and in that way the most controversial, appears in the non-negotiability of demands articulated by NSM actors. For many, particularly some neo-populists like critical theorist Paul Piccone (1993), the non-negotiability of firmly held beliefs and values, a predominant characteristic of identity-based politics, leads ultimately to retrograde dogmatism and cultural particularity which, aside from being politically impractical, undermine traditional federal solutions at reconciling difference. Piccone sees authenticity-based politics as a threat to the traditional public/private designation typical of liberal-democratic states.[6] His perspicacious deconstruction of identity or authenticity-based politics raises the dire specter of a renewed authoritarian state resurrected to bring law and order to a rhizomatic lifeworld confounded by axiological heterogeneity. It should be said that while much of Piccone's criticism can be applied to various components of NSMs, his focus is primarily those organized groups that attempt to have their axiological particularities constituted as social policy. His most acerbic criticism is leveled against gay activists who, "having adopted the Maoist belief that the private is public," have sought the legislation of personal behavior.

In contradistinction, theorists of NSMs suggest that the non-negotiability of demands articulated by movement actors serves two primary goals. First, it is a seminal component of collective identity formation, and second, it is perceived as an integral part in deconstructing axiological sedimentation. Collective behavior must be viewed as a dialectical relationship consisting of collective identity formation and collective action. Cohen (1985) goes further by arguing that: "contemporary collective actors see that the creation of identity involves social contestation around the reinterpretation of norms, the creation of new meanings, and a challenge to the social construction of the very boundaries between public and private, and political domains of action" (694).

A dualistic politics with an emphasis on collective identity formation and collective action (oriented in both civil society and the state, as well as economic institutions) is necessary since the liberal-democratic state, heralded as the great arbitor by Piccone, must also be recognized as gendered, class-specific, and, as with reference to Piccone's primary subject of criticism, vehemently heterosexual.[7] Specifically, the non-negotiable demands of NSM actors confront the apparent "neutrality" of existing axiological beliefs often codified in law.[8] Further, it could be argued that an ardent defense of authenticity characteristic of NSMs stems not from some inability to comprehend the strategic possibilities suggested by rationalizing the organization through the pursuit of state-based political solutions (inevitably an effort to straddle the Michelsian paradox),[9] but from recognition by movement actors, many of whom have worked within organized politics, of the incompetence of legislative officials and the liberal-democratic edifice itself. While it may prove impossible to maintain authenticity while simultaneously negotiating lifeworld and system (Habermas, 1989; Cohen and Arato, 1992), it is clear that a self-reflective politics of identity, with an emphasis on consciousness raising, self-help and local empowerment, has a place in the dialectical relationship that constitutes democratic politics.

Contextualizing New Social Movements

New social movements have emerged at a historically significant moment, driven primarily by what Claus Offe has referred to as a "broadening, deepening, and irreversibility of forms of domination and deprivation" (1985: 845). Theorists of NSMs have generally acknowledged the historical significance of two global political, economic, and cultural transformations that have led to new forms of collective action: the transformation from industrial to postindustrial society including the increasing inability of the state, especially the welfare state, to effectively counter global economic and political crises, and the intensification of domination by contemporary power-knowledge regimes (Foucault, 1979) due to an increasing need to coordinate control and consumption.

According to theorists of NSMs, we are currently living in a postindustrial society in which the effects of the capitalist mode of political and economic rationalization are not limited to specific classes, times, spaces or kinds (Melucci, 1988; Offe, 1985; Touraine, 1971, 1988; Boggs, 1985; Brand, 1990; Klandermans, 1990). That NSMs have emerged as a product of the economic and technological contradictions of capitalism is a theme shared by most NSM theorists, who offer a laundry list of crisis characteristics to undergird their critique. I list here those offered by Boggs (1985: 31):

- an end to industrial growth
- decay of traditional manufacturing sectors
- massive fiscal problems and currency instability
- the erosion of the welfare state
- increased poverty
- declining living standards for most working families
- plant closings, with their disruption of community life
- decaying cities
- erosion of social services
- a general sense of alienation and powerlessness

Capitalist development can no longer rest solely on the increasing international exploitation of labor, or the hyper-exploitation of natural resources. Instead, capitalism must aggressively penetrate previously acknowledged but less pursued avenues of cultural capital, symbol systems, social relations, identity construction, and needs.[10] Thus, as Melucci suggests, "[S]ocial conflicts move from the traditional economic/industrial system to

cultur   . they affect personal identity, the time and space in everyday lif   .otivation and the cultural patterns of individual action" (1988:
826).[11] Melucci argues, as did Eric Fromm (1947) a generation earlier, that,
paradoxically, complex social systems emerge to encourage individual
empowerment, self-realization, and autonomy, since our contemporary age
is more dependent on the consumption and interpretation of information.
However, state and economic interests, requiring ever more coordination,
integration and control over these complex systems, must penetrate the daily
activities and personal lives of people.

This point garners further support from Taylor and Whittier (1995) who,
in their discussions of the relevance of postmodern theory in deconstructing
contemporary symbols of resistance, argue (consistent with NSM theorists
generally) that our contemporary postindustrial age has unleashed multiple
modes of domination leading to a broader array of resistance targets. Along
with the "media-zation" of society are numerous sites where a seemingly
endless shifting of grounded meaning produces ever greater opportunities
for social control, for example, in the workplace, school, medicine, law, and
science. Examples of contemporary modes of domination include

the rise of increasingly rationalized and abstract professional discourses of medicine, science, education, and therapy that frame and monopolize issues; the ascen-
dence of massive and reflexively monitored organizations that coordinate and
control social relations across indefinite time and spaces; and the increasing
commercialization of life experiences (1995: 181).

Melucci (1994), following Foucault, stresses the relevance of an increasing
dissemination of information which, on the one hand, offers numerous
alternatives for self-definition and creativity while simultaneously penetrating beyond the public realm into the lives of individuals, offering ever more
diffuse methods of social control. Since this is also the cultural space in
which individuals endeavor to (re)construct identity, it will inevitably be
the space where movement actors will turn to re-establish control, having
in many ways usurped the workplace as the ultimate expression of contested
terrain. For Melucci, social movement actors must engage the mainstream
distribution of information with a new discourse of alternatives.

Both Taylor and Whittier (1995) and Mellucci contend that postindustrial
actors must seek and have sought transformations within civil society,
paying particular attention to institutions, such as schools, families, media,
and religion determined as primarily responsible for the transmission of
dominant cultural codes. As an "emancipatory politics" (Giddens 1991) of
cultural transformation emerges from the ranks, not of the working class,

but of the new middle class of higher educated actors, a different kind of social movement will evolve that seeks rearticulation of identity rather than, or sometimes in addition to, reconstruction of the economic and political edifice of the country. And for Melucci, it is clear that NSMs, by their attention to the degradation and consequent realization of daily life and personal identity, have changed the look of social movements, which now seem to "detach themselves from the traditional model of political organization, and increasingly detach themselves from political systems" (1994: 103).

It is worth mentioning that while recognizing the efficacy of these claims, Brand (1990) proceeds from a cyclic and structural angle to explain the onset of NSMs. Brand deviates from the postindustrial model by associating his conjunctural analysis with the *Zeitgeist* or "cultural mood" of a particular historical period. Here Brand approaches Tarrow's (1989) emphasis on "cycles of protest and reform" in which collective action is an integral component of society and not considered pathological. From this schemata Brand hypothesizes a fairly uniform cross-cultural *Zeitgeist* emerging during the 1950s and into the 1980s, which serves as the backdrop for the NSMs of the 1990s.

In sum, the contradictions of the postindustrial age that have given way to new modes of action and new actors. They involve people who have been most heavily influenced by technological, informational, and symbolic systems. Contemporary social movement actors can no longer be thought of solely in the classical terms of social class. Their activities are increasingly seen as temporary where their primary endeavor is to reveal the stakes of our contemporary, historically specific, systemically mediated crises. Actors in NSMs are organizing over symbolic and cultural meaning, the preservation and decolonization of the lifeworld. This is what Cohen and Arato (1992) mean by a "self-limiting" revolution, or what Gyani (1993) refers to as "self-reflexive" revolution, in which NSM actors have relinquished the classical call of a "classless society." They believe that we can, √ at once, preserve our immediate lifeworld while simultaneously working toward changes at the level of state policy. We are now positioned to look more closely at characteristics that have become the hallmark of NSMs.

Elements of New Social Movements

In the following section I will discuss what is "new" in the new social movements. I will present the constituent elements of NSMs through an evaluation of their values, issues, and actors.

Values

Before we address the value system of NSM actors, it would be beneficial to return to our discussion of resource mobilization, more specifically, to Olson's articulation of the "free rider" problem. Olson held that without selective incentives, rational actors have no reason to contribute resources or time to collective action. Rational actors will weigh the relative costs and benefits of participation and, rather than engage in what is potentially harmful behavior, will allow others to carry on making both group and individual sacrifices. But while there are clearly additional considerations (e.g., organizational resources, skills, objective social problems, and so forth), it must be recognized that one's value system plays a significant part in decisions to engage social movement activities. Moreover, it is the public articulation of values—values that differ from those of other groups and organizations—that distinguishes movement actors. To be considered a social movement, actors must share at least one overriding value. Often, and this is the case with NSMs, a very abstract but nonetheless recognizable value expression appears to "name" the movement, as, for example, in the peace, environment, feminist, anti-war, and pro-choice movements (Lofland 1995: 196). Furthermore, values "call attention to the positive goals that movement members want to achieve—to realize in the 'real world' " (196).

It is clear that NSM actors distinguish themselves and the contemporaneousness of their actions by what Cohen (1985) has referred to as self-understanding, what Nedelmann (1984) has termed self-referential interest formation, and Barnes (1982) calls the new citizen. In general the belief is that contemporary actors have become increasingly autonomous in articulating their own interests, a point presented in theory by Sassoon (1984) and discussed in greater detail in Chapter 5. Actors no longer depend solely on representation by larger organizational bodies, and their modes of association are historically new, relative to both the old and new left. Whether couched in the rhetoric of classical sociological theses on modernization and the increasing cult of individuality (Nedelmann), or in the transformation of society from industrial to postindustrial (Cohen), there remains the recognition that the value systems of contemporary actors differ in substantial ways from those of preceding generations.

Perhaps the most notable contribution to the study of value transformations as they relate to NSM actors has been that of Ronald Inglehart (1977, 1990). Briefly, Inglehart argues that Western industrialized nations have witnessed a significant shift in value systems, beginning with the birth cohort 1946–55, from one characterized as materialist to one identified as postmaterialist. Basing his argument primarily on the presence of the postwar welfare state, Inglehart argues that people born prior to 1946 will tend to identify more closely with materialist values given their childhood experiences with scarcity. Relying on human development models, Inglehart hypothesizes that since personality is largely shaped during the pre-adult years, the specific epoch in which one grows to maturity will significantly influence adult political, economic, and cultural choices and activities. He confirms his hypothesis that those identified as having post-materialist values will be more likely than those without to participate in NSMs. Postmaterialists, he believes, place less emphasis on economic growth and more on the "non-economic" quality of life, have a greater regard for nature, and seek less hierarchical, more intimate and informal relations with people (Inglehart, 1988: 45). Others, including Cotgrove and Duff (1980, 1981), Kriesi and van Praag, Jr. (1987) Muller-Rommel (1985), and Feitkau (1982) have noted similar postmaterialist characteristics in NSM actors in the women's, student, environmental, and peace movements.

Other values shared by NSM actors and recognized by nearly all NSM theorists include: a belief in anti-hierarchy, anti-market, and self-government (Gundelach, 1984); self-actualization, harmony with nature, participative structures, and decentralization (Cotgrove and Duff, 1981); anti-modernism—that is, NSM actors do not accept a society based on economic growth; they seek new relationships to one's own body, the opposite sex, to work, and to consumption (Klandermans and Tarrow, 1988); and the defense of identity, continuity, and predictability of personal existence along with the reappropriation of time, space, and relationships (Melucci, 1980). In his effort to document value-based expressions in social movements, Lofland (1995) makes it clear that very few social movements endeavor to combine the list of value demands indicated above within their singular movement. That is, while there is considerable overlap between movement actors who share multiple values, the typical case has movement actors concentrating on a specific institution. Intentional communities, however, offer a glimpse of the atypical. It is likely, for example, that members of ICs will attempt to address each of the values indicated above and more. Members of ICs perceive their choice to live in community as their opportunity to craft alternative living conditions. As such, they engage the full panoply of inter-personal, intra-personal, spiritual, organizational, institutional, environmental, and agricultural and craft-based production opportunities as a matter of course. This places them at the more comprehensive end of the social movement spectrum; it also should serve notice to students of social movements that ICs require reconsideration.

To further clarify what is new relative to the values expressed by NSM actors, it is important to recognize the caveat raised by Offe (1985). Offe contends that the least "new" of the components of NSMs is their values. Indeed he quite correctly suggests that declarations of personal autonomy, individual freedom, and the like are firmly ensconced in modernity, inherited from progressive movements leading back to the Enlightenment of two centuries ago. What is unique, according to Offe, is not the values themselves, but the means with which these values will be implemented. NSM actors no longer believe that economic, political, cultural, or intra-personal reparations will emerge from technological growth, market-based production and distribution, or liberal democracy.

Issues

Dominant issues pervading NSMs have their common grounding in the values previously identified: autonomy (self-government, decentralization, self-help), identity, and opposition to manipulation, control, dependence, bureaucratization, regulation, and so forth (Offe, 1985; Kriesi, 1989; Melucci, 1985, 1985; Touraine, 1988). Issues are determined by systemic contradictions providing specific historical opportunities for conflict. Activation of contemporary issues reflects these value orientations through conflicts over the reappropriation of physical, biological, psychological, and inter-personal territory. Offe (1985) suggests that what NSM actors are claiming is the "preservation and reconstitution of civil society or lifeworld (indicating the "space of action"), such as body, health, and sexual identity; the neighborhood, city, and the physical environment; the cultural, ethnic, national, and linguistic heritage and identity; the physical conditions of life, and survival for humankind in general" (829).

Further, Melucci (1980, 1994, 1995) consistently remarks that NSMs are seeking not only the reappropriation of the material mode of production, but also symbolic and cultural production, that is, the reappropriation of time and space, and of relationships.

Speaking directly to issues confronting civil society and the reconstitution of the lifeworld, Cohen (1985) contends that NSM actors should be characterized as self-limiting. She suggests that NSM actors differ dramatically from classical social movements in at least four ways. First, they no longer believe in an undifferentiated lifeworld free of all forms of power and inequity. Second, NSM actors "limit themselves vis-a-vis one another"; that is, they actively pursue autonomy, plurality, and difference without sacrificing the "egalitarian principles of civil society or the universalistic principles of the formally democratic state (a point directed to the concerns of Piccone discussed earlier)." Third, Cohen suggests that NSM actors are more willing to negotiate with others within "their movement" concerning goals and consequences. Finally, with what is perhaps the cornerstone of her rearticulation of civil society (Cohen, 1985; Cohen and Arato, 1992), Cohen argues that contemporary actors have adopted a form of self-limiting radicalism, accepting the existence of the democratic state and market economy. Activists have engaged the reappropriation of civil society as a way to reinvigorate decentralized, representative democracy rather than articulating revolutionary rhetoric since the historical experience of the latter has typically meant the breakdown of steering mechanisms and production, followed by authoritarian attempts to establish order (Cohen and Arato, 1992; Arendt, 1958a, 1977). Here, Cohen (1985), and Cohen and Arato (1992) share their distinction with Melucci (1985), who insists that NSMs "do not fight for material goals, or to increase their participation in the system. They fight for symbolic and cultural stakes, for a different meaning and orientation of social action" (797).

Actors

Klandermans and Tarrow (1988) have identified two significant population groups predisposed to NSMs. The first group comprises those who have been marginalized by changes from modernity to postmodernity. They argue that this category of actors cannot be defined solely by class or status since the problems experienced are not limited to any particular social strata. The second group, argues Klandermans and Tarrow, comprises members of the new middle class. Additional support for the contention that the participants in contemporary collective action have emerged from the new middle classes can be found, among other places, in Cohen (1985), Offe (1985) (who agrees with the significance of the new middle class and includes members of the old bourgeoisie), Klandermans (1988), and Gundelach (1984). Moreover, Jamison and Eyerman (1991) discuss the significance of intellectuals to the successful articulation of movement demands. Following Gramsci, they argue that, while established intellectuals played a significant role in the formation of both the European and American environmental movements, organic intellectuals emerging within the movement also played a crucial role.[12]

Summary

In the paradigm of the NSMs there has been a significant shift in movement actors, issues, and values. This change has emerged as a product of postindustrial transformations in nations throughout Western Europe and the United States, producing new modes of social control and identity formation. Contemporary resistance movements have emerged to reclaim the lifeworld (to be discussed in the next section) so as to redefine self, inter-personal interaction, time, space, sexuality, love, play, work, child care, decision-making, and the like. Actors within NSMs are not organizing within traditional social movement bodies or directing their angry voices at the halls of political power; indeed, they often openly rebuke them as unable and/or unwilling to address their concerns. Rather, they have turned to civil society and lifeworld for a reconstituted cultural, political, and economic experience. I will devote the following section of this chapter to a review of each of these concepts, for it is within these two realms that the greater part of NSM activism, and in particular the mode of resistance characteristic of ICs, has been concentrated.

Conceptualizing Civil Society

Before we begin, it is worth reiterating at this point that recognition of ICs as an NSM is more than a mere intellectual exercise. Actors in NSMs are aggressively confronting postindustrial commodification, bureaucratization, and homogenization by attempting to rearticulate, primarily at the level of the lifeworld, alternate ways of living. This is especially the case for those who have embraced intentional community living. Members of ICs, like their counterparts in other NSMs (there is considerable crossover among members of ICs who are also participants in Green, feminist, peace, and civil rights organizations), began rearticulating self-identity, love, sexuality, work, conflict resolution, child care, and the like during the 1970s. Theirs is a progressive rebuke of postindustrial commodification and alienating social relations. But a similar phenomenon is apparent in other social movements throughout the United States, and indeed the world. There has been increasing evidence of a global proliferation of identity-based political, cultural, and economic movements.[13] The urgency with which I contend that a reformulated conceptualization of social movement theory is warranted, and I share this with others (e.g., Laclau and Mouffe: 1985), stems from the increased proliferation of particularisms emerging within the lifeworld and the ways in which they are perceived politically. Should those on the left (regrettably, in the United States at least, a somewhat amorphous signifier) continue to ignore the persistence and relevance of the forms of resistance emerging within the lifeworld, they risk a rearticulation of these meanings within the frame of what Laclau and Mouffe have termed "a discourse of the Right." To do so would, in my estimation, revisit the worst of the populist rhetoric unleashed during the late 19th and early 20th century.[14] The lack of recognition by the left in the United States of various opportunities for political, economic, and cultural mobilization has left some, like sociologist Todd Gitlin (1995), wondering if there even is a left in America. To address the urgency of the moment, and ferret out the conceptual details of civil society, this chapter will proceed with an analysis and discussion of Laclau and Mouffe's "radical democracy," a theoretical proposition with many parallels to my own efforts articulated here, but with significant differences. Leaving Laclau and Mouffe I will move to a discussion of civil society, particularly the innovative work of Cohen and Arato (1992), to establish the significance not only of the local, but also recognition of the needed persistance of those state-based rights that ensure protection for continued pursuit of hightened humanity. In the end, I will argue that members of ICs provide us with a state of fractured consciousness. Their persistent example of alternative constructions of public and private space, and political, economic, and cultural relations serves as a sort of counter-hegemony.[15]

Radical Democracy: Revisiting Laclau and Mouffe

While there are many similarities between the work of Laclau and Mouffe and my own, more than there are differences, differences do exist. This section offers a portrait of their most significant collective contribution to social movement theory (although it was not presented as such), established in their 1985 book, *Hegemony and Socialist Strategy*. In my estimation there are really two significant contributions to be culled from this work. The first is their effort to rearticulate Gramsci's conceptualization of hegemony consistent with their observations of "new" national and international conflicts. But their primary contribution to social movement theory and to my endeavor here is found in the chapter dedicated to "radical democracy." It is within their fourth chapter, dedicated to the explication of radical democracy, that I shall loiter longest.

While there are significant points of convergence between the emphases of Laclau and Mouffe and my own, particularly as they pertain to the relative weight granted to NSMs, and their attention to anti-essentialist theorizing, what separates us, among other things, is their relative inattention to the relevance of civil society, lifeworld, and dialogical method as contributing in significant ways to the proliferation of multiplicitous voices of resistance. Moreover (and in some ways related), they continue within the subject-object frame characteristic of dialectical thinking. It is my belief that chaos theory (or non-linear dynamics) and deconstruction, to be discussed in Chapter 4, will enhance their conceptualization of movement potential by opening their model at the level of civil society, allowing for heterogeneity rather than dualistic, primarily state-directed, oppositional voices, articulated in their work via the Gramscian "war of position."

In the previous section I presented the literature addressing the collective behavior, resource mobilization, and NSM theories. There is, to my knowledge, no recognition in any of this literature of the contribution of Laclau and Mouffe, either collaboratively, or in their prolific individual publications. Perhaps most interesting, and from my perspective most disturbing, is the fact that the NSM literature has been silent on their work, for it is NSM theory that would benefit most from integration of their insights. It is with this dearth of recognition that I begin this discussion of some of the more significant propositions emerging from within *Hegemony and Socialist Strategy*.

From the opening pages of Chapter 4, Laclau and Mouffe distinguish their vision of radical democracy from the current work of social movement theorists, and in doing so, explode the persistent foundation upon which social movement theory has rested. Recognition of modes of resistance persisting at the level of the lifeworld requires the elimination of one crucial facet of social movement theory: the traditional reliance upon state-directed conflict as a necessary component of social movement organizations. It is this "test of relevance," a litmus test of sorts for social movement theorists, that has precluded recognition of alternate forms of resistance. The theoretical origins privileging singular points of rupture can be found, argue Laclau and Mouffe, in vestiges of Jacobin and Marxist suppositions regarding the emergence of historically significant actors. Their critique is leveled at the leftist belief in "the postulation of *one* foundational moment of rupture, and of a *unique* space in which the political is constituted" (1985: 152 emphasis added). Both instrumental and structuralist Marxists, who continue to agonize over the question of class consciousness, are blind to degrees of heterogeneity constituting their "subjects." Even E. P. Thompson's (1963) classic book on the English working class, as Calhoun (1982) suggests, is guilty of glossing over significant differences among workers. This point must be made more broadly.

Articulation of a homogenous revolutionary body is fundamentally at odds with the way subjects are constituted in a postmodern/postindustrial age.[16] I have discussed elsewhere the significance of subject constitution as it relates to the proliferation of medicalization and employee drug testing.[17] Here suffice it to say that there are multiple ways in which subjects are constituted, discursively assembled through what Knights (1990) has called "a plurality of disciplinary mechanisms, technologies of surveillance, and power-knowledge strategies" (319). Following Lacan, subjects engage in a process of subjectivation at the level of the imaginary where the subject is immersed in a plurality of discursive processes of identification. Foucault goes further, using his concept of subjugation. Again according to Knights, "subjugation occurs where the freedom of a subject is directed narrowly, and in a self-disciplined fashion, towards practices which may be seen or thought to secure the acknowledgement, recognition and confirmation of self by significant others" (1990: 319).

The loss of self as described here has evolved from the individualizing effect of contemporary power-knowledge techniques, and the ubiquitous commodification of all aspects of our lives. Put another way, practices experienced at the point of production, for example, that fragment and atomize workers are significant for their apparent exacerbation of the subject's concern for security and preoccupation with control (Knights 1990: 311). Owens (1983: 67) argues that one sympton of our postmodern condition is a loss of mastery over our lives, giving way to numerous therapeutic programs (e.g., TM, biofeedback, employee assistance programs) designed to instill a renewed sense of control. Further, subjugated workers turn inward to their private lives to deflect constraints inherent in their work experiences. Here, maintenance of self is expressed through the exchange relationship (i.e., consumption), and through the sign value represented by those purchases. For Baudrillard (1981), sign values are the hierarchically ascribed attributes of status, prestige, and position associated with the acquisition of certain commodities. When placed within the theoretical context of Bourdieu (1984), sign values can be analyzed relative to their signification of the tastes and influences of dominant cultural capital.

Workers are in part constituted by a work environment that exacerbates the detrimental effects of individualization by declaring those issues directly affecting them at the point of production (e.g., types of products produced, materials used, working conditions, pace of production, and so on) beyond the parameters of negotiation. The product is an ideologically reified individualization, perpetuation of a belief in the self as a free and independent agent, but one for whom only consumption is offered as the primary means for exercising their independence and consequently attaining gratification. Recognition of the multiple ways in which subjects are constituted enables us to move beyond the static debate over the emerging revolutionary class, to focus more clearly on the multitudinous ways in which people reconstruct their reality, sometimes in unison, sometimes not. Moreover, the core of contemporary ICs centers on addressing those very issues raised by Lacan, Foucault, Baudrillard, and Bourdieu concerning identity construction, non-commodification of economic and social relations, and the like.

Returning now to the relevance of state-directed conflict as a prerequisite component of social movements, a more heterogeneous model, one sensitive to subject constitution, recognizes those social movement actors who participate in a "type of action whose objective is the transformation of a social relation which constructs a subject in a relationship of subordination" (Laclau and Mouffe 1985: 153). This emphasis clearly resonates with NSM theorists like Taylor and Whittier, and Melucci, who contextualize NSM activism in terms of resistance to the cultural diffusion of information and its consequent social control functions. Indeed, Laclau and Mouffe recognize NSMs as the bearers of a new movement potential, suggesting that they "articulate the diffusion of social conflictuality to more numerous relations which is characteristic today of advanced industrial societies" (159). In addition, NSM actors, products of "postindustrial capitalism's modes of domination," have as a significant component a responsibility to "call into question new forms of subordination." Thus far, few differences appeared to separate other NSM theorists from Laclau and Mouffe. It is at this point that their interpretations begin to separate.

In an effort to contextualize the emergence of NSMs as a product of the historical maturation of capitalist social relations, Laclau and Mouffe refer to Michael Aglietta's (1976) conceptualiztion of intensive regimes of accumulation. For Aglietta, the introduction of Fordism led to the penetration of capitalist logic into all facets of social relations. This is most remarkably seen in the proliferation of advertising during the 1940s and 1950s to initiate en masse the creation of needs to promote increased accumulation. As a result, the commodification of social life "destroyed previous social relations, replacing them with commodity relations through which the logic of capitalist accumulation penetrated into increasingly numerous spheres" (Laclau and Mouffe 1985: 161). The product, as Laclau and Mouffe recognize, has not been, as Marcuse (1964) first suggested in *One Dimensional Man*, increasing domination and subordination, but rather, a proliferation of struggles within civil society, at the level of the lifeworld, to promote life-enhancing modes of interaction.

The remainder of Chapter 4, dedicated to of Laclau and Mouffe's explication of radical democracy, emphasizes more thoroughly propositions they had been reformulating throughout *Hegemony and Socialist Strategy*: the theoretical futility and political encumbrance of searching for a singular historical agent to carry the banner of socialist revolution, and the establishment of an alternate space for the rearticulation of identity.

Almost as if anticipating the contemporary debate circulating around Amitai Etzioni (1995) and his brand of communitarianism, Laclau and Mouffe suggest that the decade of the 1960s marks a significant global clarion call constituted by the discourse of the "democratic imaginary." Neo-conservatives, suggest Laclau and Mouffe, are particularly attuned to the emergence of what they perceive to be a wave of excess democracy emerging during the 1950s and 1960s with the undesirable consequence of making the populace nearly ungovernable. Recognition of this particular period of transition is of course not unique to Laclau and Mouffe. As was indicated in the previous section, at the hub of NSM theorizing is macrostructural contextualization of those political, economic, and cultural factors differentiating our epoch from that preceding the 1960s. Where Laclau and Mouffe differ from, and in my opinion improve upon, NSM theorizing is in their description of the significance of the emergence of liberal-democratic discourse. This initiates their move closer to Cohen and Arato's (1992) emphasis on civil society, and to Habermas's (1987) and Benhabib's (1992) exposition of discourse ethics. What emerges from their recognition of the wave of democratic discourse marking the postindustrial era is their promotion of a radical pluralism. More specifically, Laclau and Mouffe are arguing for the avoidance of a theoretical return to the constitution of subjects around a unitary foundational principle. Thus, radical pluralism consists of real recognition of the uniqueness and legitimacy of independent identities. It becomes a radical and plural democracy to the extent that each societal sphere is constitutive of equivalence and egalitarian logic (1985: 167).

Having established an emphasis on the plural, Laclau and Mouffe inch closer to articulating a theoretical conceptualization of social movements similar to what I will offer in the next chapter. That is, in expanding on the "character" of radical democracy, its particular shape and feel, Laclau and Mouffe contend, as I will, that there are no guarantees as to which direction the democratic revolution will carry particular political logics, that "the discursive compass of the democratic revolution opens the way for political logics as diverse as right-wing populism and totalitarianism on the one hand, and radical democracy on the other" (1985: 168). It is apparent that what Laclau and Mouffe refer to as the "democratic revolution" is in more specific theoretical and conceptual terms defined by Cohen and Arato as civil society. This is especially clear when Laclau and Mouffe claim "the democratic revolution is simply the terrain upon which there operates a logic of displacement supported by an egalitarian imaginary" (168). Moreover, in addressing the left specifically, Laclau and Mouffe challenge those who would dismantle the liberal-democratic state, arguing instead that the left should be seeking to "expand it in the direction of a radical and plural democracy." Here they take a page directly from Cohen and Arato who, anticipating a discussion to ensue below, following the Polish independence movement, illustrate the need for self-limiting revolution around issues emerging within civil society. The revolution is self-limiting in that it seeks not to dismantle democratic provisions guaranteed by the constitution, but to strengthen those that enhance the pursuit of renewed identity construction, to decrease commodification of social relations and enhance communication with members of differing geographic locales, and so forth. It is worth mentioning at this point, although I will elaborate on it in detail in the next chapter, that provisions ensured by a democratic constitution signify one of the wings of the butterfly attractor in theories of chaos. Dynamical systems can be visualized as producing two separate but interrelated outcome basins (what chaos theorists refer to as a phase space) generating what in essence appears as two wings of a butterfly. In this instance, the other wing signifies recognition of immutable competing representations of meaning constituting the lifeworld, what Laclau and Mouffe have referred to as the proliferation of the "polysemic character of antagonisms." The emphasis, as it is in chaos theory, is on the persistence of heterogeneity bounded by order. Order is procured by the recognition and expansion of those provisions in democratic constitutions identifying the parameters of social intercourse (e.g., free speech, free assembly, and the like).

Laclau and Mouffe conclude this chapter by contending that the primary obstacle confronting efforts to establish radical democracy, particularly for the traditional left, appears in the persistent a priori search for "agents of change, levels of effectiveness in the field of the social, and privileged points and moments of rupture" (1985: 178). I have applied this same critique to theorists of ICs (e.g., Kanter, Zablocki) who, in their efforts to document specific moments of rupture, perpetrate essentialism. Literature addressing the historical emergence of communitarian "experiments" typically conceive of them in terms of fixed moments of socio-political rupture. That is,

as a historical phenomenon they have an identifiable morphology constituted by birth, growth, and decay. The problem with such an essentialistic
perception of any movement actors or organizations, but particularly intentional communitarians, is that efforts to fix a singular nodal point of rupture
ignores the "constant displacement of the nodal points structuring a social
formation."[18] Ultimately the ramifications of morphological representations of social movement actors appear in the stunted ability of the left
to effectively recognize the persistence of oppressed and subordinated
peoples sempiternally contributing to a rearticulated construction of meaning at the level of the lifeworld. More specifically, these representations
have drawn sociologists and others who study ICs to the misleading
conclusion that the success of ICs can be determined solely by their ability
to outlive a few generations of researchers. Representative of both literal
and symbolic cultural phenomena, the meaning of ICs, their practices and
behaviors, has an impact that cannot be measured with any exactitude
beyond the effect it has for the members themselves. As actors interacting
at the level of the lifeworld, members of ICs are but one of a plethora of
competing discourses seeking a rearticulation of sedimented identity. Do
their innovations in farming, sexuality, work, gender relations, conflict
resolution, ecology, child rearing, and the like spark interest from the
surrounding communities? Sometimes yes, sometimes no. But to cast them
off as "utopian" while continuing to search for the working-class revolutionary agent seems intellectually shortsighted and politically dangerous.

Indeed, once essentialism has been removed from the scope of identifying a unified working class, once we accept the unique ways in which
workers perceive themselves, their antagonisms, their relationship to trade
unions, the state, and so forth, a more heterogeneous portrait of workers'
struggles unfolds. It then becomes possible to articulate more thoroughly
the resurgence of "independence movements" within the labor movement
itself, such as emerged during the 1960s and 1970s in Europe, and in the
1980s in the United States. The New Directions Movement, Black caucuses,
Latino caucuses, women's caucuses, gay and lesbian caucuses, and environmental caucuses, all play a significant role in the articulation of what is
conceived as organized labor in the United States.

In sum, Laclau and Mouffe initiate a stimulating polemic around possible
directions for social movement theory. They clearly perceive the need to
explode the dominance of essentialist theorizing (often taking penetrating
aim at their kindred colleagues on the left) as it relates to privileging a priori
historical moments of rupture and those revolutionary agents who will see
us to socialism. By doing so they reveal the terrain of discourse as multitu-

dinous and competing. Their application of Gramsci's conceptualization of hegemony indicates their recognition of the "war of position" over which competing actors and interests struggle for preeminence in the explication of issues and events. This is why, they suggest, the left must pay closer attention to those struggles identified as NSMs which have attempted to rearticulate identity. Ignoring them or rebuking them as just so much particularism leaves these groups open to the hegemonic articulation of the right. Clearly this is the concern of many who have witnessed the rise of Etzioni's brand of communitarianism. While many on the left have shunned communitarianism as right-wing ideology, it is clear that communitarianism plays to concerns of people at the level of the lifeworld. Rightists pleas for a rejuvinated public morality around community responsibility, child care, family, work, and the like identify, in the writings of some communitarians at least, similar passions for a humanist usurpation of capitalist social relations raised by many leftists, particularly Greens. Communitarians, however, with a few notable exceptions, lack the theoretical sophistication to put forth a coherent critique of capitalist social relations. But my point is that despite their lack of theoretical clarity, they have spoken to seminal concerns expressed in various ways among American people. ICs have engaged many of these same concerns; indeed they are what constitute their existence. They could represent for the left a real alternative to the proliferation of Etzionian Republican communitariansm, which, despite protests to the contrary, smacks of authoritarian oppression and restraint. Whether the left begins to recognize ICs as worthy of consideration, I believe, depends on the reconceptualization of social movement theory to include alternate forms of resistance.

Laclau and Mouffe initiate a move away from a purely NSM analysis by conceptualizing multiple avenues to realizing radical democracy. In so doing, they offer a conceptual bridge to shift our discussion in the next chapter on chaos theory away from what is now a fairly solid base in NSM theorizing toward a theory of social movements that explodes conventional conceptualizations. But this will have to wait.

Having recognized in Laclau and Mouffe considerable contributions to a rearticulated theory of social movements does not mean that they have captured in totem the essense of what must be done. Indeed, what is most unfortunate in this work is the neglect of a more coherent conceptualization of civil society. Laclau and Mouffe seem forced to return too often to convoluted and sometimes abstract language to describe the characteristics of democratic revolution. A theory of civil society accompanied by some discussion of discourse ethics would have provided a more lucid rendering and, in my opinion, would have strengthened their articulation of radical democracy. It is to this discussion that we now turn.

Contemporary Civil Society as a Locus of Change

Academics generally hold that the contemporary re-emergence of the debate over civil society was initiated in and around recent struggles for liberation in Eastern Europe.[19] This concluding section will address the contemporary articulation of civil society to identify those social spaces conducive to the emergence and proliferation of resistance at the level of the lifeworld. This is necessary since social movement theorists have recognized that actors participating as members of NSMs are demanding political, economic, and cultural changes, not primarily from the state, as with traditional social movement actors, but rather from institutions constituting civil society, and that we are witnessing now the perpetration by movement actors of self-limiting or self-reflexive revolution. Below is a brief historical explication of the evolution of the concept of civil society to locate its contemporary version within some historical context. This section will conclude with an emphasis on the more recent work of Cohen and Arato and the publication of their influential book, *Civil Society and Political Theory*. Cohen and Arato have established a move toward a synthesis of civil society and discourse analysis that addresses the limitations of Laclau and Mouffe's theoretical contribution just discussed. It is, in my estimation, the most lucid and theoretically precise account of the concept of civil society and it stimulates recognition of the multiplicitous modes of resistance resonating there.

The idea of civil society has experienced two significant historical transformations, one emanating from its eighteenth-century conceptualization as a realm of social mutuality, and the other from its nineteenth-century explication as a social space separate from the state. More recently, civil society has been variously conceived as a complex of autonomous institutions, relationships, and civil manners,[20] as the "terrain of democratization,"[21] and as the "third realm," or "societal community."[22] What each of these conceptualizations of civil society possess in common is a persistent nagging and seemingly paradoxical struggle to mediate between the public and the private. That is, that articulations of civil society originating in the nineteenth century and continuing in contemporary literatures and debates[23] have as their primary endeavor the explication of the parameters of influence generated by autonomous institutions and relationships external to the state.[24] Thus, common in the nineteenth century, in each of its Enlightenment forms (French, Scottish, and German), was the "problematic relation between the private and the public, the individual and the social, public ethics and individual interests, individual passions and public concerns" (Seligman, 1992: 5).

The contemporary revival of civil society as a locus of semi-autonomous modes of resistance follows in the wake of Eastern European efforts to restate the relevance of the "Public Man." While occidental nations have retained paramount recognition of civil society in its relationship to the state, Eastern European countries, forced for so long to subsume civil society to the interests of the state, view the contemporary proliferation of civil society (political parties, limited rights to assembly, speech, and the like) as paramount to a new freedom. This can be seen most vividly in the Polish struggle for freedom beginning in the 1970s, and in the emergence of the "Second left" in France.

The history of Poland from the late eighteenth century through the mid-twentieth century is riddled with occupations by Prussia, Austria, Russia, and Germany, leaving Poland without an autonomous state in modern times.[25] As a consequence, the idea of civil society offered the only viable political alternative to political repression (Seligman, 1992).[26] Faced with the limited success of revolution from below or reform from above, Polish theorists like Adam Michnik (1985) suggested a middle ground, what Michnik refered to as "new evolutionism."[27] According to Michnik, the juxtaposition of civil society and to the state reconfigures modes of resistance formerly directed at the transformation of society as a whole to now encompasse only those institutions constituting civil society. To achieve the "new evolutionism" Michnik called for, Poles would be encouraged to follow the politically efficacious path of self-limiting revolution initiated by Jacek Kuron (1981). I will return to this concept later, but a few words here should provide a clearer sense of how interpretations of civil society have changed over the past two hundred years.

In making their case for the legitimacy and manifestation of the concept self-limiting revolution, Cohen and Arato (1992), inspired by work of Hanna Arendt (1951, 1963), argue that "[a]ll major revolutions from the French to the Russian and the Chinese not only demobilized the social forces on which they originally depended but also established dictatorial conditions that were meant to block the reemergence of such forces at their very root for as long as possible" (32). In more thoroughly probing the meaning of self-limiting revolution within the Polish context, Cohen and Arato also cite Michnik, who views his activism as being stirred by the ability to mobilize activity from below by "constructing a highly articulated, organized, autonomous, and mobilized civil society" (Cohen and Arato, 1992: 32).

But in Poland there was, and continues to be, significant theoretical and political debate regarding conceptual problems over the actual meaning and literal translation of civil society. For example, would the Polish model of civil society according to Michnik fuse well with the liberal model of economic individualism adopted following the political successes of Solidarity? Since the model of civil society espoused by Polish intellectuals was to be pluralistic, was there any contradiction when an organizational oversight body was temporarily accepted? Would it be dismantled? Cohen and Arato suggest that there was no clear consensus on whether the Polish model of civil society would, following the example of Solidarity, be apolitical in matters of the state, or whether it would expand its efforts toward the construction of a separate republic. Examples of both could be found in the prevailing rhetoric. Despite dramatic successes in the construction of a stable model of civil society, Poland, Michnik contends, did establish a foundation for the construction of an independent sociocultural space for the proliferation of lectures, publications, teaching, and discussing. The French case offers additional insight.

While the historical experience with liberal democracy in France may at first pass seem to preclude any correlation between French interests in a rearticulated civil society and that of Eastern Europeans, there are certain similarities. French intellectuals and political activists affiliated with the second left have largely been responsible for the increased attention to civil society in France. Authors like Andre Gorz, Alain Touraine, Michel Foucault, Cornelius Castriadis, Pierre Rosanvallon, Patrick Viveret, Pierre Bourdieu, and Claud Lefort have each, in their own way and with their specific emphases, referred to the increasingly "totalitarian" nature of the French state. It is totalitarian to the degree that, relative to their occidental contemporaries in Europe and in the United States at least, the French state subsumes with greater voracity those aspects of private and public life considered to fall within the realm of civil society. Much like the penetration of capitalist social relations into all aspects of public and private life discussed in the previous section, the state now wields significant controlling influence over day-to-day activities, particularly through its adiministration of social services.[28] For Pierre Rosanvallon, for example, the welfare state destroys "social networks and forms of mutuality, self-help, and lateral cooperation by systematically organized functions." It does so by "disorganizing social networks, associations and solidarities," replacing them with "state-administrative relations." As an answer to the increasing encroachment of the welfare state, Rosanvallon (1981) offers neither liberalism nor statism but rather those efforts constituting "privately based collective service and underground forms of non-market, non-state-oriented structures of economic life." While he refers to these efforts as significant in themselves, he primarily recognizes them as the stepping stones of a much larger program to develop a renewed public sphere.

For the French, civil society is separate from political society and each is differentiated from the state, a conceptual line of theorizing that can trace its roots to Tocqueville. According to Cohen and Arato, the French view civil society as "social associations cutting across class relations: neighborhood groups, networks of mutual aid, locally based structures providing collective service (1992: 38). Furthermore, and this is where the relevance of civil society for our concerns becomes apparent, the French conceive of civil society as that social space responsible for the incubation of nascent forms of social experimentation.

With this revised conceptualization of civil society, struggles for democracy previously directed toward the disparate poles of revolution or democratic reform now appear on the terrain of civil society carried by semi-autonomous "groups, associations, and public spaces." Or, echoing the refrain of Kuron and the Solidarity movement, we see in France an evolving interest in the energetic promotion of self-limiting revolution. Moreover, following Lefort (1986), Lipset (1983), and Seligman (1992), actors are no longer conceived of in terms of a privileged class, but rather as participants in social movements.

The American experience with civil society differs dramatically from both the Eastern and Western European experience. According to Seligman, American culture was embued with the two most significant philosophical, political, and economic constructs necessary to realize civil society: "Reason (as the equality of citizens), and the individual—as well as the locus of these ideas in the traditions of ascetic—Protestantism" (1992: 111). Add to this the absence of a feudal tradition and you have not only a uniquely articulated civil society in America, one in which socialist efforts to expand political, cultural, and economic freedoms were largely stifled, but also the persistence of social movements as indicative of historically relevant political perturbations. Seligman contends that articulation of political participation in terms of social movements and not political parties is uniquely American, and that it stems from our unique mixture of "metaphysical equality," individual autonomy, Protestantism, and a historical context free of feudalism. Efforts in France to reconceptualize political participation and self-limiting struggles for democratization as consisting primarily of social movements and not classes exemplify the French dedication to the separation of civil and political society, which in a sense may be viewed as a move away from the classical nineteenth-century European model of civil society toward a model more like the American experience.

Other considerable efforts to reconstruct civil society have emerged over the last twenty years in Germany and Latin America. The German case has primarily revolved around the theoretical accomplishments of Claus Offe, and to some extent Andre Gorz, and the political organization of the Greens. Much of the radical left critique in Germany, as was also the case in France, centered on the intrusive and sometimes manipulative welfare state policies directed at various spheres of civil society: family, schools, or cultural institutions, (Cohen and Arato, 1992: 42). Moreover, welfare state policies proved an ineffective means for the administration of economic steering. This, coupled with the fiscal constraints produced by hefty public expenditures, has propagated two decades of both radical and neo-conservative critique.

Neo-conservatives proposed a reconstruction of civil society in the image of laissez-faire capitalist economic relations, a vision of the lifeworld uncontaminated, not by the state, but by political society. In an effort to re-establish authoritative relations within the cultural sphere. The radical left, particularly the Greens,[29] on the other hand, initiated their critique of the welfare state by echoing the deleterious consequences of state-based steering on local associations, solidarity, and the like. For Offe (1985), NSMs are viewed as the progenitors of what he refers to as "non-statist socialism," an alternative to liberal democracy and the welfare state. That is, NSMs reclaim the realm of civil society as the locus of reconstituted identity.

In Latin America the case is more complicated. It is clear that Latin American authors have recognized civil society as a crucial component of democratization processes. Generally, however, the conceptualization of civil society in Latin America corresponds to its East, East Central, and Western European counterparts. Careful references to Guillermo O'Donnell et al. (1986) *Transitions From Authoritarian Rule* identify a proliferation of associations, church groups, and local governments persisting in the face of authoritarian regimes. Recurring themes in this literature include declarations of the right to assembly, to freedom of expression (including, but not limited to, speech acts), and the presence of social movements. Here, civil society is viewed as the cultural sphere comprising semi-autonomous associations mediating between individuals and the state, the public and the private.

Having suggested through the brief discussion of four different "cases" the re-emergence of the concept of civil society, I would like now to step back and consider, also in brief, the contemporary origins of the concept. This will by no means represent a thorough rendering, but rather a schematic presentation of the concept of civil society which can then be applied in Chapter 5, to our interest in resistance and intentional community.

Prior to the eighteenth century, references to civil society constituted a series of interpretations and often misleading translations of the original Aristotelian conceptualization. Aristotle conceived of civil society as the realm of the *zoon politikon*, the political animal. The concept was first conceived under the heading *politike koinonia*, or political community, and consisted of "a public ethical-political community of free and equal citizens under a legally defined system of rule" (Cohen and Arato, 1992: 84). There was no separation between the state and society; all interactions, regardless of how private or public, fell within the purview of *politike koinonia*, thus moving closer to our perception of "society." From all appearances it is the Aristotelian conceptualization that, according to Cohen and Arato, entered into the tradition of political philosophy.

Between the ancient Greek and the eighteenth-century renderings of civil society was the period of monarchical autonomy that opposed the republic to the *Standestaat*, which "balanced the new powers of the prince with that of the organized, corporate estates that assembeled all those having power and status in feudal society" (Cohen and Arato, 1992: 86). This period has typically, and mistakenly, according to Otto Brunner, been compared with the appearance of civil society against the state. However, as Cohen and Arato insist, following Marx, the old corporate society was predominantly political, bringing it closer to Aristotle's *politike koinonia* than even eighteenth-century configurations. What is interesting, and I'll elaborate more on this later, is that Cohen and Arato see the irruption of civil society throughout Europe during the medieval period following the emergence of the modern state. They contend that the disintegration of the *Standestaat* as a product of the consolidated power and authority of the prince did not eliminate those corporate interests formerly constituting its politically legitimate counterweight. It produced instead a "society of orders." Through the creation and proliferation of associations and private interest groups (religious and economic), corporate and estate interests reassembled to challenge the reign of monarchical authority, producing in effect a "countermovement" of the "society against the state." Resulting forms of independent association led Cohen and Arato to the conclusion that "there is no doubt that the 'society' of the Enlightenment, constituting a new form of public life, was the prototype of the early modern concept of civil society" (87). Here, they appear to challenge Seligman's articulation of an "American Exceptionalism," citing instead evidence of an embryonic civil society in Western Europe. Consider France, where the anti-absolutist theorizing of Montesquieu, the critique of extreme wealth and privilege in Voltaire, and still some remnants of the conflation of civil society with political society found in the writings of Rousseau resonated with the cultural emergence of independent publications, political assemblies, and coffee shop, club and salon conversation, each indicative of a semi-autonomous sphere of cultural and political activity separate from the state. So unlike Seligman,[30] who argues for a uniquely American conceptualization of civil society, Cohen and Arato recognize in France, especially in the publication of Thomas Paine's *Common Sense* and the French *Declaration of the Rights of Man and Citizen*, an expression of an independent sphere of legitimate authority separate from even the constitutional state.

In England, despite the erosion of Locke's ambiguous formulation of society separate from the state, civil society came to be associated with civility, manners, and a moral code for high society. The contributions of Ferguson, Hume, and Smith, evolving as they did from the Scottish Enlightenment, incorporated the English emphasis on civility and added the procurement of economic and material security. For example, Adam Ferguson's articulation of civil society in *An Essay on the History of Civil Society* primarily referred to "a society of less barbarous manners, a society which practised the cultivation of the mind by arts and letters. Civil society was seen as one in which urban life and commercial activities flourished" (Shils, 1991: 5).

What is most significant in the work of Locke, Ferguson, Smith, and Hume is their epistemological break with theological prescriptions of the social order. The classical vision was unique in that its conceptualization of civil society presented the "social space of human interaction as a moral sphere," rather than a neutral space comprising competing groups and associations. What made their vision truly unique, according to Seligman, was their "coupling of a vision of society with that moral field implied by the term civil society while, at the same time, rooting this field in an inner-worldly logic and not in a transcendent reality" (1992: 31). Transcending Locke, Ferguson articulated this difficult relationship as one characterized by the balance of reason and interests, the pursuit of the common good while remaining cognizant of passion. He did so by retreating from the transcendent components of Lockean natural law, the belief that human agents are godly subjects, and articulating a more positivistic conceptualization of the agent/society continuum; that is, "the knowledge of the universal was to be attained through a collection of particulars under general headings" (Seligman, 1992: 35). Here Enlightenment thinking "managed to articulate a representative vision of civil society where the particular and the universal, the private and the public, were indeed united within one field of meanings" (Seligman, 1992: 35). Ferguson's attempt to establish the unity of reason and moral sentiment would later be critiqued by a host of philosophers and political theorists, most poignantly by Hume. Hume is notable in this section for the absense of a theory of civil society. Hume rebuked the very grounds Ferguson and others writing in the Scottish Enlightenment had established to construct their image of civil society by declaring the unification of moral sentiment with reason inherently contradictory. Hume argues:

Since morals have an influence on the actions and affections, it follows, that they cannot be deriv'd from reason; and that because reason alone, as we have already prov'd, can never have any such influence. Morals excite passions, and produce or prevent actions. Reason of itself is utterly impotent in this particular. The rules of morality, therefore, are not conclusions of our Reason. (in Seligman, 1992: 37)

So it is for Hume, as for Adam Smith, that reason exists solely as the "calculus of individual or particular goods." The perceived selfishness that characterizes humanity, enjoined by the scarceness of resources, seemed to Hume the most significant reasons for pursuing common interests in the form of justice.

In Germany, the scope of civil society was even more sharply focused primarily due to the theoretical innovations of Kant and Fichte. While clearly influenced by English, Scottish, and French configurations of civil society, influences that become more apparent in Hegel, Kant and Fichte distinguished their portrait of civil society in the way in which they juxtaposed it to the more self-absorbed, rationalistic, and commercial activities of dominant culture. For Seligman, it is only in the writings of Kant that the traditional preoccupation with the series of dualisms characteristic of the public/private dichotomy (i.e., particular/individual and universal/social) is fully articulated (1992: 41).

Kant is notable for his designation of the agentic individual constituted by a transcendent reason. An articulated universality of a subject-centered pursuit of reason surmounted the traditional bifurcation of public/private, individual/social. But perhaps most important, practical reason, for Kant, was fully realized only in communion with "the juridical community of citizens." That is, it was only in the public realm that "the workings of

Reason could be substantiated" (Seligman, 1992: 43). Here we also have the first fully enunciated differentiation between civil society and the state. Civil society appeared as a separate cultural sphere constituted by rigorous, informed public debate, a sphere noticably different from the state or political society. The Kantian vision of a juridically composed sphere of reason distinguished itself from traditional theorizing on civil society by separating the sphere of morality from the sphere of the juridical community.[31]

In Fichte, as with Kant, one sees the separation of civil society from the state, as well as recognition of the coexistence of the individual and the universal subsumed in the social. In general, the German Romantics offered a more thoroughly articulated conceptualization of "folk" society. For German theorists the folk society represented "a small local society, dominated by tradition and history; it was a society in a condition where "status" governed action: the individual had no standing on the basis of his individual qualities and achievements. It was a society of agriculturalists and craftsmen in small communities largely self-contained" (Shils, 1991: 5).

These ideas appear later in the work of Tonnies (1957), Durkheim (1984), Weber (1976), Wirth (1938), and others to capture the often deleterious consequences of the occidental accent on individualism, urbanization, commercialism, and rational thought.

The eighteenth-century innovations of Kant and Fichte gave way to the nineteenth-century contributions of Hegel and Marx who, while recognizably different, returned in their own ways to the Scottish Enlightenment for a conception of civil society that sought to reconstitute it of both the moral and juridical.

For Hegel, civil society comprised the economic activity of the social, the heteronomous convolutions of the market, its institutions and social relations, in addition to affiliated associations and group representations of super-individual interests. Perhaps Hegel's most compelling and controversial addition (particularly among Marxist and utilitarian theorists) to the traditional literature, established the individual procurement of private property as an "indispensable feature of civil society." Hegel's conceptualization of civil society rested on three pivotal syntheses:

First, Hegel took over from the natural-law tradition and from Kant the universalist definition of the individual as the bearer of rights and the agent of moral conscience. Second, he generalized the Enlightenment distinction between state and civil society in a manner that also involved their interpenetration. Third, he took over from Ferguson and the new discipline of political economy the stress on civil society as the locus and carrier of material civilization. (Cohen and Arato, 1992: 92)

Civil society, for Hegel, was the site of conflicting interests that would inevitably invite its destruction. Participation within civil society in "Corporations" comprising representations of individual interests and desires served, for Hegel, to cement the private with the public, thereby overcoming the conundrum confounding the antinomies of Ferguson. However, participation in corporations was limited to those organized into "Estates," effectively occluding day laborers and the poor. Their fate would befall the state wherein the moral and the ethical, and so too, freedom, were constituted. Unlike the Scottish philosophers who sought to locate the moral and ethical within the realm of society, Hegel imbued the state with moral and ethical oversight. The full realization of civil society could be attained only in its sublimation to the benevolent state, in Hegel, the paragon of freedom. Marx, like Hegel, imbued civil society with a moral and ethical component; however, in genuine Feuerbachian fashion, Marx inverted Hegel's juxtaposition of civil society and state.

In his evaluation of Marx's articulation of civil society, Hunt (1987) contends that Marx's thinking on the topic traversed three distinct periods of his political and intellectual development. Only the first and second (transitional) stages are relevant to our concerns here. Hunt suggests that the concept of civil society is integral to the work of the young Marx, particularly in publications preceding his economic work (*Critique of Hegel's Doctrine of the State* and *On the Jewish Question*) in which he inverts Hegel's conceptualization of the juxtaposition between civil society and the state. In the transitional period Marx perceives civil society ideologically; it represents "social relations in general."

For the young Marx, civil society necessitates the attention of radical critiques, like the one professed in the *Declaration of the Rights of Man and of the Citizen*, because it is there that social relations have severed the ties between human beings. Marx is particularly critical of the preservation of private property as a component of liberty since it merely promotes the "right of self-interest." In contrast to Hegel, Marx vehemently opposes any notion that the state will defend the interests of the unrepresented within civil society. He argues, with specific reference to the 1793 declaration and much like contemporary European welfare-state critics, that the independent and often "political" realm of civil society has given way to the affairs of state which has "necessarily smashed all estates, corporations, guilds and privileges," and has "raised state affairs to become affairs of the people" (Hunt, 1987: 24). Despite his critique, Marx, at this time, was unable to provide a "positive" conception of civil society as the locus of species-being. For this we would await publication of the *German Ideology*.

In what is perhaps the most often cited passage referring to civil society, Marx and Engels (1975: 50, 89) declare the following:

The form of intercourse determined by the existing productive forces at all previous historical stages, and in its turn determining these, is *civil society*. It has as its premises and basis the simple family and the multiple, called the tribe.

Civil society embraces the whole material intercourse of individuals within a definite stage of the development of productive forces. It embraces the whole commercial and industrial life of a given stage and, insofar, transcends the state and the nation, though, on the other hand again, it must assert itself in its foreign relations as nationality and inwardly must organize itself against the state. Civil society as such only develops with the Bourgeoisie; the social organization evolving directly out of production and commerce, which in all ages forms the basis of the state and the rest of the idealistic superstructure, has however, always been designated by the same name.

Two competing interpretations have emerged from this passage. First, it is conceivable that Marx and Engels are suggesting, much like Cohen and Arato, a three-tiered model in which civil society as the realm of social relations is differentiated from the "productive-forces" and the "state" (a component of the superstructure). The second interpretation stems from Engels's conflation of civil society with the economic base. Hunt (1987) suggests that Engels has "read the base-superstructure distinction of the mature Marx back into the civil society-state distinction of the early Marx" (28). Here, civil society represented a "society in which the propertyless mass of the population was coercively held in subjugation by the owners of the instruments of production" (Shils, 1991: 6). What constituted civil society were those class-based social relations historically determined by the mode of production.

Three persistent themes characterized nineteenth-century articulations of civil society: recognition of a cultural sphere distinct from the state; a sphere that provided for the preservation of individual rights, particularly rights granting individual procurement of private property; and recognition of the existence of numerous associations of sometimes divergent opinions and interests interacting without the intrusion of the state. The final section of this chapter will provide an account of contemporary theorizing on civil society. It is my hope that recognition of a cultural sphere uniquely constructed and preserved for dialogical intercourse by agentic individuals over political, economic, and cultural issues will move us closer to appreciation of the implications of activities and modes of resistance within this sphere.

Contemporary Articulation of Civil Society:
The Synthesis of Cohen and Arato

Among the seminal contributions to our contemporary understanding of civil society, Cohen and Arato (1992) have advanced perhaps the most lucid and the most synthesized account since Hegel. Their predominant influences are sociologists Talcott Parsons and Niklas Luhmann, political theorists Hannah Arendt, Jurgen Habermas, and Antonio Gramsci, and poststructuralist Michel Foucault. While interesting, explication of this theoretical lineage is beyond the scope of our concerns here, so this concluding section will be reserved for a review of Chapter 9 in their book *Civil Society and Political Theory*. In this chapter Cohen and Arato offer their synthesis of the theorists referred to above, and in so doing offer an Archimedian point of departure.

At the heart of their analysis lies the primary concern expressed by Etzionian communitarians, Rawlsian liberals, and members of NSMs alike: how to construct a cultural sphere imbued with rights and responsibilities, separate from the state (and in Cohen and Arato, the economy), where agentic actors can interact in dialogical intercourse to produce truly democratic, perhaps radically democratic, societies.

Cohen and Arato take their first step in synthesizing the work of twentieth-century theorists by recognizing the contributions of Gramsci and Parsons to the construction of a tri-partite conceptualization of civil society-state-economy. This distinguishes them from pre-twentieth-century theorizing, which presented a dichotomous model of civil society emphasizing in various ways a distinction between it and the state. The antinomies of Gramscian and Parsonian thought, however, have propelled their move to a more diversified conceptualization of civil society, one that neither regresses into the state-civil society model (Gramsci) nor methodologically equates each sphere, as Parsons did with his conceptualization of the societal community. Gramsci relegates the role of civil society to an extension of the state, each with the responsibility for reproducing the economy. Unlike Gramsci, Parsons clearly designates the societal community as a distinct sphere separate from state relations and the economy. However, his insistence that they be treated as methodologically equal subsystems ignores the deleterious impact on civil society of an expanding welfare state and the increasing commodification of social relations stemming from seemingly uncontrollable capitalist expansion. The answer, for Cohen and Arato, is Habermas's "critique of functionalist reason" found in his two-volume compendium *The Theory of Communicative Action*. They begin by turning to Habermas's conceptualization of the distinction between lifeworld and system.

Lifeworld for Habermas realizes a synthesis of Durkheim's conscience collective, Parsons's societal community, and symbolic interaction of George Herbert Mead. The primary emphasis for each of these theorists is on the institutional socialization of subjects where social integration is the primary focus. Habermas's contribution to these earlier efforts is his emphasis on a multidimensional communicative action. Habermas initiates his exploration of the lifeworld with references to the phenomenological notion of the *Lebenswelt*, which Habermas referred to as the "always already" present horizon of cultural codes for guiding human interaction. Believing this conceptualization still too embossed in consciousness, he pushes further the relevance of communicative interaction by identifying the lifeworld as "taken-for-granted background assumptions and naively mastered skills" and "a culturally transmitted and linguistically organized stock of interpretive patterns." In his translation of the second volume of *The Theory of Communicative Action*, McCarthy (1989: xxvi) suggests the following interpretation of the lifeworld:

In the form of "language" and "culture" this resevoir of implicit knowledge supplies actors with unproblematic background convictions upon which they draw in the negotiation of common definitions of situations an indeterminate and inexhaustable background of unquestioned presuppositions, a shared global preunderstanding that is prior to any problems or disagreements.

Cohen and Arato, in their interpretation of lifeworld, acknowledge those components suggested by McCarthy, arguing further that the lifeworld "refers to a resevoir of implicitly known traditions, the background assumptions that are embedded in language and culture and drawn upon by individuals in everyday life" (1992: 428). Actors are never completely free to withdraw from or to question the totality of the lifeworld.

What is most interesting in the work of Habermas as it pertains to his conceptualization of the lifeworld is recognition of the structural differentiation that has emerged as a product of the modernization process. Following Weber and Parsons, Habermas establishes the presence within the lifeworld of three structural components: culture, society, and personality. In combination, the structural components ensure the acceptance by an aggregate social group of normatively held prescriptions for behavior. System integration, cultural reproduction, and socialization occur to the extent that the stock of cultural capital (Bourdieu) or the "reservoir of known traditions" is sempiternally engaged in a communicative process of evaluation and reevaluation. Most important for Cohen and Arato is that this structural differentiation of the lifeworld occurs due to the emergence of institutions responsible for the "reproduction of traditions, solidarities, and identities." Habermas's innovation is to envision within the lifeworld the requisite structural components of social life necessary for a rearticulated democratic sphere of communicatively based interaction. But to promote a conceptualization of civil society sensitive to hermeneutic and pheno-menological experiences required "reconstruction" of the structural com-ponents of the lifeworld. That is, Habermas sought a return to culture, society, and personality in an effort to reconstruct those long sedimented cultural codes constituting traditional knowledges, solidarites, and person-alities. Here, the Habermasian "third way" becomes apparent because the institutions recognized as comprising the lifeworld involve neither the modernist steering mechanisms of money (economy) or power (rationlized organizations). So while Habermas clearly articulates a tripartite model of civil society, he avoids the methodological functionalism of Parsons by recognizing the obvious influences that the steering mechanisms of money and power have on institutions within the lifeworld. For him, these steering media penetrate the lifeworld through the vehicle of the law.

Cultural Modernization

For Habermas, following Nietzsche, Weber, and the neo-Kantians, cul-tural rationalization is the only possible road to modernization of the lifeworld generating "reflexive associations, publicity, solidarity, and iden-tity." Much like the emphasis in chaos theory and deconstruction, a (post)modernization of culture would "open up" cultural capital to reflexive interpretations of core values, traditions, and norms.[32] For Habermas the product is a non-normatively constructed consensus derived from commu-nicatively informed debate where communicative action refers to "a linguis-tically mediated, intersubjective process through which actors establish their interpersonal relations, question and reinterpret norms, and coordinate their interaction by negotiating definitions of the situation and coming to an agreement" (Cohen and Arato, 1992: 435).

Here, Etzioni's communitarian concern with the flight of tradition is mediated by a communicative process that actually modernizes tradition. The result is a reflexive "nontraditional relation to tradition." From the rationalization of culture circulates in Durkheimian fashion a collective effervescence cultivated by a sphere of activity, encouraging the prolifera-tion of voluntary associations and often unconventional identity construction, morality, spirituality, artistic expression, literary critique, science (chaos theory?), and so on. Perhaps in a way returning to pre-twentieth-century concerns, "the modernization of the lifeworld is the foundation for the parallelism between individual, social, and cultural forms of moral consciousness" (Cohen and Arato, 1992: 436). A discursively constituted, expanded, and increasingly differentiated lifeworld would facilitate the constitution of autonomous and reflexive individuals transcending boundaries between contemporary and traditional role responsibilities. The legitimacy of tradition, rather than being bound in unquestioned role expectations, is determined by its inventive appropriation when juxtaposed to contemporary political, economic, and cultural meanings.

Habermas initiates exposition of an expanded comprehension of political participation through his articulation of "discursive will formation." Unlike Arendt's (1968, 1973) conceptualization of public space as the terrain of agonistic intercourse directed toward political advantage, or Bruce Ackerman's (1980) pleas for a public space bound by neutrality, Habermas envisions a public space constituted by open public debate involving all who might be affected by the ramifications of public policy decisions or local and super-local normative content. Habermas's version of public space is unique relative to the republican or liberal models. His emphasis is on the construction of an "ideal speech situation" capable of engaging divergent actors in dialogical intercourse to perpetually validate political, economic, and cultural mandates. Participants in ideal speech situations must be constituted by two normative constraints: universal moral respect and egalitarian reciprocity (Habermas, 1989: 105). These constraints serve to stay majoritarian dominance.

Opposition to Habermas's conceptualization of ideal speech situations often centers on precisely what is and what is not open for public debate. Kenneth Baynes (1988), much like Rawls, argues for the imposition of "substantive constraints" on discourse as a way of avoiding the disintegration of our "most deeply held moral convictions." Baynes suggests that preservation of the U.S. Constitution would serve to contextualize most public discourse, a belief shared by Cohen and Arato. But in her (1992) treatise, *Situating the Self*, Seyla Benhabib goes further in establishing the parameters of discursive will formation by arguing that a truly ideal speech situation would explode all barriers to public scrutiny and perforate all sedimented federal, state, and local constitutions. This does not mean (as she is quick to point out) the total abrogation of rights and responsibilities, but rather that "in the game of democracy the rules of the game no less than their interpretation and even the position of the umpire are essentially contestable" (1992: 107). This position approximates that which is proposed in Chapter 4 by the chaos theory and poststructuralism, and is one I find particularly appealing as it applies to the praxis of perpetually reconstituted identity.

Having briefly discussed some of the more significant tenets of Habermasian discourse ethic, I proceed with a conceptual history of civil society by introducing Seligman's articulation of American exceptionalism. This will allow me to move from the more theoretical analyses of civil society to identification of modes of resistance emerging within civil society.

At the core of Seligman's interpretation of civil society is the conclusion that only America has realized the consummation of civil society in its "true" state. Seligman frames his position within the context of the nineteenth-century debates over citizenship, arguing that "citizenship, and with it the values of membership and participation in collective life, become, in this period, the new model for representing the values of both autonomy and mutuality within the boundaries of the nation-state" (1992: 101). To establish America as the "calm in the hurricane's eye," or put another way, as the center of an otherwise swirling vortex, Seligman addresses the extent to which socialist parties in the United States and various countries in Europe effectively mobilized sentiment on issues as well as those of citizenship thought to be a part of a thriving civil society. This included expanding participation by working people in the affairs of state by extending rights of assembly and voluntary association to unionized workers, extending male suffrage, improving working conditions, permitting free speech, allowing freedom of movement within national borders, and organizing political parties. At the root of his contention is the belief that socialism played only a minor role in the overall fabric of political and economic life in those places where there was a preexistent civil society already constituted by some majority of those characteristics just cited.

Having stated his premise, Seligman devotes the entire second half of his careful analysis to establishing what he refers to as "American exceptionalism." Seligman concludes, as have many others,[33] that the absence of feudalism signifies the initiation of what would become in still other ways a unique historical experience. In those countries throughout Europe where strong allegiance to vestiges of feudal privilege lingered long into the industrial age, and where access to civil, political, and economic participation was continually denied the working classes, therefore revolutionary movements organized around syndicalist demands for increased participation were more likely to occur. But in countries with liberal democratic and reformist polities like England and Germany, and to an even greater extent in the United States, rights of citizenship were, relatively speaking, more rapidly dispersed among the population. The resulting pacification of the syndicalist movement was a product of its assimilation into the civil, political, and economic spheres. As Seligman concludes, "[W]here civil society and citizenship existed and the working class was therefore integrated into the body politic, there was little need to advocate (or attempt to implement) the overthrowing of the existing society" (1992: 106). Since America had a more thoroughly developed civil society, the numerous socialist and anarchist parties, although influential, had a less significant impact than in other developed countries. Explanations for the relatively insignificant impact of left-wing political parties and organizations on American culture abound; political incorporation was merely one. Other reasons include: rising worker affluence and an associated social mobility; extreme forms political harassment and coercion, including physical brutality (against striking workers, socialist and anarchist organizers, and members of left-wing organizations generally), ransacking political headquarters of left-wing organizations, and political, economic and cultural blacklisting; segmented labor markets; left-wing political infighting, including sexism and racism; ideological socialization to meritocracy; and the existence of an external proletariat supplying capital with cheap labor and raw materials.

In contrast to Europeans, Americans came to perceive themselves as agentic actors, no longer respresentative of the universal, but actually constituted by both moral and ethical grace, and the universal, a cultural by-product of the Protestant Reformation.

Durkheim, for his part, challenged this belief in a dualistic individual identity, arguing instead (much like Freud) that individuals were imbued with internal conflict, consisting of a utilitarian, self-centered, self-maximizing side opposed by the sacred, moral, other-directed side exemplified in the conscience collective. Durkheim's endeavor, like that of the Scottish Enlightenment theorists before him, was to uncover a "theoretical edifice of mutual solidarity," a civil society to oppose utilitarian individualism. Durkheim argued, much like Habermas's articulation of the lifeworld, that existing within all cultures was a base of knowledge that pre-existed the individual. This conscience collective served to imbue individuals with the universal properties of the community and, as a result, led to what would become a uniquely sociological conceptualization of subjects constituted by individual ego inseparable from an "a priori structure of knowledge."

In sum, the absence of a feudal American past, with a concomitant consumption of the moral/ethical-universal subject characteristic of the

Protestant Reformation, has produced a public sphere in civil society convoluted by private interest claims. That is, in Habermasian lexicon, rather than an autonomous sphere of civil society that would encourage reflexive contemplation of traditional lifeworld codes, that public space is convoluted by the interest claims of morally autonomous subjects.

I believe that Seligman's frustration with the "negative dimensions of civil society" can be addressed with a return to Habermas. Habermas contends that the project of a fully constituted and thriving civil society has been stifled by differentiation within the lifeworld and the system, leading ultimately to the "colonization of the lifeworld." For civil society to exist and proliferate it must be protected from the vagaries of the state. Civil society is not completely separate from the state, nor could it be. Each is bound by constitutionally guaranteed rights of freedom of assembly, voluntary association, speech, and so on, and by traditions regulating moral and ethical conduct within specific communities. For example, the industrial working classes in liberal democratic states have sought juridical refuge from the deleterious effects of a self-regulated economy. The outcome, however, is ambiguous, revealing the invisible hand of the economy while simultaneously enhancing the regulatory power of the state. Put another way, "Labor legislation unambiguously protects the lifeworld against uncontrolled economic forces, but comprehensive sets of welfare-state entitlements, while they may intend to promote autonomy and rebuild social integration, have the opposite effect because of the bureaucratic, statist manner of their implementation" (Cohen and Arato, 1992: 445).

The resulting distribution of social rights produces clients instead of citizens (Cohen and Arato: 446). For Habermas, as for Weber before him, the increasing rationalization of economic and administrative subsystems intensifies at the expense of the rationalization of civil society (Cohen and Arato: 448). This is primarily experienced as the separation of expert knowledges and status privileges from the lifeworld, leading to what Cohen and Arato refer to as "cultural impoverishment." Moreover, a schism is created within the lifeworld, enabling the penetration of the media of power and money producing in a postmodern/postindustrial society, what Baudrillard has referred to as the proliferation of "sign values." Again, the ramification of the emergence of political and economic subsystems is the reification and colonization of the lifeworld. For Cohen and Arato, once communicative interaction has been displaced by lifeworld colonization and "the institutions specialized in socialization, social integration, and cultural transmission are increasingly functionalized to serve the imperatives of uncontrolled and ever-expanding subsystems," there will be, in their words, "pathological consequences." With regard to economics, these "consequences" constitute the nucleus of NSM critiques of dominant cultural emphases on increasing consumption and the penetration of monetary steering mechanisms to the detriment of worker's interests in relations of production.

When the colonization of the lifeworld manifests itself through the arm of bureaucratic rationalization, a paradoxical reification ensues that is simultaneously positive and negative.[34] Habermas, Luhmann, and Offe each conceive the penetration, manipulation, and clientization of the social body by the welfare state as latent by-products of efforts in liberal democratic and socialist countries to act in the interests of the "global subject."[35] Following the insights of Foucault, Cohen and Arato conclude: "Power is not a neutral medium; state penetration saves the lifeworld and solidarity from the medium of power and money only at the cost of futher 'colonization' " (466). The nucleus of a rearticulated civil society has as its Archimedian essence the decolonization of the lifeworld. Decolonization can occur only when the penetrating steering media of power and money are tempered by communicative codetermination.

In this chapter I have attempted to establish the literature on NSMs as a positive theoretical move toward a more comprehensive recognition of postindustrial social movements. But while NSM theory cleary offers numerous advances over the collective-behavior and resource mobilization paradigms, it still clings to traditionally argued valuations of overt, typically state-directed conflict as a crucial component of any movement body. Moreover, NSM theory maintains a fairly consistent epistemic frame opposing subject and object. To expand the conceptualization of precisely what social movements are and how they are perceived, we moved to a preliminary discussion of the work of Ernesto Laclau and Chantal Mouffe. It is their articulation of radical democracy that initiates a move toward a more vigorous exploration of a reconstituted social movement theory, which will follow in the next chapter. Finally, both NSM theorists and Laclau and Mouffe view the conceptual presence of civil society, and more specifically lifeworld, as a critical prerequisite to the cultivation of resistance groups and organizations. The relevance of civil society as a cultural space incubating heterogeneity, and a pragmatic attraction to self-limiting revolution rounds out the conceptual space necessary to prepare us to venture beyond traditional accounts of social movements. In the chapter to follow, I will make the argument that to truly recognize social movement potential, movement theorists must explode the boundaries of traditional theorizing, even that of NSMs, to allow for a further expanded articulation of multitudinous interests, identities, and political and economic configurations at the state and local levels. Throughout the next chapter we must keep in mind the value of civil society and lifeworld as conceptual spaces within a rearticulated social movement theory. This is particularly relevant in Chapter 5 as examples of modes of resistance are offered that are within this realm.

Notes

1. For a thorough review of Melucci's thoughts on the ontologization of the concept of new social movements see his "Getting Involved: Identity and Mobilization in Social Movements," in B. Klandermans, H. Kriesi, and S. Tarrow (eds.), *International Social Movement Research*, Vol. 1 (Greenwich, Conn.: JAI Press, 1988).

2. Talcott Parsons's early work suggests a theoretical fondness for symbolic interaction, particularly the work of George H. Mead. For an overview of his work and its relation to action theory and later systems theory see Jurgen Habermas, *The Theory of Communicative Action*, Vol. 2, trans. Thomas McCarthy. (Boston: Beacon Press, 1989), pp. 199–299.

3. Parsons's conceptualization of societal community claims its antecedents in the sociological tradition of Durkheim and Tonnies. His synthesis addresses the three pillars of his ancestral thought—social integration, community, and solidarity. For Parsons, the societal community is separate from the state, political, and cultural sphere, an interpretation following in the tradition of liberal conceptualizations of civil society. But oddly enough, as Cohen and Arato (1992: 119) suggest, "this synthesis, in which both individuation and integration are central . . . involves a partial, and conscious return to the Hegelian theory of civil society."

4. Tilly attempts to address the problems posed by the rational actor model by substituting the concept of rational interaction. Here, while it is possible to identify the goal-directed interests of collective actors, the addition still does not offer any insight into the construction of collective identity.

5. This characteristic of NSMs has its critics. For what is perhaps the most direct criticism I am currently aware of, refer to Ernst Wimmer (1985), "Ideology of New Social Movements," *World Marxist Review*, Vol. 28 (July): 36–44.

6. Birgitta Nedelmann (1984) confirms Piccone's emphasis on the social confrontation over instrumentalizing the previously separate public/private components of political culture. She suggests that actors in NSMs are more forthcoming than actors in earlier movements concerning those aspects of their private lives they wish to have recognized at the level of state policy, and those they wish to remain untouched.

7. References to the "heterosexuality of the state" can be found in the luminous work of M. Foucault, *History of Sexuality*, Vol. 1, trans. Robert Hurley (New York: Random House, 1978); D. Altman, *Homosexual: Oppression and Liberation* (New York: Outerbridge and Dienstfrey, 1971); P. Robinson, *The Freudian Left: Wilhelm Reich, Geza Roheim, Herbert Marcuse* (New York: Harper and Row, 1969); and J. Butler, *Gender Trouble: Feminism and the Subversion of Identity* (New York: Routledge, 1990).

8. For a thoughtful theoretical articulation of the gendered nature of law, see Zilliah Eisenstein's (1988) *The Female Body and the Law*.

9. The challenge confronting contemporary social movements is how to avoid what Roberto Michels (1959) referred to as the "iron law of oligarchy," the insipid hierarchicalization and instrumentalization of movement organizations composed of power and money. For resource mobilization theorists, this poses less of a problem since codifying organizational structures is one of the keys to successful social movements. But for actors in NSMs, the lifeworld, discursively constituted, cannot traverse the transition to system. Following Habermas (1989), Cohen and Arato (1992) argue that "movements cannot influence structures coordinated through means other than normative or communicative interaction without succumbing to the pressure for self-instrumentalization" (561). For them, success at the level of civil society appears to the extent that actors continue efforts to democratize values, norms, and institutions. This is precisely the role played by contemporary intentional communities, a point that will be taken up later.

10. See, for example Pierre Bourdieu, *Distinction: A Social Critique of the Judgement of Taste*, trans. Richard Nice (Cambridge, Mass.: Harvard University Press, 1984).

11. Clearly concerns over time, space, and the appropriation of day-to-day activities by the dominant class are not unique to our epoch. Many authors have noted similar concerns as concomitant with the rise of the capitalist mode of production (e.g., Thompson, 1963; Pollard, 1969). What separates recognition of these experiences is the pervasiveness of domination techniques designed to enhance manipulation and control. While they existed in past centuries, the techniques used were often confronted with great hostility when imposed and were simply quite crude. This differs dramatically from postindustrial experiences, where the micro-physics of contemporary power-knowledge regimes (Foucault, 1979) are so pervasive as to have been internalized by the mass of humanity to the point that there is little recognition of their existence.

12. There have been, however, both competing conceptualizations of the new middle class (e.g., Gundelach, 1984; Kriesi, 1989), and refusal to accept the new middle class as an adequate way to conceptualize NSM actors (e.g., Bagguley, 1992).

13. Readers should consider Jonathan Freidman's 1993 publication of "Order and Disorder in Global Systems: A Sketch," *Social Research*, 60 (2): 205–34; M. C. Waters, *Ethnic Options* (Berkeley, Calif.: University of Calif. Press, 1990); A.

Nandy (1987), "Cultural Frames for Social Transformation: A Credo," *Alternatives*, 12: 113–23; G. Gyani (1993), "Political Uses of Tradition in Postcommunist East Central Europe," *Social Research*, 60 (4): 893–13; M. Vautier (1994), "Postmodern Myth, Post-European History, and the Figure of the Amerindian: Francois Barcelo, George Bowering, and Jacques Poulin," *Canadian Literature*, 141: 15–37.

14. See, for example, T. Luke (1992–93), "Neo-Populism: Fabricating the Future by Rehabbing the Past?," *Telos*, 94: 11–18; C. Lasch, "Communitarianism or Populism?," in A. Etzioni (ed.), *Rights and the Common Good* (New York: St. Martin's Press, 1995) pp. 59–66.

15. For reasons that will be elaborated on later, Gramsci's conceptualization of counter-hegemony does not thoroughly capture the more amorphous proliferation of resistance within the lifeworld. It is used here to establish in an initial way the relevance of juxtaposition.

16. Indeed, as John Berger (1979) makes clear in his introduction to *Pig Earth*, this evaluation could have been applied throughout European history, particularly to peasant associations with artisans and revolutionaries during times of peasant uprising. Peasant unification with non-peasant groups was typically issue-specific and readily dissolved following resolution of the struggle.

17. Robert Schehr (1995), "Divarications of Employee Drug Testing Through Deconstruction and Discourse Analysis," *Humanity and Society*, 19 (1): 45–64.

18. In classical social movement theory see the work of Sydney Tarrow (1983), "Struggling to Reform: Social Movements and Policy Change during Cycles of Protest," *Western Societies Paper*, 15, Cornell University; and B. Klandermans, H. Kriesi, and S. Tarrow (1988), "From Structure to Action: Comparing Social Movement Research Across Cultures," in B. Klandermans, H. Kriesi, and S. Tarrow (eds.) *International Social Movement Research*, Vol. 1 (Greenwich, Conn: JAI Press, 1988).

19. See A. Seligman, *The Idea of Civil Society* (New York: Free Press, 1992) pp. 145–98; J. Cohen and A. Arato, *Civil Society and Political Theory* (Massachusetts: The MIT Press, 1992).

20. Edward Shils (1991), "The Virtue of Civil Society," *Government and Opposition*, 26 (2): 3–20.

21. Cohen and Arato, *Civil Society*, p. 16.

22. Talcott Parsons, *The System of Modern Societies* (Englewood Cliffs, N.J.: Prentice Hall, 1971).

23. Many identified with the communitarian label have returned to the essence of civil society, see Charles Taylor (1990), "Modes of Civil Society," *Public Culture*, 3 (1): 95–118; Alasdaire MacIntyre, *Three Rival Versions of Moral Enquiry* (London: Duckworth, 1990); Michael Walzer (1991), "The Idea of Civil Society," *Dissent*, (Spring): 293–304; Daniel Bell (1989), "American Exceptionalism Revisited: The Role of Civil Society," *The Public Interest*, 95: 38–56.

24. Cohen and Arato (1992) go further by presenting a model of civil society that is separate not only from the state but from the economy as well. More will be said on this matter in the remaining sections of this chapter.

25. Seligman, *The Idea*, p. 8.

26. Seligman argues throughout his treatise on civil society that the preponderance of Eastern European attention directed to civil society was limited by its emphasis on *realpolitik*, omitting the transcendent component of civil society articulated by eighteenth-century and nineteenth-century progenitors of the concept. To the extent that Seligman is correct, and I believe he is, this should not, in my opinion, detract from the perceived relevance of civil society as it has been articulated, particularly in Poland by Michnik (1985), Wojcicki (1981), Kuron (1981), and others, as a social space designated for the revival of resistance.

27. Adam Michnik, "A New Evolutionism," in *Letters from Prison and Other Essays* (Berkeley: University of California Press, 1985).

28. This theme has been developed in detail by Claus Offe, particularly in his book, *Contradictions of the Welfare State* (Massachusetts: The MIT Press, 1984).

29. For an overview of the Green Party, see Brian Tokar, *The Green Alternative: Creating An Ecological Future* (San Pedro: R. & E. Miles, 1992).

30. See especially Chapter 3. I will discuss Seligman's articulation of "American exceptionalism" in more detail below. The point here is to suggest the distinction between Cohen and Arato's recognition of the "spirit of civil society" emerging in France, England and Germany, and Seligman's contention that America's unique historical development provided for a uniquely different, and I infer, superior, version of civil society.

31. See S. M. Shell, *Rights of Reason* (Toronto: University of Toronto Press, 1980); and J. Rundell, *Origins of Modernity* (Madison: University of Wisconsin Press, 1987).

32. Since discourse surrounding the reinterpretation of tradition hinges on mimetic experiences within the lifeworld, Habermas comes closer to chaos theory than deconstruction. For it is chaos theory, unlike deconstruction, that recognizes the culmination of chaos in order. That is, even though communicative action stimulates a reflexive analysis of tradition (morals, values, norms, beliefs), tradition and the accumulated stock of cultural knowledge nonetheless shapes the terrain of discourse, resulting in a sempiternal interplay between articulated subjects and those institutions constituting the steering media associated with bureaucratic organizations, the economy, and the remaining institutions within the lifeworld. A truly deconstructive approach, on the other hand, would seek to explode prevailing occidental knowledge bases, opening the field yet again. This time, however, tradition plays but a minor role as but one of many possible steering mechanisms and constitutive discourses in a rhizomatic cacophony of competing knowledge claims.

33. See, for example, Werner Sombert, *Why There Is No Socialism In the USA* (London: Macmillan, 1975); Seymor Martin Lipsit, "American Exceptionalism in

the North American Perspective: Why the United States Has Withstood the World Socialist Movement," in G. Adams, ed., *The Idea of America* (Cambridge, Mass.: Harvard University Press, 1977). For an analysis that focuses specifically on the correlation among the rise of socialism, the American labor movement, and capitalist social relations in America see Mike Davis, *Prisoner of the American Dream* (London: Verso, 1986).

34. Foucault has produced the most lucid account of the simultaneous positive and negative ramifications of power in his *Discipline and Punish: The Birth of the Prison* trans. Alan Sheridan (New York: Vintage Books, 1979); and *The History of Sexuality* trans. Robert Hurley (New York: Vintage Books, 1980). Several compelling applications of this theme can be found in works addressing medicalization. See, for example, Robert Crawford (1978), "You are Dangerous to Your Health: The Ideology and Politics of Victim Blaming," *Social Policy* 8: 10–20; Peter Conrad and Joseph Schneider, *Deviance and Medicalization: From Badness to Sickness* (St. Louis: Mosby Co., 1980); and Schehr "Divarications of Employee Drug Testing."

35. What Michael Walzer has most recently referred to as the global adoption of a "thin" or "minimal" morality based on vaguely articulated beliefs in, for example, justice. Walzer makes this point in his *Thick and Thin: Moral Argument at Home and Abroad* (Notre Dame: University of Notre Dame Press, 1994).

4

CHAOS THEORY, METAPHOR, AND SOCIAL MOVEMENTS

This is a world in which one wanders within and between multiple borders and spaces marked by excess, otherness, and difference. This is a world in which old certainties are ruptured and meaning becomes more contingent, less indebted to the dictates of reverence and established truth.

Henry Giroux, *Fugitive Cultures*

As we saw in the previous chapter, social movement theory can generally be said to comprise one of three contemporary paradigms: collective behavior, resource mobilization, and in what is referred to in Europe as new social movement theory (NSM) or the identity paradigm (Jamison and Eyerman, 1991). I would like to initiate in this chapter a discussion of a possible fourth approach to social movement theory, one that builds primarily upon the insights of the NSM literature, especially those of Italian sociologist Alberto Mellucci and French sociologist Alain Touraine, but endeavors to move beyond what is conceptualized here as a still limited articulation of movement potential. For while it is true that NSM theory has advanced conceptualization of movement actors, issues, environments, and demands, it continues to cling to conventional articulations of social movement, resulting in a still restrictive ontologization. That is, while Touraine (1985, 1988), Offe (1985), Mellucci (1980, 1988, 1990, 1995), and others associated with NSM theory have expanded the field of conceptualization regarding NSM status and significance, they reproduce the emphasis on state-directed conflict or other modes of political organization as a defining moment in its morphological composition, a proposition it shares with the resource mobilization and classical traditions.[1] This is, in my view, too narrow a conceptualization of social movement. Remaining within the confines of traditional theorizing on social movements limits our capacity to identify forms of resistance occurring within civil society at the level of the lifeworld. We do so at the risk not only of poor scholarship but also of the potential danger involved in not identifying the issues, actors, circumstances, and cultural capital (e.g., indigenous constructions of folklore, myth, language, song, and the like) constituting the cultural milieu of oppressed peoples. As Laclau and Mouffe (1985) have argued, inefficacious attention to alternate modes of resistance and movement potential from left-wing academics leaves the discourse of opposition, identity formation, alienation and anomie to those traditionally on the political right who, as we have witnessed particularly in the recent surge of interest in the communitarianism of Etzioni (1995a, 1995b) and Bennett (1984), may appropriate the language of pain offering a regressive return to tradition. So while a sociological interest in the everyday lifeworld behaviors of people is not new, I contend that even where this emphasis does exist within the literature analyzing of social movements (e.g., Evans and Boyte, 1986; Fantasia and Hirsch, 1995; Flacks, 1988; Hirsch, 1990; Jenson, 1995), overt action-oriented political activity is privileged.

I contend in this chapter that our zest to categorize, label, and thereby ontologize collective behavior as befitting one or the other paradigms referred to above serves to launch perhaps the most prodigious segment of movement potential—that activity occurring within the lifeworld—into theoretical obscurity. What is called for, I believe, is a reconceptualization of social movement theory. Most radical and potentially contentious in my proposition is to explode the boundaries constituting previous conceptualizations to eliminate morphological accounts of social movements that privilege incidences of collective behavior that are both historically rare and relatively recent (Cohen and Arato, 1993; Scott, 1990; Welch, 1985). What is needed is a theory of social movements capable of capturing the potential of actors hovering in the lifeworld, a theory that can capture the persistence of resistance. What is needed, I contend, is a sociological adaptation of the theory of chaos.

While anthropologists have long lamented the neglect of peasant rebellion, not merely the recognition of them but also (and equally as important) the ways in which they rebel, as a serious omission in sociological scholarship on social movements. Sociologists, for their part, have traditionally shaped their analyses of social movement phenomena by drawing upon the influential but flawed work of the collective-behavior school initiated by Herbert Blumer (1946), Talcott Parsons (1937), and Turner and Killian (1972), but were catapulted to disciplinary prominence in the early 1960s by Neil Smelser (1962).[2] Resource mobilization theory (e.g., della Porta, 1988; Jenkins, 1989; Klandermans and Tarrow, 1988; McAdam, 1988; McCarthy and Zald, 1977; Tilly et al., 1975; Tilly, 1985), while an advance over the collective-behavior paradigm in its reassurance that collective behavior is not irrational but a normative component of human interaction, nevertheless perpetuates the collective behaviorist's exposition of social movements as vying primarily for political recognition at the level of the state, and has tended to neglect the construction of collective identity, that is, the multiple ways in which actors interpret images within and beyond the lifeworld, leading them to participate in social movements.

Neglected in this literature is the wide spectrum of resistance by oppressed peoples directed not at the state but at the level of the lifeworld. As Scott (1990) clearly demonstrates in his work on peasant rebellion, the oppressed, by virtue of their status as oppressed people, have constructed forms of resistance that intentionally deflect attention away from state-directed activities to focus on issues emerging within civil society. Crucial in this work, and that of others (Benjamin, 1969; Bernal, 1994; Bloch, 1995, 1988; Bond and Gilliam, 1994; de Certeau, 1984; Foucault, 1976; Gilmore, 1987; Gross, 1992; Gyani, 1993; Heehs, 1994; Laclau, 1990; Nandy, 1987; Rao, 1994; Scott, 1990; Welch, 1985), is the historically relentless preservation of local myth and folklore, including what Hobsbawm and Ranger (1983) refer to as the act of "inventing tradition," procured by the oppressed and reinscripted in daily activities to buffer the intrusion of dominant cultural capital (Bourdieu, 1984). The active interpretation and reinterpretation of the habitus of oppressed people, by and for oppressed people, is overlooked in classical application of social movement theory. Indeed, to the extent that it is recognized, as, for example, when Tilly (1985) argues that there is "nothing new in new social movements," that the demands and activities of NSM actors can locate their origins in past movements, it is clear that he and others within the resource mobilization paradigm neglect the preservation and rearticulation of the lifeworld. It seems clear that our contemporary moment differs, in some ways dramatically, from our pre-1960s predecessors (Boggs, 1985; Brand, 1990; Johnston and Klandermas, 1995; Melucci, 1988, 1990; Offe, 1985; Touraine, 1971, 1988). Whether it is perceived as postmodern, postindustrial, or hypermodernity (Luke,

1991), sociological analyses of social movements must be reconceptualized to absorb a broader array of resistance potential.

Actors in ICs, operating at the level of civil society and without state-directed conflict as their *modus operandi*, can be recognized as participants in a social movement only if the boundaries of the classical social movement tradition are transformed. To that end, the focus of this chapter will be the rearticulation of social movement theory consistent with recent sociological interpretations of chaos theory and poststructuralism. If I am successful, we will be left with a theory of social movement that is at once heterogeneous, non-linear, and perhaps most important, radically morphological. I mean by "radically morphological" an abandonment of the classical social movement emphasis on birth, growth, decay—an Enlightenment inspired evolutionary model (Bernal, 1994; Bond and Gilliam, 1994; de Certeau, 1984; Nandy, 1987)—to be replaced by a rhizomatic articulation of structure and form that recognizes in global actors a resounding mosaic of resistance. Perhaps it is true that it is not deviance that needs explanation, but order.

Enter Chaos: Butterflies and Fractals

It is useful to initiate discussion of chaos theory with a reference to Nietzsche, perhaps the first postmodern modernist. Much like Alain Touraine, Alberto Mellucci, Carl Boggs and other authors of NSM literature who have derided contemporary political, economic, and cultural arrangements as alienating and oppressive, embedded as they are in the manufacture and distribution of information (what Foucault (1979) would identify as power knowledge regimes), Nietzsche, writing in *The Will To Power*, sounds ominously similar.

Disintegration characterizes this time, and thus uncertainty: nothing stands firmly on its feet or on a hard faith in itself; one lives for tomorrow, as the day after tomorrow is dubious. Everything on our way is slippery and dangerous, and the ice that still supports us has become thin; all of us feel the warm, uncanny breath of the thawing wind; there we still walk, soon no one will be able to walk. (Miller, 1978: 27)

For Nietzsche, history is chaos, a collection of pseudo-sedimented recollections emanating from a multiplicity of competing interests. He may well be among the first of the new historicists. Nietzsche, argues James Miller (1978: 31), perceived history as "an energy field where conflicting interpretations are perpetually in play, organizing themselves through mutual antagonism; [where] only the momentary outcome of these conflicts determines the local sense of history, a provisional meaning that is never univocal, always revocable." It is his emphasis on the multiple causal strands of historical confrontation and their consequent fluidity that marks Nietzsche as the philosophical forebearer of those post-Marxist and post-structural articulations of social movement to be discussed below. For him, there were no essentialisms seductive enough to thoroughly constitute the human mind, body, and spirit. As long as human beings retained the cognitive capacity for skepticism, there would always remain a hermeneutic buffer between dominant ideologies and the practical interpretations of those ideologies at the level of the lifeworld. Nietzsche's anti-Enlightenment critique of essentialist truth claims and worldviews emerged coincidentally with his articulation of individuated and secularized polytheism. The fully self-situated human being free to choose from among a multiplicity of belief systems, norms for behavior, and so on, was Nietzsche's ideal.

Fond of aphorism and metaphor, Nietzsche likened the gift of theistic deontologization to a solar eclipse. Once the ontologizing presence of the monotheistic sun had been shielded in the sky, "the world can appear illuminated by a variety of constellations, many suns providing many perspectives, with no single standpoint privileged any longer" (Miller, 1978: 29). Of course, Nietzsche did not believe that "commoners" possessed the boldness and daring necessary to aggressively embrace a multiplicity of life choices. His gravest concern, most clearly articulated in *Thus Spake Zarathustra*, was for the persistence of the "last man," human beings driven by the fear of *living*. Nietzsche believed, much like Fromm (1941) and Foucault (1976, 1979, 1980), that the experience of oppressive social relations and consequent disempowerment constituting most human beings made them docile and that they were happiest, not when exposed to multiple lifeworld options, but when they could simply be left alone.

Nietzsche's analysis of multiplicity and fear offers significant points of departure both for this book on chaos and social movements, and for the ways in which he critiques philosophical conceptualizations of progress and immanence. Nietzsche openly criticized socialist articulations of alternative conceptions of reality based on a transformation of the mode of production. He believed that, rather than leading to the realization of species being, human beings would continue to become more efficient "machines" tied to ever more efficient means of production. But perhaps more important for us, Nietzsche was critical of the "herd mentality" produced by yet another ontology—socialist—that professed allegiance to its articulation of the truth principally as it concerned the notion of "progress." While it is safe to conclude that Nietzsche, much like Marx and Engels, would have viewed utopian efforts of the nineteenth century and earlier as perpetrating one or more forms of essentialistic thought, I argue that ICs attempting to reconstruct the lifeworld come much closer to his articulation of heterogeneity and multiplicity, and in that way are pushing beyond the docile fear-driven "last man."

While there have not, to my knowledge, been any attempts to enjoin the nineteenth-century philosophical works of Nietzsche with the initial stages of the development of chaos theory[3] (although it was not yet referred to as such), in the latter part of that century, it is apparent that their conclusions are remarkably similar. Below is a brief history of chaos theory and a discussion of its primary components. I will conclude this section by identifying recent sociological efforts to apply chaos theory to contemporary social problems, followed by ways in which chaos theory informs a reconceptualization of social movement theory.

The science of chaos was born in 1890. While attempting to derive the precise calculations of the earth's orbit around the sun, Henri Poincaré determined that "a solution was not possible using Newtonian physics" (Hayles, 1990: 1). Poincaré and others had discovered that small perturbations in the relationship between the earth's attraction to the moon meant changes in the earth's orbit around the sun, which in turn altered the moon's orbit around earth. Newtonian physics, guided as it was by linear calculations of cause and effect, was insufficient to the task of accurately predicting these orbital deviations; a new science of non-linear dynamics was required. But despite the inaugural work of Poincaré, scientists in Europe and the United States were committed to continuing the tradition of Aristotle and Newton by establishing the hegemony of mathematics through the inauguration of rigorous positivistic methods. It wasn't until the 1960s and 1970s and the proliferation of supercomputers that serious attention was directed at advancing knowledge of complex non-linear mathematical models.

The idea of non-linearity and heterogeneity, had also begun to capture the imaginations of artists and academics working during the 1970s. This was particularly true for poststructuralists dedicated to the deconstruction of literature. It was during this period that magnificent philosophical treatises emerged to challenge the classical, essentialistic, and totalizing perspectives that had dominated the discipline since the Enlightenment. While poststructuralism found its voice in Derrida, Lacan, de Man and others, it could locate its roots in the works of Nietzsche and Heidegger. This chapter will attempt to explore the strands of association between chaos theory and poststructuralism as they apply to the articulation of a new theory of social movement.

Two significant strands of chaos theory within the scientific literature have been adapted to work in the humanities and social sciences. The first strand, as N. Katherine Hayles (1990) suggests, refers to the "order out of chaos" phenomenon first articulated in the work of Ilya Prigogine and Isabelle Stengers (1984). Prigogine and Stengers noted in their research that systems comprised both linearity and non-linearity, with neither being causally prior. Their primary contribution, however, was to suggest that emerging from entropic perturbations within systems was stasis, order. Life, and Prigogine and Stengers' book, *Order Out of Chaos*, was in some ways a treatise on metaphysical illuminations of time, was a process of *becoming*.

The second strand of chaos theory differs in its attention to the persistence of chaos in various systems rather than the return to order emphasized by Prigogine and Stengers. For theorists like Mandelbrot, Lorenz, Feigen-baum, and Shaw, chaotic systems are sempiternal; they persist over time. Emphasis is placed on the order that exists within typically chaotic systems, an order determined by phase space and attractors. To identify the level of predictability in dynamical systems, scientists attempt to plot repetitive motion in a geometric space called phase space. Attractors are simply points within a phase space that attract the system to it. Linear models, like those founded on the principle of Newtonian physics or Euclidean geometry, can be identified in phase space as having fixed point-attractors, those systems that tend toward equilibrium regardless of their initial conditions.[4] But chaos theory offers the social sciences, sociology in particular, a theory of non-linearity, and non-linear systems behave in uniquely variable ways. In fact, non-linear systems of three dimensions or more are characterized by what Hayles has referred to as a combination of simplicity and complexity, determinism and unpredictability, each the product of "strange attractors." Strange attractors are unique since there is no way to predict, based on initial conditions, where the system orbit will end up. And yet, in the end, there is order. Strange attractors do possess a fixed-point symmetry; that is, numer-ous micro-level deviations produce large, but patterned changes in the system's orbit. Numerous systems have been effectively modeled via strange attractors. Hayles suggests that they have been used to "describe outbreaks of infectious diseases, variations in cotton prices and in the number of lynxes caught by trappers, the rise and fall of the Nile River, and erratic eye movements of schizophrenics" (1990: 150).

Articulation of strange attractors draws attention to the crux of chaos theory: recognition the fact that small perturbations in initial conditions can be amplified into magnificent and unpredictable products. During the 1950s and 1960s Kolmogorov in Moscow and Smale in the United States each recognized that it was possible to approach random-like conditions when considering non-linear systems of three or more dimensions (Kamminga, 1990). Their research suggested that while perturbations and measurement errors exist in all levels of research, they tended to produce relatively insignificant ramifications for systems with two or fewer dimensions. But it wasn't until the early 1960s and the publication of Lorenz's study on atmospheric convection that the presence of three or more dimensions, initial conditions, was seen as having an important impact on predictive capacity. Lorenz realized that "systems of three or more dimensions can have the property of sensitive dependence on initial conditions" (Kamminga, 1990: 55). Any errors in measurement or perturbations in initial conditions initiate a process of orderly disorder in which errors are magnified, uncontrollably making prediction of future behavior impossible. To highlight the significance of non-linearity and initial conditions in climatology, Lorenz referred to the metaphor of the butterfly. He asserted that a butterfly flapping its wings in Brazil could produce a tornado in Texas. Similarly, Gleick (1987), in his book on the evolution of chaos theory, suggests that even if sensing devices were placed at one-foot intervals on poles as high as the atmosphere, and these poles were placed one foot apart all over the earth and the results fed into a supercomputer, the weather could not be accurately predicted. Between the sensing devices, fluctuations in temperature and wind velocity would go unrecorded, and these fluctuations could soon affect global weather patterns (21). The point is that, unless all aspects of the initial state of a system are known from the start, its initial conditions and prediction about its future are impossible.[5] Application of chaos theory to the social sciences amplifies this concern since system complexity and the total degrees of freedom are far greater and far less predictable.

Lazlo (1987) suggests that even when initial conditions have been precisely calculated, there are numerous possible products. This is because "physical systems are not constrained to follow a single evolutionary path" (White, 1991: 263). They proceed for the most part on what Lazlo refers to as "bundles of trajectories," acted upon and interacting with countless exogenous and as yet unpredictable strange attractors each altering the course of the other. But the product is a bounded chaos. Lazlo, following Prigogine and Stengers' articulation of dissipative structures,[6] argues that from the chaos percolating at the local level emerges a highly differentiated but nonetheless ordered state.

What is perhaps most compelling for sociologists, is the degree to which the recognition by chaos theorists of the non-linearity of systems, the correlation between numerous unpredictable occurrences at the microlevel and their consequent patterned emergence at the macro or system level, can be reconceptualized to include variables relating to, for example, social movements. Is it conceivable that Wilson's (1983) metaphor of the transition from boiling water to steam has applications to such seemingly unrelated subjects as the relationship between localized forms of resistance and the preservation of civil society via state-based preservation of rights of assembly, speech, and so on? Has the sociology of social movements ignored micro-level diversity due to its commitment to positivism? Following Shaw (1981), who comes dangerously close to Nietzsche, isn't it conceivable that sociologists, who have traditionally busied themselves with the construction of conceptual boxes in which to locate and analyze cultural phenomena, are partially to blame for impeding the proliferation of cultural forms at the level of the lifeworld? For as Shaw would suggest, it is chaos that produces all new forms of information, and, I would add following Nietzsche, myriad diverse lifeworld options where creativity, opportunity, and alternatives, emerge from the unpredictability of the microlevel.

Consider Benoit Mandelbrot's (1983) articulation of fractal geometry as a case in point. Mandelbrot argued that nature was constituted by non-linearity, complexity. Positivistic science (including social science) has endeavored to capture, encase and explain natural phenomena; unpredictability is perceived as extraordinary. To prove otherwise, Mandelbrot invented fractal geometry. Fractal (taken from the Latin adjective *fractus*, meaning broken), exemplifies the juxtaposition between Euclidean and non-Euclidean geometry. According to Hayles, "[I]n Euclidean geometry one equilateral triangle is taken to be similar to any other equilateral triangle, regardless of their relative sizes" (1990: 165). There are no strange attractors. But for Mandelbrot, nature is replete with fractal geometry in cloud formations, mountain contours, and tree grains (1983: 165). Euclidean geometry cannot explain these variations in nature, this chaos. As opposed to the frustration characteristic of positivistic science, the chaos of nature is perceived by Mandelbrot, Shaw, Serres, and others affiliated with the strange attractor analysis of chaos theory as what constitutes its beauty, its majesty. Serres (1977) has identified in the work of Epicurean physicist Lucretius the application of chaos to illuminate the origin of the universe. According to White (1991: 265), "Lucretius images this state of disorder as the eternal fall of atoms through space. At uncertain times and indefinite places, the universal fall of the atoms is interrupted by what Lucretius calls the *clinamen*, 'the smallest conceivable condition for the first formation of turbulence.'"

As the atoms begin to collide and spiral, we have the beginning of the universe and, subsequently, the world. Lucretius proposes a theory of chaos to resolve the most prodigious philosophical question in occidental philosophy: Why is there something rather than nothing? It all happened by chance. A state of negentropy emerges from the volatile sea to render the manifest, "pockets of local order in rising entropy" (Serres in White, 1991: 265).

Finally, as if he were directly addressing our concerns for IC and heterogeneity, White (1991: 265), following Serres, asserts:

We ourselves must become improvisational artists, *bricoleurs* who live close to the clinamen, where Nature is born, close to the fertile chaos from which form is continually emergent" (original emphasis). This is what Serres refers to as the "wisdom of the Garden," the significance of the local, the improvisational. Here Serres's work, particularly his publication of the *Parasite*, begins to round out the correlation between chaos theory and my critique of classical social movement theory, resource mobilization, and some components of the NSM conceptualization of social movements.

In *La Naissance* (1977) Serres contributes further to the distinction between indigenous knowledge and master narratives by conceptualizing the mythological figure of Venus as the manifestation of the wisdom of the garden. Venus, the goddess of love, emerged as the product of the torrid flux of the sea. If we are to expand the parameters of sociological theorizing on social movements, that is, if we are to embrace the wisdom of the garden and promote an alternative vision of social movement consistent with recognition of local (i.e., lifeworld) autonomy and forms of resistance, we must battle that other formidable mythological figure, Mars the war god, who, according to Serres, "proposes a science and an ethics of totalization, force, mastery, and empire" (1977: 236). Venus and Mars are antithetical. Venus promotes the value of stochastic processes, while Mars promotes the " 'science of death' according to which reality can be reduced to deterministic trajectories" (White, 1991: 266). To ensure system predictability, Mars must resort to violence and control; control over identity construction, sexuality, leisure, work, nature. For Serres, Mars initiates a "thanatocratic" world order in which "there is nothing new to be learned, to be discovered, to be invented" since hegemonic ontologization has reduced in theory what exists as diversity to the status of anomaly. What follows is the "reduction of difference to sameness" where there exists a prevailing belief that there is "nothing new under the sun."

Serres offers us a convenient transition enabling us to document the evolution of intentional communities. It is my contention that prevailing sociological analyses of communes and the commune "movement" as originally conceived in the work of Zablocki (1980), Kanter (1973), Berger (1981), and others shared a similar conclusion. This initial section on chaos theory and the following section on post-Marxism and poststructuralism contend that these sociological interpretations, particularly the extensive research of Zablocki, are limited in their exposition of the social movement potential of ICs due to their conceptualization of social movement within the classical tradition. Classical social movement theory and resource mobilization are both constituted by the Enlightenment-based positivistic search for truth. They hover, much like Mars, in the linear milieu of deterministic predictability and cause and effect. What they miss, and what chaos theory and post-Marxism and poststructuralism alert us to, is the myriad diversity of organic interaction sempiternally constructing and reconstructing lifestyle options: flirtations with identity, alternate expressions of sexuality, innovative forms of consensus decision-making, renewed respect for the earth, for life, for peace.

What emerges in the theory of chaos is recognition of the life-giving force of heterogeneity, multiplicity. Just as with physical systems, in cultural systems, too, chaos enhances opportunities for creativity. In Serres's novel *Parasite*, closed cultural systems are destabilized by the parasite lurking within. The ensuing turmoil created by the introduction of the parasite produces innovative options, or, as White (1991) suggests, "alternative logics," to address the perceived instability. This means for us and for our efforts to reconstruct an alternate theory of social movement, particularly as it applies to ICs, a reliance upon "parasitic dissonance" (White, 1991) at the level of the lifeworld.

While it is perhaps an unfortunate choice of metaphor, since parasites are usually perceived as organisms drawing life from another without offering comparable return, members of intentional communities do perceive themselves as purveyors of the possible. And since they exist for most of us at the fringe of society, they are well positioned to exemplify effective alternatives to the numerous components of cultural capital constituting our national popular (Gramsci).

Perhaps a more efficacious metaphor can be located in Pirsig's (1991) *Lila: An Inquiry Into Morals*. In attempting to ascertain the distinction between Static good and Dynamic good, Pirsig refers to a passage in Ruth Benedict's (1934) *Patterns of Culture*. To establish the pervasiveness of culturally specific deviance designations, Benedict relates the story of a charismatic Pueblo Indian living in Zuni, New Mexico, in the nineteenth century: "In a society that thoroughly distrusts authority of any sort, he had native personal magnetism that singled him out in any group. In a society that exalts moderation and the easiest way, he was turbulent and could act violently on occasion. Zuni's only reaction to such personalities was to brand them as witches" (in Pirsig, 1991: 110). Accused of witchcraft by the war priests, the man was hung by his thumbs on rafters to compel him to confess to being a witch. However, as his good fortune would have it, a messenger was sent to summon government troops who later arrived to remove him from the rafters. War priests responsible for the punishment were imprisoned by the government troops, and among those imprisoned was a priest considered to be "the most respected and important in Zuni history." Upon returning to the Pueblo following his imprisonment, this formerly most celebrated of priests was reduced in status and power, never again to resume priestly office.

For Pirsig, this tale foretold considerably more than cultural relativism. Pirsig concludes that the man accused of being a witch was actually a *shaman*, or more precisely, a *brujo*, "a Spanish term used extensively in that region that denotes a quite different kind of person." A *brujo* is a person who "claims religious powers; who acts outside of, and sometimes against local church authorities" (1991: 112).

The story of the *brujo* related here is significant for us on two levels. First, the *brujo* is a more accurate metaphorical figure than Serres's parasite to exemplify the complicated role played by members of ICs in contemporary American culture. To genuinely encompass the significance of ICs, a metaphor must communicate the imagery of an organism that is of, but not of. That is, ICs must be conceptualized as having emerged from dominant culture, but as, standing in many ways opposed to it, simultaneously viewed as exogenous actors sempiternally engaged in a process of agitation and integration. The *brujo*, by challenging the authority of priests, stood on the cultural fringe, offering alternative interpretations of traditional cultural capital. The image of the *brujo*, the cultural critic, presents us with a metaphorical character possessing attributes that contribute to the vitality and heterogeneity of civil society. In his capacity as critic and contributor to the vivacity and enrichment of his culture, the *brujo* approximates members of ICs.

The metaphor of the *brujo* equally offers us a critique of essentialism. One of the more interesting components of Pirsig's work is his effort to promote subjectivity while being mindful of deterministic systems. In his effort to define quality, Pirsig, drawing upon the tale of the *brujo*, determines that there are two distinct forms of "the good," one static and the other dynamic. Static good refers to sedimented cultural practices: language, folkways, mores, myth, norms, and values. Static good makes the persistence of culture possible, predictable. In this context, the *brujo*, one who challenged tradition, was viewed as deviant, dangerous, deserving of punishment. The priests, in contrast, are the embodiment of tradition. They are good. This classic Derridean bifurcation of good and evil holds a lesson for students of social movement theory.

It is my contention that neither classical social movement theory nor resource mobilization considers the significance of actors acting at the level of the lifeworld due to their allegiance to positivistic interpretations of social scientific phenomena. In the metaphor of the *brujo*, Pirsig cites the work of anthropologist E. A. Hoebel to confirm the restrictive power of sedimented interests:

[I]n the more highly developed cultures in which cults have become strongly organized churches, the priesthood fights an unrelenting war against shamans. Priests work in a rigorously structured hierarchy fixed in a firm set of traditions. Their power comes from and is vested in the organization itself. They constitute a religious bureaucracy. Shamans, on the other hand, are arrant individualists. Each is on his own, undisciplined by bureaucratic control; hence a shaman is always a threat to the order of the organized church. (in Pirsig, 1991: 113)

In this sense, ICs present classical social movement theory with a curious problem. They do not fit the mold of classical conceptualizations of movement actors. Indeed, they signify chaos at the level of the lifeworld. As such, they are morphologically perceived by social scientists as perhaps amusing historical phenomena possessing an uncanny capacity to surface during various historical epochs. This interpretation would certainly satisfy the structural concerns of social movement theorists like Tarrow (1989, 1994), and sociologists like Kanter (1973) and Zablocki (1980). But the metaphorical interpretation of the *brujo* corresponds nicely with my efforts to reconceptualize social movement theory by focusing greater attention on potential movement actors contemporaneously perceived as existing on the fringe (and therefore not in need of serious attention), and relatedly in the way that it enables us to see that an academic commitment to specific Enlightenment-inspired methodological assumptions leads us to overlook cultural phenomena occurring at the level of the lifeworld.

Applications of Chaos Theory in the Humanities and Social Sciences

Among the expanding literature attempting to apply the principles of chaos theory to the humanities and the social sciences, perhaps the most compelling are works of George A. Reisch (1991) in history, Jonathan Freidman (1993) in political science, Dragon Milovanovic (1993a, 1993b, 1994) and T. R. Young (1992) in criminology, and a collection of twelve lucid interpretations of the application of chaos to literature in N. Katherine Hayles's (1991) edited work *Chaos and Order: Complex Dynamics in Literature and Science*. Since most of the emphasis in this genre has showcased literature, in this concluding discussion I will consider the lesser known work of historian Reisch, political scientist Friedman, and criminologist Milovanovic, with greatest attention given to Milovanovic and his efforts to integrate chaos theory with Lacanian poststructuralism.

In "Chaos, History, and Narrative," George A. Reisch (1991) attempts to grapple with the same philosophical and methodological demons confronted in this book, namely, the impact of logical empiricism on the philosophy of history. Reisch initiates his analysis by confronting Carl Hempel's "covering-law" history, the view that the only acceptable explication of historical and scientific phenomena must be derived from "deductive-nomological" explanation. To contrast the views of Hempel, he cites Mandelbaum (1961), Danto (1985), Mink (1987), and Roth (1988) as initial sources of support, arguing that each shares a commitment to a "pluralism in historical episteme which holds that accounts of events need not answer to any singular and supreme model of explanation" (1). While these earlier efforts to expose Hempel's determinism still serve as reservoir of fertile ideas, Reisch offers a theoretical critique of Hempel's efforts that draws upon the insights of chaos theory. In doing so, Reisch catapults theorizing on the philosophy of history to another dimension.

Unlike Hempel, Reisch asserts that "history is chaotic" (1991: 2). But to establish his thesis he first constructs a view of historical phenomena using Hempel's covering—law history. In my view there are clear correlations between the methodological assumptions articulated by Hempel and his tradition in history, and the classical and resource mobilization paradigms of social movement theory. To further elaborate on these similarities I would like to present Hempel's thesis in greater detail.

Reisch initiates his analysis of Hempel with reference to Hempel's essay "The Function of General Laws in History" originally published in 1965. In this essay, Hempel determines "proper" historical explanation to be composed of "covering laws, initial conditions, deduction of *explananda* from *explanans*, [and] symmetry of prediction and explanation" (Reisch, 1991: 3). Hempel, according to Reisch, continues to assert that such covering laws, once discovered, "govern processes that span years, generations, even centuries" (3). Reisch problematizes this thesis through his application of chaos theory.

Referring to the literature on chaos cited previously, Reisch defines chaotic systems as those sensitive to perturbations in initial conditions. As such, he commences his application of chaos theory to history with reference to "history as biography." But history, he admits, is more than biography; it includes structural impediments to articulation of individual motivations and indeed shapes conceptualization of motivations. Political, economic, cultural, and environmental structures each serve to constrain the behavior of individuals and groups. Perhaps, Reisch concedes, structuralists are correct in their assertion that "history is actually quite insensitive to the ripples on its surface, to the particular details of historical circumstance, and that history, therefore, is not chaotic at all" (1991: 8).

While conceding to structuralists the significance of institutions for constraining individual and group behavior, Reisch contends that they confuse constraint with determination, and that lurking within and about all systems of constraint are organisms actively creating and recreating their own lived experiences. Hegemonic ideological expressions of power and cultural superiority are confronted at the level of the lifeworld by counter-hegemonic interpretations of dominant culture rearticulated in the language of the oppressed through the vehicle of folklore, myth, song, each constituting what Welch (1985) has referred to as "dangerous memory," and Benjamin (1969), drawing on Marx, labeled "nostalgic utopia." Following Nietzsche, then, Reisch concludes that "history—writ large—is still chaotic," since there are times when effervescent activities of civil society penetrate the thick layers of cultural constraint, transforming both. Reisch contends:

There are times when circumstances and their inherent possibilities give rise to very unstable situations whose outcomes are selected by what might seem at the time the most trivial of factors. Often enough, the state of the world is hypersensitive to the conditions of the past. Or, put differently, the present might well be wholly different if the past were just slightly different. (1991: 9)

I find this a most appealing illustration of the seemingly endless interethnic struggles initiated with the retreat of Soviet influence over activities in the former Yugoslavia. The geo-ethnic rivalry that engulfed the Serbs and Croats in bitter conflict has its roots in a struggle initiated some 600 years ago. While the dominating influence of Tito created a facade of order uniting these disparate peoples, "critical memory" preserved generations of hatred. Here again the question emerges: Will there be order out of chaos?

Reisch concludes his discussion of chaos theory and history with a reference to economic historians and narration. He contends that the market is chaotic; that is, it is extremely sensitive to initial and intervening conditions. Without precise knowledge of the behavior of every trader, journalist, CEO, and investor, and all possible environmental, political, economic, and cultural events, there is no possible way to accurately construct covering laws. Finally, and returning again to Nietzsche (although Reisch curiously avoids mentioning him), Reisch concludes by articulating via chaos theory the essence of new historicism. He contends that "provided the laws which govern a chaotic system are known, the greater the temporal distance between initial (and intervening) conditions on the one hand and the event on the other, the greater the accuracy with which those conditions must be known" (1991: 17). However, since it is probably impossible for historians to reconstruct with absolute certainty events that occurred at some point in our historical memory, we should avoid interpretations based on covering laws. Ernesto Laclau states:

Society as a sutured space, as the underlying mechanism that gives reasons for or explains its own partial processes, does not exist, because if it did, meaning would be fixed in a variety of ways. That is to say, the order of society is the unstable order of a system of differences which is always threatened from the outside. (1988: 254)

In his 1993 essay, "Order and Disorder in Global Systems," Jonathan Friedman contends that global social relations have been moving toward entropy for at least the past two decades. His explanation for this transformation resides in the global decentralization of capital accumulation away from the "old centers" in the West to parts of Southern and Southeastern Asia resulting in "increasing competition and increasing instability." What is unique in Friedman's interpretation of these events is his recognition of the simultaneous global transformation in cultural politics. He suggests that the decentralization of capital accumulation has meant the waning of modernity and its promise of universal progress and development, to be replaced by a new politics of cultural identity, a politics of the local. Referring to the United Nations declaration of 1993 as the Year of Indigenous Peoples, Friedman cites a vast array of indigenous voices clamoring for recognition. From "those indigenous peoples persisting within the margins of national states" (e.g., American Indians, Maori, Sami), to older Euro-ethnic subdivisions now irrupting in segregated voices of difference (e.g., the former Yugoslavia, Quebec, the Basques in Northern Spain), "ethnification," argues Friedman, "is a global process and not a mere coincidence" (1993: 213).

To contextualize this phenemenon, Friedman turns to the poststructural insights of Frederick Jameson's interpretation of Lacan. Briefly, Friedman contends that individual identity is tied to modernity. Perceptions of individual self-construction based on the utilitarian conceptualizations of self-motivation and development were intricately interwoven with essentialistic prescriptions of core nations and their articulation of political, economic and, cultural success. But with the decentralization of capital accumulation has emerged a fractured modernist ego, leaving us postmoderns (or post-industrials) without an ontologizing subject, without a center. This has created what Friedman refers to as a "crisis of personhood" and a general state of depression, or, following Alberoni (1984), a "depressive overload." Individuals not plagued by narcissism will move to eradicate the sense of ego loss and subsequent reconstitution of identity through participation in social movements or other group-based projects. It is this recognition of a re-established order out of "identity chaos" that firmly locates Friedman's analysis within of chaos theory.

The last of the applications of chaos theory to the social sciences to be discussed here is the work of sociologist Dragon Milovanovic. Three publications have established the work of Milovanovic as the progenitor of applications of chaos theory to the field of sociological research. In 1993 there was publication of "Borromean Knots and the Constitution of Sense in Juridico-Discursive Production," and "Lacan's Four Discourses, Chaos and Cultural Criticism in Law." The year 1994 saw publication of "The Decentered Subject in Law: Contributions of Topology, Psychoanalytic Semiotics, and Chaos Theory," wherein Milovanovic initiates what he refers to as "a foray into the realm of the imaginary," an effort to articulate a virgin language necessitated by the inception of a new episteme. In this discussion of Milovanovic's application of chaos theory to sociology, more precisely, to criminology, I will direct my attention to "Lacan's Four Discourses." This article seems to capture the spirit of Milovanovic's efforts to epistemologi-cally reconstruct our conceptualizations of penology and the study of crime. Later, when I discuss efforts to combine chaos theory with poststructural-ism, I will revisit Milovanovic, especially his article "The Decentered Subject in Law."

For Milovanovic, Lacan's psychoanalytic semiotics resembles chaos theory in that it marks a parallel effort to construct an episteme,[7] comprising both order and disorder. Indeed, he contends that in order "to understand his [Lacan's] writings the reader must loosen her/himself from the centripetal pull of conventional discursive practices which tend to produce what chaos theorists refer to as *limit* or *point* attractors" (1993b: 4–5). In order to free psychoanalytic interpretation from "spatiotemporal frameworks" we must pursue alternative explanations and "discursive practices," which in the lexicon of chaos theory would be referred to as pursuit and recognition of strange attractors. Milovanovic offers Lacan's four discourses for consideration.

In the late 1970s Lacan introduced in a seminar, the four discourses of the Master, University, Hysteric, and Analyst. Milovanovic contends that the four discourses were intended to identify relatively stable intersubjective structures that account for the generation of discursive practices (1993b: 5). Furthermore, the four discourses were said to account for "educating, governing, desiring and protesting, and transforming or revolutionizing" (Brecher in Milovanovic, 1993b: 5). Among the four discourses, the language of the Master corresponds to a point attractor, an essentialism or ontology. Like the language of the University, a limit attractor, the language of the Master is static or, as Milovanovic argues, "devoid of a sensitivity to fluctuating social conditions (i.e., far-from-equilibrium conditions) and hence resistive to change"(12). Milovanovic applies chaos attractors to the study of law by suggesting that it is the signification of the Master (point attractor) and University (limit attractor) discourses first encountered by neophyte law students. Master and University discourses provide students with the perception of clearly articulated and only gently debated paradigmatic structures for practicing law.

Next, Milovanovic juxtaposes the point and limit attractors characteristic of Master and University discourses with the torus and strange attractors he associates with the discourses of the Hysteric and Analyst. It is here that Milovanovic returns us to our preliminary discussion of chaos theory, in particular the two specific strands represented on one end by Prigogine and Stengers (the "order out of chaos" strand) and on the other by those making use of strange attractors (e.g., Mandelbrot, Shaw, Serres).

Recall that for Prigogine and Stengers, order emerged as a product of chaotic systems. Diagrammatically, chaos theorists have portrayed these "dissipative structures" as torus attractors or Poincaré sections. A cross-sectional image is extracted from a tube (order or structure) and portrays, at the local level, instability. Milovanovic argues that torus attractors are useful in articulating the significance of initial conditions in the exegesis of legal cases. That is, as court cases move through their assorted iterations, small evidentiary perturbations can produce vastly contradictory legal decisions.

Milovanovic's explication of strange attractors follows Mandelbrot's articulation of fractal geometry. Here, as with torus attractors, slight changes in initial conditions produce substantial macro-level consequences. Also like torus attractors, strange attractors tend, at the structural level, toward order. However, strange attractors are conceptualized diagrammatically as two wings of a whole, a butterfly attractor, constituted by "infinite variation within a finite space" (1993b: 13). In practice this has been interpreted as suggesting the presence of "two (or more) outcome basins within which any accurate prediction is impossible" (1993b: 13), and that while order reigns at the global level, there is disorder at the local. In law, reference to strange attractors has been found in the work of Brion (1991) who argues that one basin or butterfly wing could be conceptualized as constituting legal heritage, while the other contains heresy, alternative or subversive legal views. Strange attractors offer judges alternatives at the level of decision-making, but once a decision has been reached it constitutes a point attractor in the adjudication of law via *stare decisis* ("law of precedent").

Milovanovic's and Brion's adaptations of chaos theory to criminology and law suggest possible avenues for our conceptualization of social movement theory and my articulation of the role played by members of ICs as social movement actors. Let us return for a moment to the butterfly attractor. Contemporary communitarians constitute a heterogeneous rearticulation of dominant cultural capital. Innovations in sexual relations, gender and race/ethnic relations, conflict resolution, modes and means of production, child rearing, play, relationship to the environment, commitment to organic and holistic (diversified agriculture, aquaculture) food production, planetary consciousness, education, spirituality, and the like distinguish contemporary communitarians not only from dominant culture, but when taken holistically, from their communitarian predecessors. In the lexicon of chaos theory, members of ICs are hovering at the Archimedean nucleus of the two wings of the butterfly. One wing represents dominant cultural capital, the familiar. The other wing signifies the unfamiliar, the entropic, a torrent of possibility—Nietzsche's dancing star. It is here in this instability that creativity flourishes, where the cultural revolutionary emerges to rearticulate critical memory, or quite possibly to activate nostalgic utopia.

Now it becomes apparent that this is the possible link between essentialism and civil society, between daily ritualized forms of resistance to oppression expressed at the level of the lifeworld, and those social movements indicated by sociologists as having a morphological composition. Operating in the entropic wing of the butterfly attractor, cultural revolutionaries articulate a new master signifier (counter-hegemonic), founded on local knowledge, myth, folklore, and the like. This new knowledge is qualitatively different from the master discourse of dominant culture since only critical memory "can avoid excluding [intense enjoyment], because it offers not absolute, clearly established, self-referential identities, but rather a system of oppositions embodied in images and fantasies that offer no unequivocal identities, meanings, or values" (Bracher in Milovanovic, 1993: 18). That is, conceptualizing social movements within the context of chaos theory enables us to do is recognize the relevance and continuity of those social movements most clearly identified in the work of collective behaviorists and resource mobilization theory, one wing of the butterfly attractor, all the while we remain aware of the entropic other wing. For if my interpretation of the postindustrial or postmodern malaise as represented in the NSM literature is accurate, those "disenfranchised, marginalized, colonized, and repressed subjects" hovering at the archimedean nucleus of the butterfly attractor have the capacity to (re)create meaning consistent with critical memory or nostalgic utopia. More specifically, the entropic wing of the butterfly attractor offers no specific direction for the disenfranchised. It is out of entropy that negentropy has arisen in the form of intentional community. A new master signifier materializes to act as a counter-hegemonic alternative to dominant cultural capital. The fragmented and unsituated self returns to an ordered state.

Enter Poststructuralism

To suggest that the mathematical science of chaos theory does not parallel in all its assumptions and conclusions the evolution over the past two decades of poststructuralism and deconstruction in literature is no surprise. Indeed, as I will attempt to show in this concluding section, deconstruction theorists aspire to propel randomness in meaning and interpretation far beyond even Mandelbrot. For many deconstructionists (e.g., de Man, Derrida, Saussure, Barthes), the value of multiple interpretations of texts is the culmination of infinite meanings. Their endeavor is to lean on the boundaries of classical interpretations and systems while privileging entropy, the milieu of creativity.

The most significant distinction between the science of chaos and deconstruction lies in their conceptualizations of order. Where scientists value the order emerging from chaotic systems, deconstructionists seek to explode the shackles of order. Derrida's (1976) *Of Grammatology* has stood as an exemplar of deconstructive efforts to destabilize meaning. In many ways parallel to the work of Feigenbaum (1980) in chaos theory,[8] Derrida challenges occidental assumptions that truth emerges in speech through articulation of his neologism "differance." For Derrida, a search for the origins of truth as expressed in writing gives way to recognition of the "always already, acknowledgment of a subconscious warehouse of child- hood experiences preceding the written. As a consequence the " 'always already' formula implies that there is no origin, that the very idea of origin is an illusion" (Hayles, 1990: 181). To more resolutely establish his premise, Derrida turns to the process of iteration.[9] He contends that words spun in multifarious contexts lose their ontological meaning. Furthermore, as Hayles suggests, "the boundary between text and context is not fixed. Infinite contexts invade and permeate the text, regardless of chronology or authorial intention" (1990: 180–181). It is through the process of iteration, slight alterations in the placement of words, that "indeterminacy inheres in writing's very essence."

The point here is to extend the significance of the intrusion of "noise" into the sphere of interpretation and meaning. At bottom is recognition of the fact that any presumption of "correctness when confronting texts as regards, for example, syntax, sentence structure, and the like, emanates from what Hayles, following Derrida and Barthes, refers to as "an illusion perpetrated by centrist philosophy to control texts, language, and power structures within society" (1990: 187). Barthes (1974) elaborates on the necessity of rereading texts to uncover new meaning as a counterweight to capitalist consumptive habits.

Rereading, an operation contrary to the commercial and ideological habits of our society, which would have us "throw away" the story once it has been consumed (or "devoured"), so that we can then move on to another story, [or] buy another book, rereading is here suggested at the outset, for it alone saves the text from repetition (those who fail to reread are obliged to read the same story everywhere). Rereading is no longer consumption, but play. (Hayles, 1990: 192)

Here again the iterative process, initiated by the reader who rereads her texts, generates the "noise" necessary to introduce new meaning and enable continued interpretation and insight.

For our purposes, perhaps the most compelling deliberation of decon- struction can be found in the work of Gilles Deleuze and Felix Guattari. What follows is a brief discussion of their collaborative work *A Thousand Plateaus: Capitalism and Schizophrenia*, published in 1987. It is here that many of the strands of deconstruction and chaos theory begin to merge. It is also clear in this book that a rearticulation of social movement theory, founded on the premise of entropy, can be reformulated.

Let us return for a moment to an earlier effort to establish the significance of entropy as it relates to social movement actors through the use of metaphor. You will recall that I offered to replace the metaphor of the parasite, suggested in Serres's novel of the same name, with that of the *brujo* found in the philosophical work of Pirsig. It was the *brujo* who stood on the periphery of dominant culture, simultaneously a product of that culture, and potentially its most threatening iconoclast. Now it is possible to further loosen conceptually the metaphorical constitution of social movement actors. Doing so explodes the dissipative structures established by chaos theory to articulate a perpetual state of *not order*.

A Thousand Plateaus is a masterful work of near entropy. Any plateau, or chapter of the book, can be read (the authors recommend), with the exception of the conclusion,[10] in any order. It is most important that the reader builds on preceding plateaus, regardless of the order in which they are read, leading to imminent crescendo.

Conceptualization of plateaus is esential to our efforts to understand the role played by social movement actors who resist, not by directing their energy at the level of the state, but rather, through a multifarious juxtaposition of resistances at the level of the lifeworld culminating in a multiplicitious weave. These forms of resistance generally go unnoticed in contemporary social movement research. In the Translator's Foreward, Brian Massumi illuminates the derivation of Deleuze and Guattari's use of the concept of plateau from an essay on Balinese culture by Gregory Bateson. In his research, Bateson "found a libidinal economy quite different from the West's orgasmic orientation." Massumi contends:

In Deleuze and Guattari, a plateau is reached when circumstances combine to bring an activity to a pitch of intensity that is not automatically dissipated in a climax. The heightening of energies is sustained long enough to leave a kind of afterimage of its dynamism that can be reactivated or injected into other activities, creating a fabric of intensive states between which any number of connecting routes could exist. (Deleuze and Guatari, 1987: xiv)

Perceiving global social movement actors as comprising myriad plateaus sempiternally acting and interacting at the level of the lifeworld, and occasionally the state, liberates social movement theory from confounding and, in my estimation, deleterious constraints. As we will witness in Chapter 6, it is more likely, and probably more efficacious (as they seem well aware), for movement actors to resist oppression in ways producing the afterimage of a plateau rather than to try to confront images of power directly through the use of force. In this way movement actors, as those in ICs, constitute one of the numerous strands producing the complex weave of resistance that indelibly designates for current and future generations an alternate path, a counter-hegemony. It is in the afterimage of the plateau that oppressed people rely upon myth, folklore, tradition, and the like to (re)construct critical memory (Welch, 1985). Articulation of the plateau will also be an important foundational concept in Chapter 6 when I introduce and elaborate on Walter Benjamin's reference to nostalgic utopia.

Conceptualization of the plateau is only the inauguration of Deleuze and Guattari's contribution to this section. It is as close as they will come to articulating any form of synthesis, fusion, order. We are now better positioned to return to our discussion of metaphor, which is being revisited to address and further expand upon the subject-object duality persisting in much of poststructural and Marxist thought. Rather than conceptualizing ICs, or any social movement actors within a dialectical context, I propose the construction of social movement theory predicated on the work of Deleuze and Guattari and their articulation of the rhizome.

In the first chapter of *A Thousand Plateaus*, Deleuze and Guattari establish the constitution of "rhizomatic," or "nomadic" representation. Their world metaphor is arborescent; they set out to critique essentialist thought by comparing it to the tree. The tree, as they explain, "is the classical book, noble, signifying, and subjective organic interiority (the strata of the book)" (1987: 5). Modernity inaugurated recognition of the second form of the book, the radical-system or fascicular root. Here, at various places where the tree had been pierced, punctured, or severed, an "indefinite multiplicity of secondary roots grafts onto it and undergoes a flourishing development" (5). Contrary to the claims of modernists, however, unity resounds as a totalizing principle. Deleuze and Guattari refer here to the work of William Burroughs. They contend that "the folding of one text onto another, which constitutes multiple and even adventitious roots (like a cutting), implies a supplementary dimension to that of the texts under consideration. In this supplementary dimension of folding, unity continues its spiritual labor" (6).

One could conceivably include the artistic efforts of cubists, surrealists, dadaists, or, in jazz, the music of Charles Mingus. The point is that elaborating on or adding additional dimensions to the existing tree is and has been a requisite step in fractured consciousness but moves us no closer to conceptualizing the multiple. We must, Deleuze and Guattari inform us, look in the other direction. We must confront "the dint of sobriety" through our recognition of lifeworld activities. It is here that we discover the rhizome, the bulb and the tuber, not roots and radicals. The remainder of this discussion will focus on Delueze and Guattari's six characteristics of the rhizome.

The first two principles identify a strand of thought very similar to that referred to in the work of Bracher and Milovanovic. As heterogeneous entities, rhizomes can be affiliated with multiple semiotic chains as diverse as political, economic, and cultural systems. Or, following Deleuze and Guattari (1987: 7), "a rhizome ceaselessly establishes connections between semiotic chains, organizations of power, and circumstances relative to the arts, sciences, and social struggles." This semiotic chain comprises a colorful array of "dialects, patois, slangs, and specialized languages," but unlike Habermas (1989), Benhabib (1992), and perhaps Cohen and Arato (1992), Deleuze and Guattari insist that there are no ideal speech situations. Rather, and this is the primary affiliation I see with Bracher and Milovanovic, heterogeneous language organizes around a centralized power, "a parish, a bishopric, a capital." It forms a bulb in that it organizes around critical memory. It becomes a language of the people, a language of the oppressed.

The third principle is that of multiplicity. Deleuze and Guattari are emphatic in arguing that it is only when multiplicities are viewed as substantive—not in relation to the tree, to ontology, as marginality theory would have it—that we are truly rhizomatic. Perhaps most important as regards our efforts here, Deleuze and Guattari (1987: 8) confirm that "there are no points or positions in a rhizome, such as those found in a structure, a tree, or root. There are only lines." This points to the seminal proliferation of the persistence of resistance, recognition of the plateau.

One of the most intriguing correlations between Deleuze and Guattari's deliberations of rhizomes and my interests in intentional community can be found in their fourth principle. They contend that the proliferation of multiplicity referred to above stems from the capacity of rhizomes to emerge from events that splinter or shatter a particular strand by grafting onto vestiges of weaves spun in historical memory, or by constructing entirely new strands. That is, "every rhizome contains lines of segmentarity according to which it is stratified, territorialized, organized, signified, attributed, etc., as well as lines of deterritorialization down which it constantly flees" (9). There are obvious correlations here between contemporary intentional communities and their predecessors. While contemporary ICs are presented here as unique relative to their pre-1960s predecessors (primarily based on a more total, holistic agglomeration of communal living skills), there remain, without doubt, vestiges of past communal efforts. Moreover, the data discussed in this book, as with all data presented in aggregate form, are less sensitive to the differences persisting within the IC movement. Recognition of similarity and multiplicity strengthens sociological comprehension of movement actors and issues.

Finally, the fifth and sixth principles amount to a concluding clarion call for movement activists. Citing American pop singer Patti Smith's suggestion, "Don't go for the root, follow the canal," Deleuze and Guattari follow with, "We're tired of trees." While they fully admit that to be rhizomorphous may, at historically significant times, require some penetration of the trunk, they do so only to put the trunk to new uses (15). Furthermore, they suggest, trees have made us suffer too much: "Nothing is beautiful or loving or political aside from underground stems and aerial roots, adventitious growths and rhizomes" (15). In America, "everything important that has happened or is happening takes the route of the American rhizome: beatniks [I would add ICs], the underground, bands and gangs" (19). Deleuze and Guattari offer a fertile conceptual model within which to locate a rearticulation of social movements, and recognition of specific manifestations of rhizomatic resistance.

In sum, I have sought to illuminate possible insights offered by chaos theory and poststructuralism as theoretical alternatives to prevailing social movement theories. It is my contention that through the privileging of one or another mode of overt conflict and the construction of social movement organizations and political lobbies, prevailing social movement theory is incapable of capturing the full panoply of diverse modes of resistance sempiternally operating within the lifeworld. This, I argue, is due in part to a continued effort on the part of social scientists to ontologize movement actors, and to view movement successes through a narrowly defined and delimiting morphological lens.

Application of chaos theory and poststructuralism to an abreviated analysis of intentional communities serves to punctuate my interest in elevating indigenous modes of resistance to a position of prominence among movement theorists. That intentional communities are not viewed as constituting a social movement, I argue, is due primarily to the continued reliance of social scientists on tidy theoretical boxes in which to locate movement actors. In the end, chaos theory alerts us to the endless array of potential furiously moving about at the quantum level of analysis—for me, at the level of the lifeworld. It is from this frenzied activity within the lifeworld that new patterns emerge at the level of the system. Here, while it was not thoroughly addressed in this essay, it is conceivable that the persistence of indigenous modes of resistance mobilizing, for example, over greater community autonomy on issues ranging from recycling programs to education and health care, will spiral upward and outward, effecting broader structural level changes. While this could mean, on the one hand, the preservation of those political spaces necessary for free expression of local issues and activities—that is, the preservation of civil society—it may equally mean structural level policy innovations in education, environmental healing, dispute resolution (as with victim/offender reconciliation projects, which typically emerge as community efforts), work generation projects, and so forth. Like chaos theorists, poststructuralists encourage us to value the rhizome, the creative, the unpredictable as the true source of social change. I am convinced that doing so requires social scientists studying social movements to move beyond prevailing theoretical paradigms. This is indeed an uncomfortable proposition. While not relinquishing entirely the numerous insights offered by prevailing theory, it means moving beyond contemporary theory to privilege actors, issues, and activities that may not fit so nicely into our more familiar theoretical boxes. Intentional communities stand as but one of many examples of social movements that defy contemporary social movement theory. Having little interest in structural-level confrontations, they work to bring about social change within the lifeworld. They operate with very little organizational infrastructure; indeed, they often proudly perceive themselves as a working antithesis of organizations. And yet they persist. Recognizing intentional communities as a social movement requires exploding the boundaries of social movement theory.

Having now set the course for an expanded conceptualization of social movement theory, I turn now in Chapter 5 to a detailed discussion of the multiple historical manifestations of "utopia," followed by a survey of resistance centered within the lifeworld. It is here that I believe we can finally begin to see the relevance of ICs as they appear as the contemporary bearers of the utopian mantle to rearticulate lifeworld concerns.

Notes

1. In fairness, Mellucci has recently begun to "expand" his conceptualization of movement composition to include a broader array of movement potential. Readers should refer to his "A Strange Kind of Newness: What's New in New Social Movements?", in E. Larana, H. Johnston, and J. Gusfield, *New Social Movements: From Ideology to Identity* (Philadelphia: Temple University Press, 1994, pp. 101–130).

2. For a discussion and critique of the collective-behavior, resource mobilization, and new social movement paradigms, please refer to Chapter 3.

3. A possible exception here would be the work of N. Katherine Hayles who, while not elaborating specifically on the correlation between Nietzsche and chaos theory, does mention him in relation to the evolution of postmodernist and post-structuralist thought. In her (1990) book *Chaos Bound*, Hayles devotes Chapter 7 to the similarities and differences between chaos theory and poststructuralism.

4. Fixed point attractors are also referred to in the literature as *periodic attractors*, or *simple attractors*. Wherever there are systems of two or fewer dimensions, there will be only fixed point attractors.

5. For a more detailed discussion of the significance of initial conditions, see Hayles, *Chaos Bound*, pp. 143–174.

6. Following Porush (1991: 59), dissipative structures can be viewed as a "dynamic system which undergoes the sudden transformation from *apparently chaotic* to *increasingly ordered* on the other side of the bifurcation point" (original emphasis).

7. Foucault refers to the episteme as historically sedimented discursive formations manifested in numerous disciplinary mechanisms.

8. Feigenbaum argued that chaos was generated from numerous iterations, but that over time, with repetition, differences in initial conditions gave way to a recognizable pattern. Derrida makes a similar case with the numerous word-based iterations possible in texts.

9. Readers may want to refer to the work of Deleuze and Guattari, particularly their *A Thousand Plateaus*. In this book Deleuze and Guattari articulate their conceptualization of the rhizome.

10. In the Authors' Note, Deleuze and Guattari state that *A Thousand Plateaus* "is composed not of chapters but of 'plateaus.' We will try to explain why later on. To a certain extent, these plateaus may be read independently of one another, except the conclusion, which should be read at the end" (1). I would add only that the first plateau, the Introduction, should be read first.

5

THE UTOPIAN IMAGINARY: CRITICAL MEMORY AND THE PERSISTENCE OF RESISTANCE

The word survivor has two meanings. It denotes somebody who has survived an ordeal. And it also denotes a person who has continued to live when others have disappeared or perished.

John Berger, *Pig Earth*

In our search for a rearticulated theory of social movements we have travelled very far. But there remains one significant element, an arborescent strand, if you will, yet to be discussed which I believe is crucial to satisfying concerns within social movement theory and which has direct application to ICs. Specifically, we must address in this last of the theoretical chapters the dubious and misleading signification of ICs as "utopian." For it is clear, as we have seen in reference to Marx and Engels as well as classical and contemporary social movement theorists, that efforts to realize "alternative" modes of living through the construction of ICs has been relegated, where it is recognized at all, to the status of insignificance. I will attempt to show through a historical analysis of the evolution of the concept of utopia. I will also discuss more recent efforts to resurrect the concept that, like Mannheim (1936), without some conceptualization of utopia, without the cultivation of alternative perceptions of reality, society would be dead. Moreover, and this is directed at those who would dismiss utopian conceptualizations as regressive, it could equally be argued that these propositions are in themselves ideological, a point pursued more thoroughly below. My endeavor in this section will be to establish elements of utopia applicable to contemporary ICs as but one link in the well-established chain of efforts to realize alternate modes of living.

The second section of this chapter seeks integration of utopic qualities with actual efforts at either creating ICs or, as is the case in most regions of the world today, modes of resistance to oppression or postcolonial rearticulations of localized identity. This section will be relevant on two counts. First, acknowledgement of the sempiternal proliferation of peasant resistance requires serious consideration from social movement theorists, particularly in sociology. An expanded definition of social movements, like the one established in the preceding, chapter enables us to do so. Furthermore, it will reiterate the significance of lifeworld activities in the preservation of peasant modes of resistance. Most pertinent to our concerns here is recognition of the fact that when scanning the literatures addressing peasant and other forms of resistance persisting at the level of the lifeworld, one notices the indispensable relevance of myth, folklore, and tradition. We are familiar with the ambivalent perceptions of ICs held by social theorists and activists. They are perceived to be constituted by an annoying and potentially arresting proclivity for "looking backward" (Bellamy) or as Melluci scolds, as constitutive of "regressive utopia." I will argue, with the help of Scott (1990), Welch (1985), Benjamin (1969), de Certeau (1984), and others, that when juxtaposed with contemporary social conditions, traditional references to "critical memory" or "nostalgic utopia" can and have emerged as peasant modes of resistance. That is, reference to tradition, "invented traditions" (Hobsbawm and Ranger, 1983), to history, or even to mythistory (Heehs, 1994), which conjure images of a more egalitarian past, serve as potential wells of inspiration for resistance. I argue, that members of ICs provide us with a state of fractured consciousness. Their persistent example of alternative constructions of public and private space, and political, economic, and cultural relations serve as a sort of counter-memory.

Establishing the Concept: The Etymology of "Utopia"

Historical record is replete with cross-cultural references to efforts at constructing this or that form of alternative cultural arrangement. In their book on the history of utopia, Pamela Neville-Sington and David Sington (1993) locate the predecessor to utopian thought in what they refer to as a near-universal and enthusiastic reference to "the Golden Age." Here, romantic voices as distinct as the Greek poet Hesiod, Roman poet Ovid, the Bible, and the Sumerian epic of Gilgamesh refer with passion and reverence to antiquity free from want of basic necessities. Often these reminiscences centered on the bounteous and indulgent procurement of food, as in Hesiod's proclamation: "With hearts free from sorrow and remote from toil and grief, the fruitful earth spontaneously bore them abundant fruit without stint."

In the imagination of Ovid, the Golden Age was the

first age, which, with no one to compel, without a law, of its own will, kept faith and did the right. The earth herself, without compulsion, untouched by hoe or ploughshare, of herself gave all things needful. Anon the earth, brought forth her store of grain, and the fields, though unfallowed, grew white with the heavy, bearded wheat. Streams of milk and streams of sweet nectar flowed, and yellow honey was distilled from the verdant oak. (Neville-Sington and Sington: 3)

Contemporary anthropological explications of pre-agricultural bands[1] (up to 10,000 B.C.) seem to offer evidence of hunting and gathering communities that worked, on average, no more than twenty-five hours per week gathering food and procuring shelter. The Kung San of Southwestern Africa offer a good example. The Kung San work seventeen hours per week gathering a portion of the over 500 edible plants that constitute their daily diet, extending gathering periods to twenty-five hours per week during the rainy seasons (Sahlins, 1972). This led, when compared with early-agricultural and agricultural periods, to a superior diet (of fruits, nuts, berries, and occasionally, meat) and increased leisure. To punctuate the juxtaposition of contemporary work habits with those of the hunters and gatherers, Sahlins referred to hunters and gatherers as the original affluent society, based on the minimal effort they required to satisfy their material needs and wants.

References to the Golden Age were not without their detractors, of course, and were countered by the satire of poets writing from the fifth century B.C. through the second century A.D. Hesiod and Ovid were ridiculed by comic poets like Athenaeus (second century A.D.), Teleclides (fifth century B.C.), and Crate (fifth century B.C.) for their efforts to mythologize the Golden Age. Through satirical references to the abundance of food and gentility of daily life, these early critics chided references to a chimerical past as illusory and diversionary.

In the fourteenth century, and in direct contradistinction to the image of the Golden Age portrayed by priests and poets, peasants constructed their own version, perhaps the most well-known representation of a utopic vision prior to the publication of More's *Utopia*. It was during this century that a poem, inspired by the dire straits of peasants, commanded references to an unbounded somewhere that catered solely to the wants and desires of the unremarkable. In "The Land of the Cockaigne,"[2] peasants furnished their own critique of "gluttonous monks" and opulent displays of wealth while envisioning a place where

> There are rivers broad and fine
> Of oil, milk, honey and of wine;
> Water serveth there no thing
> But for sight and for washing.
> There is a mighty fine Abbey,
> Thronged with monks both white and grey,
> Ah, those chambers and those halls!
> All of pasties stand the walls,
> Of fish and flesh and all rich meat,
> The tastiest that men can eat.
> Wheaten cakes the shingles all,
> Of church, of cloister, bower and hall.
> The pinnacles are fat puddings,
> Good food for princes or for kings.
> Every man takes what he will,
> As of right to eat his fill.
> All is common to young and old,
> To stout and strong, to meek and bold.
> Everyman may drink his fill
> And needn't sweat to pay the bill.
>
> (Neville-Sington and Sington: 6)

Peasants openly confronted the pious and austere renderings of the Golden Age with Cockaigne, a place Kumar (1991) describes as "a land of extravagance, exuberance and excess. It evokes words like Falstaffian and Gargantuan. Its master themes are abundance and freedom from work. Everything is free and available for the asking" (6). American literary references to the land of the Cockaigne include *The Big Rock Candy Mountains* and *Poor Man's Heaven*. Most importantly for us, however, is recognition of the fact that what began as a literary genre articulating a sort of counter-hegemonic hedonism later manifested itself in the form of peasant-centered festivals celebrating non-normativity.

References here would include the medieval Feast of Fools, the Roman Saturnalia, and in America, the Mardi Gras held every year in New Orleans. These festivals and thousands of others like them held annually around the world are characterized by their open disregard for normative behavioral prescriptions, and by their "popular license, and uninhibited indulgence." Crucial here is the extent to which fanciful representations of alternate modes of living represented in literature found their way into popular expressions of peasant disgust. The Land of the Cockaigne symbolizes an everpresent alternative construction of reality percolating at the level of the lifeworld. Determining whether it is actually indicative of a utopian vision is a more difficult matter.

While fanciful renderings of bounteous victuals posed by peasants rebuking disparities in wealth and power approximate utopian juxtapositions, they are *not* utopian. Absent from visionary reminiscences prior to the sixteenth century were efforts at "constitution building." For this, sixteenth-century authors would have to turn to Greece and Rome and the innovations in political, economic, and cultural engineering inspired by Salon, Lycurgus, and Plato. For this reason, mythological accounts prior to the sixteenth century, while representative of the requisite "wish imagery" (Mannheim), nevertheless lacked the characteristic coherence offered by later utopians who fused these earlier folk images with analytical efforts to calculate daily political, economic, and cultural matters. Thus, the image of the Cockaigne, while a seminal component of utopian thought, captured only a portion of its visionary potential. Two centuries later, Thomas More would endeavor to fill the void.

Unlike the poetic Cockaigne, Salon, Lycurgus, and Plato catalyzed numerous political and economic innovations that inspired utopian thinkers nearly two millennia later. Among Salon's credits is the elimination of serfdom in sixth-century Greece, the introduction of legal codes, encouragement of trade and industry, establishment of property and not birth status as the criteria for political power, and creation of a people's assembly of 400 to counter the aristocratic council. He is referred to by Neville-Sington and Sington as the most reform-minded of the three. In contrast, Lycurgus engaged more radical methods in his reconstruction of Sparta. For example, he redistributed land throughout Sparta to eliminate wealth inequity, abolished gold and silver coinage to deter financial corruption, made the selection of marital partners one of mutual choice, promoted "free love" to eliminate jealousy, and encouraged the practice of eugenics to selectively breed children. Each in his own way influenced emerging utopian thought.

Plato's *Republic*, however, stands as perhaps the most significant classical account of utopic imagery. In 386 B.C. Plato founded the Academy in Athens to initiate the education of would-be politicians in the art of philosophical thought. His interest in founding the Academy drew directly from his own apparent involvement and disgust with Athenian politics, so much so that it led him to conclude:

that all existing states were badly governed, and that their constitutions were incapable of reform without drastic treatment and a great deal of good luck. I was forced, in fact, to the belief that the only hope of finding justice for society or for the individual lay in true philosophy, and that man will have no respite from trouble until either real philosophers gain political power or politicians become by some miracle true philosophers. (Neville-Sington and Sington: 9)

It was during his initial years in the Academy that Plato penned the *Republic*, a dialogue with Socrates on the principles of a society governed by two classes, the rulers and the auxiliaries. The rulers and the auxiliaries together constitute what Plato referred to as the guardians. The guardians, according to Neville-Sington and Sington, are "committed communists. They have no possessions, property, or family, and like the Spartans, follow military-style discipline. They are entirely supported by the state, and their life is austere in the extreme" (10). Austerity, argues Neville-Sington and Sington, prevents corruption and disunity. Perhaps most startling, particularly by contemporary standards, is the extremely "liberated" proposition advanced by Socrates that among the guardians there be no marriage, that all women be available to all men, and that all children be raised in common. This, he proposed, was necessary since the affairs of family would impede those of the state. In many ways analogous to the efforts by John Humphrey Noyes to enhance the occupational opportunities of women, Plato's suggestion that women be emancipated from the responsibilities of marriage and child care emanated from his concern that the Greek state was only "half a state" so long as women were not participating fully. Female guardians actively engaged in both physical and intellectual training. But like the Oneidas, the primary responsibility of women was child rearing. The selection of suitable partners was managed through a eugenics program designed to produce the "most suitable leaders" for the state. Furthermore, there was to be no sex without permission from the rulers, or more specifically, no intercourse without the intention of procreating for the greater good of the state. Here, parallels to Noyes's Oneida community are compelling.

Plato's *Republic* has many detractors. In his own time his student, Aristotle, chided any attempt to articulate a vision of an ideal state. Aristotle was especially unreceptive to Plato's communism, arguing that humams are by nature bound to their possessions, "caring less for what is common." In the twentieth century, Plato has found his most sardonic critic in Karl Popper who, writing in *The Spell of Plato*, argues that the *Republic* is "the original philosophical charter of fascism." It is true, as Neville-Sington and Sington (1993) acknowledge, that as the political force of National Socialist rhetoric gained recognition from academics in Germany, references to similarities between the platform proposed by the Third Reich and Plato's *Republic* were advanced. But in their account, Neville-Sington and Sington wish to salvage the "constitutional quality" of Plato's work, not insofar as it is a blueprint for the ideal state, but because Plato openly rejected this kind of philosophizing. Rather, because they believe his ideas concerning the preparation and proliferation of philosopher kings represented the first systematic effort to combine an imaginative explication of "another way" based on a re-evaluation of political, economic, and cultural constructs. With the innovations of Salon and Lycurgus, and the passionate peasant rendering of Cockaigne, we realize the foundation of utopic thought leading to the twentieth century. Standing between these momentous historical achievements and the twentieth century, however, was an effort in literary muse that would transform the realm of utopian imagery.

Contemporary articulations of utopia identify their origins in the publication of Sir Thomas More's whimsical yet poignant tale, *Utopia,* originally published in 1516. Through the neologism "utopia," More was able to capture the dualistic tension he perceived to permeate his time, as utopia referred simultaneously to "no place" (*ou topos*) and "good place" (*eu topos*). More's utopia captured the imagery of the possible at the same time it denied it. It is, as Kumar (1991) would proclaim, "to live in a world that cannot be but where one fervently wishes to be" (1).[3] It is to perceive the zenith of human cohabitation—for More, communism, a disdain for precious jewels and gold, and the absence of monarchy—while simultaneously acknowledging its unrealizability. The utopian imagination is inspired by myth and folklore, most apparent in the work of Ernst Bloch (1955, 1959), and by fantasy, daydreams, fairy tales, tales of travel, and literary utopias.[4]

Concomitant with the proliferation of sea travel during the sixteenth and seventeenth centuries was the emergence of a literary genre poised to engage the imaginations of the politically oppressed, economically exploited and dispossessed masses of More's Tudor England. It was the height of the Renaissance, the time of discovery. The voyages of Christopher Columbus and Amerigo Vespucci, undertaken in More's lifetime, had an electric effect on the European imagination. It was also during this period that classical texts, like Plato's *Republic*, found a rejuvenated audience ready to untangle the mysteries of the ancients, while challenges to the authority of the Catholic Church were manifested in criticisms of an alleged distortion in the Latin version of the New Testament, criticism brought primarily by Erasmus's inaugural publication of the New Testament in Greek.

It is within the context of exploration and possibility that More concocted his chimerical farce. An accomplished lawyer, More was valued by King Henry VIII for his ability to negotiate trade relations with international merchants. In 1515, write Neville-Sington and Sington, More traveled to Bruges at the behest of Henry VIII "to negotiate a commercial treaty with Flanders concerning the wool trade." During July, and with negotiations at a stalemate, More left Bruges to visit a friend of Erasmus named Peter Gilles living in Antwerp. It is here that his fantasy takes shape. A dialogue unfolds between More and Peter Gilles around the constitution of utopia and the introduction of the book's protagonist, Raphael Hythloday.

More's *Utopia* was inspired by the exploration of Amerigo Vespucci. Vespucci's travels to the New World and his enthusiastic reminiscences upon his return stimulated European imaginations beyond the realm of the New World uncovered by the earlier expeditions of Columbus. According to More, Raphael Hythloday accompanied Vespucci as he made his fourth expedition to the New World. Rather than returning to Europe with Vespucci, Hythloday pushed beyond the known lands until he came upon the island of Utopia.

While there remains some debate concerning More's intentions, it is clear that the book, written in two parts, advances a searing indictment of Tudor depravity. Krishnan Kumar claims that while Part 2 of *Utopia*, written first and almost entirely while More was in Antwerp, is an intelligent and playful[5] reminiscence of the constitution of political, economic and cultural relations on the island. Part 1 establishes his critique of bourgeois England. Kumar argues that having cultivated the chimerical qualities of Utopia, More realized the need to commit their inspiration to an indictment of contemporary social relations. While his fanciful articulation of Utopia was not unlike other accounts in the Renaissance humanist tradition, his juxtaposition of Utopia with contemporary English vice was. But most relevant for our purposes is the way More advances, in his arraignment of England and conceptualization of Utopia, a transcendent (un)reality that is neither reformist, nor entirely unrealizable. It is, as with the *brujo*, of but not of.

The genius of More's *Utopia* (and this pertains to subsequent uses of the concept), is the creative construction of a seemingly unrealizable, unattainable *somewhere*. It exists by virtue of its naming and yet there can never be any manifest record of it. The product is a sempiternal searching, pursuit, journey.[6] Much like Mannheim (1936), who will be discussed in greater detail below, More perceives the utopic function as the gift of the possible. In Mannheim this manifests itself in historically contextualized and unique acts of refutation driven by the juxtaposition of contemporary status-preserving relations with alternative configurations. Mannheim perceives the Anabaptists, who found their voice in Thomas Munzer, as the first cultural confrontation shrouded in a utopic imagination. Historically, utopic imaginings always seem to have one foot in reality, with the other suspended (never sedimented) somewhere over the possible.

The same can be said of More's juxtaposition of the two parts constituting *Utopia*. Had he produced a novel based solely on the exploration of the island that is both "no place" and "good place," his legacy would, I believe, be that of the Cockaigne: intelligent, witty, fanciful, but lacking the requisite bite needed to conjure critical imaginings in the minds of the oppressed. The juxtaposition of Part 2 with Part 1 at once infused *Utopia* with political expediency and the creative imagination necessary to engage the construction of alternate modes of living. In the end, it can be argued that *Utopia* served as a predecessor for many aspects of contemporary occidental life, including the articulation of social and economic equality, rational thought, and religious tolerance (Neville-Sington and Sington, 1993). That More's *literary* utopia inspired nineteenth and twentieth-century experiments in communal living is generally well accepted, but it is important to remember that his imagination was catalyzed by real living conditions in his period of Tudor England. This point should be pursued further.

There is a peculiar parallel between existing cultures, subcultures, charismatic personalities, and counter-hegemonic practices, and the utopic visions of eighteenth, nineteenth, and twentieth-century utopian visionaries. Whether one is referring to the influence of Lycurgus's Sparta on the composition of Plato's *Republic*, or that of the Incas on Thomas More's *Utopia* and Edward Bellamy's *Looking Backward*, the norms, values, and institutions of these cultures have inspired the utopian imagination. Religion, more precisely, monasteries, constitute a persistent historical referent for utopians as distinct as Gerrard Winstanley and the Diggers, More, Campanella, Bacon, Saint-Simon, Compte, and Bellamy.[7] Monasteries symbolized a life of disciplined hard work, sacrifice, communal living, and, not insignificantly, a rebuke of the emerging competition and denigration of social relations associated with the ascending dominance of money and wage-based labor. There was and is, moreover, an environment imbued with love, friendship, peace, and harmony. That this image of monastic life continues to inspire communitarian efforts should come as no surprise.[8]

Ernst Bloch (1988), to whom I will refer in greater detail below, offers the compelling proposition that it is death, or more precisely, our mortal fear of it, that propels humans toward utopic thought and action. Death, for Bloch, depicts the "hardest counter utopia." As he puts it, "[N]ailing the coffin puts an end to all of our individual series of actions at the very least" (9). Religion exalts death as the *eschatological other*, offering eternal life as its negation. Of course, eternal life requires the miracle of divine intervention, and resurrection, a transcendent act capable of cheating the abyss. This act, too, according to Bloch, "belongs to utopia." Theodore Adorno (1988), in conversation with Bloch, adds,

> to be sure, I believe that without the notion of the unfettered life, freed from death, the idea of utopia, the idea of *the* utopia, *cannot* even be thought at all. Where the threshold of death is not at the same time considered, there can actually be no utopia. (original emphasis)

Here, Adorno alludes to the same contradiction recognized by More, that whether it is symbolic or literal, "utopia cannot be conceived without the elimination of death." It is on this point that Adorno and Bloch converge in their agreement that utopia is essentially a "critique of what is present." Here, particularly in religious imagery, utopia emerges as the negation of what is.

Where utopians have confronted opposition to their ideals by critics' claims that they are unrealizable and even reactionary, they have frequently sought references to (myth) history as a way of confirming the legitimacy of their endeavors. There are numerous representations of this phenomenon, which will be elaborated on in detail below. Of pressing importance at this stage—in my attempt to establish the relevance of utopian thought for sociologists interested in social movements—is discussion of a more elaborate articulation of those theoretical attempts to root the utopian imagination within the historical memories of the oppressed. Specifically, where much of the scholarly attention devoted to studies of utopia has emphasized form, content, and function, theorists like Georges Sorel, Karl Mannheim, Ernst Bloch, Walter Benjamin, Paul Ricour, James Scott, and Sharon Welch, to name but a few, have transcended morphological accounts through their recognition of the transformative puissance of utopian visions (Mannheim, Benjamin, Ricour) and mythological reminiscences (Sorel, Scott, Welch) once juxtaposed with actual social conditions. In the paragraphs below I would like to briefly elaborate on the theoretical insights of Sorel, Mannheim, and Bloch, for they have set a more "progressive" tone for a critical appropriation of utopian efforts.

Sorel wrote most extensively of utopia in *Reflections on Violence*, a work, along with others during the five year period 1904–1909, heavily influenced by an emerging syndicalist movement in France. His support for both

Mussolini and Lenin has brought him praise and criticism from the Left and Right. What interests me is his theoretical juxtaposition of utopia with myth. Sorel conceptualizes the transformative power of myth in the same way that Mannheim attributes it to utopia. For Sorel, "ideas in the form of myths, could potentially perform a mobilizing and transformative function" (Levitas, 1990: 59). However, utopias, in virtually all of their manifestations, appear in Sorel as deficient political-economic miscalculations of social reformers. Chided by Sorel as a merely intellectual exercise rather than product of the will, utopia is nonetheless constituted by the capacity to promote alternate visions of the future regardless of the immature analysis of the "processes of social change." Sorel classifies utopian efforts into three ideal types: literary utopias, utopias characterized by their radical revolutionary potential, and those absorbed into political programs. Literary utopias, those proposed by More, Bacon, Bellamy, and the like, are dismissed for their efforts to "reverse economic history." Sorel, much like Lenin, believed that the emerging factory system, inspired to the degree it was by Taylorism and scientific management and later by Fordism, was the most perspicacious organization of productive activity known to humanity. He concedes that "everything must proceed on the model of the factory running in an orderly manner, without capriciousness or waste of time" (Levitas, 1990: 61). Although he may have appreciated Saint-Simon, Fourier, or even Robert Owen for their vision of an alternate future he remained quite critical of their apparently naive (for Sorel) recognition of the economic force of history, appearing as it did in the emergence of capitalist labor process. Failing to appreciate the capitalist mode of production resulted, for Sorel, in an immature and completely academic proposition for the construction of an alternate future. While Sorel conceded that all utopias offered a critique of contemporary social conditions and a plan to improve them, a vision necessary for any change to occur, he was equally stern in his repudiation, as is evident in his lament: "all utopias can do is express desires and regrets" (Levitas, 1990: 63), leaving untouched the oppressive social conditions.

Stepping back for a moment, recall that classical and contemporary social movement theories dismiss ICs from their accounts of social movement organizations and actors based on the contention that they are "utopian," or as Melucci suggests, they engage in the practice of "regressive utopia." Because IC activities are not solely (and often not at all) directed at state-based social change, because they may extract from their utopian predecessors modes of living that by contemporary standards, recalls an umbilical dependence on the past (particular references are made here to the agrarian character of many ICs), for these reasons and others left unexplored, members of ICs should not be given the mantle of social movement. But let's concur for the moment that ICs *do* resemble in many ways their nineteenth- and early twentieth-century predecessors (not an incorrect assumption, to be sure). And let's agree that what separates my analysis from those offered by other social movement theorists is the particular frame or interpretation offered in evaluating contemporary ICs and their appropriation of modes of living characteristic of these earlier epochs. That is, what current social movement theory perceives as regressive in the historical reminiscences constituting alternate modes of living offered by intentional communitarians, I perceive as constitutive of a complex arborescent historical weave of liberating potential. Specifically, when juxtaposed with contemporary social conditions, alternate modes of living exemplified by ICs evoke notable contrast. Determining with any accuracy whether the clash of difference will reverberate with enough perspicacity to initiate transformations in dominant cultural behavior is difficult at best. Moreover, as is particularly the case with Sorel, the liberating potential of myth is valued for its capacity to inspire action; internal consistency and historical accuracy are irrelevant and purely academic. We return now to our discussion of Sorel, Mannheim, and Bloch, staying focused on our interest in the theoretical articulation of the revolutionary potential in utopian and mythological juxtapositions of contemporary social conditions with selective images and remembrances culled from historical memory.

Sorel identifies the liberating potential of the oppressed not in utopia but in the power of the creative juxtaposition of myth. In her interpretation of Sorel, Levitas (1990) contends that "the function of any myth is to facilitate action." Myths exist in the historical memory of specific actors and may be imbued with utopian images of alternate modes of living. But whereas myths conjure active attempts to transform social conditions, utopias offer only criticism. Myths are requisite constructs for the realization of revolution. Levitas argues further that "The superiority of myth over utopia is not just that it is more effective at changing the world. Myth is morally superior because of the state of mind which it induces and the action which it gives rise to" (66).

So it is with Sorel that mythological renderings of significant historical events provoke the possibility of transforming oppressive conditions. Myths conjure passion. They offer comprehension of a historical self in association with others perceived to be like them that is more vivid (that is not to say more accurate), than their own experiences. In contradistinction, utopia, to

Sorel, is rather pejoratively relegated to the realm of the intellect. Indeed, Sorel chides utopian visions as "reactionary" and "diversionary," more interested in ends than in process. Unlike Sorel, Mannheim (1936) promotes cultivation of a utopian imaginary as the necessary dialectical counter-weight to ideology. It is to Mannheim's conceptualization of utopia that I now turn.

Mannheim, like Sorel, believed that images expressing the will and desire of like-minded people could inspire efforts to transform prevailing social conditions. And while there are similarities in the ways in which Mannheim and Sorel conceive their concepts, their intellectual purpose and paradig-matic frames provided for distinct conceptualizations. In his most famous work, *Ideology and Utopia* (1936), originally published in 1926, Mannheim endeavored to construct a sociology of knowledge in the interpretative tradition established by Max Weber, capable of perceiving the true nature of ideology. His analysis proceeds by distinguishing ideology from utopia on the basis of their social functions. While drawing on the insight of Marx, Mannheim asserts that it is the function of ideology to *preserve* existing political, economic, and cultural relations, while utopian visions emerge to *transcend* the status quo in pursuit of alternate modes of living: "Only those orientations transcending reality will be referred to by us as utopian which, when they pass over into conduct, tend to shatter, either partially or wholly, the order of things prevailing at the time" (Mannheim, 1936: 192).

To be sure, it is not merely the existence of "wish-images" that constitute utopian status; these existed in religious imagery, for example, throughout the medieval period as but a single component of cultural capital. Rather, it is only when these wish-images are acted upon in revolutionary efforts to transform dominant cultural capital that they become utopian. With specific reference to this period, Mannheim, like Bloch, refers to Thomas Munzer and the "orgiastic chiliasm of the Anabaptists," as the utopian imagination. Mannheim's most significant contribution and most confounding problem was to balance his confluence of ideology and utopia, with their manifes-tations in concrete, identifiable reality.

The nature of "reality" or "existence as such" is a problem which belongs to philosophy, and is of no concern here. Inasmuch as man is a creature living primarily in history and society, the "existence" that surrounds him is never "existence as such," but is always a concrete historical form of social existence. (Mannheim, 1936: 193)

As others have noted,[9] Mannheim's contention that reality is a comprehen-sible, tangible entity ignores symbolic interventions at the level of the lifeworld that serve to filter and recompose dominant cultural images.[10] What Mannheim does convey in this passage, however, is the Marxist correlation among dominant ideas, utopian alternatives, and class conflict. Mannheim indirectly refers to Marx's interpretation of the dialectic and the process of negation when he suggests that every epoch produces within it the seeds of its own transcendence. He states specifically that the relationship between the existing state of affairs and utopia is a "dialectical" one: "The existing order gives birth to utopias which in turn break the bonds of the existing order, leaving it free to develop in the direction of the next order of existence" (Mannheim, 1936: 199).[11]

For Mannheim, ideology is composed of three distinct types. The first ideological type emerges from within social relationships bound by socio-historical axioms from which the thinking agent is unable to discern truth. The second ideological type involves self-deception. Although it is now conceivable to uncover the "incongruence between ideas and conduct," emotional and intellectual investments in these prevent agents from doing so. It is the third ideological type that most closely approximates Marxist articulations in that Mannheim conceives ideology here as being based on "conscious deception, where ideology is to be interpreted as a purposeful lie" (1936: 195). Here, ideology is no longer constituted by self-deception but by the conscious deceit of another. By way of contrast, utopia is similarly conceived of as transcendent but in no way ideological. That is, utopias are constituted by "counteractivity" directed at the transformation of current social conditions in keeping with the vision(s) of utopians themselves, thus leading Mannheim to profess that "the utopias of today become the realities of tomorrow." But perhaps more important, it concerns our endeavor to establish the significance of the utopian imaginary as potential source of social change is his suggestion that

it is always the dominant group which is in full accord with the existing order that determines what is to be regarded as utopian [and therefore "unrealistic," "imma-ture," "regressive"], while the ascendant group which is in conflict with things as they are is the one that determines what is regarded as ideological. (Mannheim, 1936: 203)

Clearly it is a Marxist expression of ideology. It is noteworthy that Mannheim's extremely structuralist interpretation of elite power, one that is confounded on grounds of ontological overdetermination, has been appended. Levitas contends, and I agree, that what is needed for a truly reflexive analysis of the role of class and power in the articulation of ideas and mobilization of state-based steering activities is a neo-Gramscian conceptualization of hegemony that incorporates the insights of post-Marx-ism and deconstruction discussed in Chapter 4. This would free investiga-tors to pursue the often fragmented, multiple interests constituting dominant culture, while remaining cognizant of class-based combinations.

So it is that while Mannheim exposes in rudimentary form the relevance of utopian thought for the potentially revolutionary power it wields, it is also true that his monotonically formulated conceptualization of utopia, one determined by the same conflict criteria we find in current social movement theory, ignores those groups (in his schema they would not qualify as utopians without the conflict focus) practicing alternative modes of living that also exercise their option not to violently confront dominant culture. Moreover, and following Ricoeur, when Mannheim projects the "criterion of realizability" as the true distinction between utopia and ideology, he perpetrates as fallacious an expectation of success as do Kanter and Zablocki. That is to say, is it truly necessary for ICs or any other organiza-tional manifestation of a utopian imagination to pass a sociologically contrived longevity test in order to be considered a "success"? The purpose of this chapter, and indeed this book, is to argue against such a proposition. Recognizing in Mannheim some vestige of this contention in his effort to distinguish ideology from utopia, but adding a lucid twist, Ricoeur (1986) submits:

Who knows whether what has been condemned by history will not return in more favorable circumstances? The "unreal" element in the dialectic is not defined by the unrealizable but by the ideal, in its legitimizing function. The transcendent is the "ought" which the "is" conceals. (179)

This theoretical maneuver initiates a move closer to the position I will articulate as my own: that it is not necessary for ICs to stir revolutionary impulses or converge on state legislatures in order to effectuate transcen-dence. It is similarly the case that Ricoeur anticipates my interpretation of contemporary ICs by saying, "Utopias themselves are never realized to the extent that they create the *distance* between what is and what ought to be" (179, original emphasis). In other words, utopias can never fully abrogate their association with dominant culture. As we witnessed in Chapter 2, contemporary ICs *are* relatively integrated into their communities. They participate in lifeworld activities and engage lifeworld issues all the while they continue to practice alternative modes of living.

Finally, unlike Bloch and Sorel, Mannheim dismisses myth, folklore, religion, utopian novels, and tales of travel as just so many lifeworld interpretations of "reality." While he perceives their presence as indicative of "wish-images" or dreams of a better future—absent efforts to actively engage in the transformation of the status quo—they are not considered utopian. Ernst Bloch moved beyond Mannheim in his analysis of the utopian imagination to include just such expressions of mythistory. His work will help catapult our analysis toward contemporary anthropological data on the use of myth, folklore and the like in struggles that resist oppressive social conditions.

"It is a question of learning to hope." So begins the introduction to Ernst Bloch's analysis of the "not-yet-consciousness." For Bloch, humanity is imbued with the ability to strive for a better life. Wherever people have experienced hard times, their daydreams have offered them visions of something better.

This is the manifestation of what Bloch refers to as the utopian principle. The utopian principle is constituted by "expectation, hope, intention towards possibility that has not become" (1995: 7). Cultivation of utopian consciousness is necessary, not as a diversion from the pressing difficulties characteristic of life, but as a necessary filter through which to contemplate one's immediate situation. Bloch seems to be arguing that it is only through the juxtaposition of immediate social relations with a sharp utopian consciousness that one can successfully navigate the darkness permeating day-to-day life.

Bloch conceptualizes the cultivation of utopian consciousness as occurring within the "not-yet-consciousness," the preconsciousness of what is to come. Articulation of the not-yet-consciousness emerges as a companion concept to Benjamin's (1969) nostalgic utopia, in that, consciousness of past and future is a perpetual process of recognition and interpretation. Like Marx, Bloch conceptualized the manifestation of the future as recognizable in the present and the past. Myths, songs, fairy-tales, travel tales, and daydreams, each represent the consolidation of historical images consumed and reconfigured to meet contemporary and future demands. Plaice et al. (1995) suggest that the creative appropriation of historical imagery provides for the possibility of "New meaning and fresh synthetic combinations extracted from the thinking of the past, to be discovered and inherited by each succeeding age" (xxvii). For Bloch, then, utopia was not, as it was for More, solely a place in literature. Utopia was realizable, probably in socialism.

It is Bloch's insistence on three significant components of utopia: the inevitability of its presence in the not-yet-consciousness in all people, the active way in which people appropriate images of the past through myth, folklore, fairy tales, travel tales, songs, and daydreams, and his insistence that utopia is a conscious possibility, that makes his interpretation so appealing. It is this active appropriation of the past to meet the juxtaposition of the present and future that will emerge as a persistent theme in what follows below.

Exploring the Hidden Transcript

In her analysis of the Mateel community in the Northwestern United States, Jentri Anders (1990) explains that Mateelians have adopted a "paraprimitive solution" to addressing urgent needs for planetary regeneration. According to Anders, community members "look to primitive societies as models because they are relatively ecologically stable" (1990: 7). Members regard themselves as an "embryonic paraprimitive community" characterized by reduced resource consumption (electrical, water, and the like), rejection of public utilities, home food production, owner-built homes, natural childbirth and midwifery, with experiments in kinship, marriage and family. Moreover, as Anders concedes (1990: 7–8), "approaches [to communal living] combine elements taken from mainstream American past with ideas borrowed from other cultures." And almost as if anticipating this chapter's concern for the ideological and literal weight of mythological appropriations of mythistory, Anders (1990: 8) argues that among the Mateelians

there is a yearning to recapture the past but the yearned for past is idealized and reflects contemporary environmental concerns. Their image of the past is a place where families could support themselves by virtue of their labor on small pieces of land.

However, in a long passage that directly confronts Alvin Toffler's dismissal of communal efforts as little more than "first wave reversionists," Anders makes two sweeping and confusing comments. First, she argues that Mateelians are not utopian because, she contends, utopias are/were too "inflexible." Instead, members of the Mateel community embrace a combination of "craft-based production with appropriate technology and alternative energy sources." Neither does she believe that Mateel represents a communal movement, a designation she interprets, with no elaboration, as indicative of being little more than a "fad." I do not wish to make too much of these statements as they represent only minor excerpts from a text at once insightful and rich in detail. But when combined with other accounts of contemporary ICs, Anders's narrative of Mateel corroborates my contention that, perhaps contrary to her interpretation, they *are* indeed indicative of the multiple causal strands constituting a NSM. Perhaps her conceptualization of the literal relevance of utopian thought and juxtaposition, as well as her dismissal of communal efforts as faddish, are the products of classical interpretations of each. Again, as discussed in the preceding chapter, the discourse of the left must struggle to deconstruct those concepts previously defined and in so many ways dismissed by classical interpretations of communal activities, and reappropriate them to illuminate their significance for actors seeking alternative lifeworld options.

The Mateel community is presented here as indicative of those ICs conscious of their historical reminiscences, both domestic and international, which serve as antiquated beacons of valued lifeworld experiences. These historical images inspire renewed efforts to construct meaningful lives and for this reason alone are worthy of recognition. It is to an articulation of the multifarious composition of invented traditions (Hobsbawm and Ranger)— their theoretical and practical meaning—that this final part of Chapter 5 is dedicated. It is my contention that, far from being "regressive" or "impotent" reflections on a bygone era, mythological, mythistorical, and folk-based articulations of counter-hegemony represent the amassing of subjugated knowledges (Foucault), often in cryptic compositions identified by Scott (1990) as hidden transcripts, yielding a potentially transformative counter-memory (Welch).

But what is myth? At the core of much theorizing on nostalgic utopia is an often unstated acceptance of myth as a virtually self-explanatory concept. To avoid misunderstanding I should like to clearly identify the working definition of myth utilized in this book. While an unproblematic conceptualization of myth, one often utilized by anthropologists and mythologists, could be given as "sacred narratives of traditional societies generally involving superhuman beings," more expanded definitions include "traditional stories, legends, [and] sagas."[12] But the definition of myth I will be using follows the work of Heehs (1994: 3) who, in the critical tradition of Barthes,[13] perceives myth as

a set of propositions, often stated in narrative form, that is accepted uncritically by a culture or speech-community and that serves to found or affirm its self-conception. "Myth" in this sense includes most traditional narratives as well as some modern literature, but also "texts" such as performance wrestling, certain advertisements, and so on.

To the extent that these perceptions are accepted uncritically, that is, they exhibit a certain taken-for-grantedness, they closely resemble Bourdieu's insightful articulation of cultural capital.

The function of myth has been perceived in two predominant ways. First, myths serve as modes of cultural expression, emollient deflections of popular angst in which "language would take the place of action, speech the place of motor response. This social affect would find, in the form of narrative, a secondary and symbolic exteriorization" (Marin, 1984: 36). At the same time, and perhaps more relevant for our interests here, myths can be viewed as scripts for articulating cultural history. Here, it is the process of story-telling through mythic transposition of cultural artifacts and symbols that permits, indeed encourages, the free and creative play with history. In doing so, writes Louis Marin, "mythic narrative picks up a history of the past, even one that precedes time, and gives it its own rhythm and order" (1984: 36). Myth facilitates clarification of often opaque lifeworld experiences. It is this process of presentation and interpretation that constitutes in myth a transformative capacity.

The power of myth to inspire action in defense of custom and illuminate alternate modes of thinking on contemporary issues is juxtaposed with Enlightenment-based rationalism, which directs behavior through the cognitive vehicle of logical thought. This, Habermas contends, is the essence of the distinction best represented in the dualism *doxa* and *logos*, where the former is indicative of behavioral consistency achieved through the "authoritarian normativity of tradition," and the latter through the "unforced force of the better argument."[14] Specifically, mythic representation can be viewed as the narrative juxtaposition of antinomies. And it is through the narrative process constituting myth that cultural contradictions at once locate their realization and supersession. Potent combinations of myth and tradition as expressed in contemporary struggles for liberation or, as in the case of ICs, in structural details outlining alternate modes of living, have been referred to by Hobsbawm and Ranger (1983) as invented traditions.

Invented traditions are unique in that they are fabricated mythological constructs grafted from components of historical memory to suit contemporary situations. Their value is often realized in their ability to provide direction and meaning during times of rapid cultural, political, and economic transformation. Guidance emanates from a creative composition of traditional reminiscences with contemporary cultural codes.

In addition to contributing historical examples of invented tradition, Hobsbawm and Ranger (1983: 1) also delineate its core components. Invented tradition is taken to mean "a set of practices normally governed by overtly or tacitly accepted rules and of a ritual or symbolic nature, which seek to inculcate certain values and norms of behavior by repetition, which automatically implies continuity with the past." Two themes appear in their presentation of invented tradition: the significance of repetition and ritualization, and the construction of symbols.

Repetition and ritual keep alive reminiscences of a historical memory typically, as Hobsbawm and Ranger remind us, to solidify the "national popular" (Gramsci), to socialize the anti-social to the cultural codes appropriate for full participation in a given community (real or imagined). This has been, they argue, the primary function of invented tradition since the Industrial Revolution. And while it has served well the interests of fascism (Zipes, 1992–93; Jameson, 1972), hyper-conservatism, and conservatism generally,[15] it has also been used, with revisions, by postcolonial movements the world over to promote a rearticulated national identity. Jameson, for example, is especially clear on this point. While acknowledging the conservative origins of invented traditions, he also perceives the transformative capacity of creative appropriation as is apparent in this comment directed toward Walter Benjamin's efforts to articulate a nostalgic utopia:

[I]f nostalgia as a political motivation is frequently associated with Fascism, there is not reason why a nostalgia, conscious of itself, a lucid and remorseless dissatisfaction on the grounds of some remembered plentitude, cannot furnish as adequate a revolutionary stimulus as any other. (82)

In many ways, the manipulation and digestion of historical memory operates in a way similar to the appeals made by Barthes for the sempiternal interpretation of the text. That is, there are countless ways to interpret the stock of accumulated knowledge for contemporary activation. A similar point has been made by David Gross (1992) in his book *The Past in Ruins*, and in his reply to critics in the *Telos* symposium published in 1992–1993. Gross rebukes those who dismiss critical appropriations of tradition as only so much distorted cultural baggage by arguing that "traditions, particularly defeated or marginalized ones, have become what traditions never were before: forms of alterity which, if approached correctly, can help challenge quotidian existence" (1992–93: 6).

More directly:

By juxtaposing rather than integrating the past and the present, the nonsynchronous and the synchronous, it may become possible not only to see the present from an entirely new perspective but to raise questions about some of the otherwise hardly noticed cliches of contemporary life. (1992–93:6)

In this passage, Gross hits upon a crucial distinction which merits pursuing as it applies directly to our efforts here. Namely, neo-populists who see in reconstituted communities the role of counter-hegemonic counterweights to dominant culture must also recognize the role played by traditions in cultivating collective sentiments. That is, while a reinvigorated emphasis on recapturing lifeworld activities (the decolonization of the lifeworld) lies at the root of neo-populist rhetoric, the *negativity* inherent in the critical juxtaposition of communities effectively promoting the distinction between a mythistorical rendering of cultural life through creative appropriation of traditions, and dominant culture, rounds out its transformative potential. Each is present in the analysis I have presented in this book. My obvious emphasis on ICs as a NSM points at once to the significance of a return to revitalized communities while recognizing the broader implications of often radical juxtapositions with dominant culture. I agree in principle with Gross that the importance of contemporary references to tradition lies in their "shock value," or, as he suggests, in their ability to "provoke contra-dictions and open up new ways of thinking about 'what is' in light of 'what was.' " (1992–93: 9)

As with Gross, this is perhaps the most compelling insight emerging from Hobsbawm and Ranger's account, for it recognizes the creative promise embedded in counter-hegemonic interpretations of historical memory, or what they referred to as the "well-supplied warehouses of official ritual." International, cross-cultural references to folklore, music, festivals, dinners, work processes, agriculture, *Gemeinschaft*—each of these and many more constitute the stock of cultural memory from which contemporary IC members derive their mechanisms for producing the structures of commu-nity. Members of ICs seeking to generate their own legitimating codes, in keeping with the values of non-violence, spiritual awakening, simplicity, diversified agriculture, and the like, freely appropriate relevant references to historical memory, and often its symbolic composition, regardless of its ethnic, geographic, or spiritual origin. They themselves appear to symbolize the embodiment of the postmodern. For example, elements of ancient Eastern religious teachings (e.g., Buddhism, Islam, Hinduism), Wicca (or goddess worship), American Indian spiritualism, Christianity, and Judaism are very often combined with the so-called New Age spiritualism (e.g., crystal and gem stone ceremonies, Tarot readings, numerology) producing a postmodern spiritualism at once traditional and contemporary. Moreover, contemporary gatherings of intentional communitarians celebrating fall harvest or spring planting are reminiscent of their pre-twentieth-century predecessors. While in detail they are often as different as the communities themselves, these occasions and numerous others throughout the year typically consist of music and dancing, colorful craft displays, and the sharing of food to round out the symbolic association of each to each other, and the community.

Concomitant with ritual is the symbiotic appropriation, revitalization, and/or creation of symbols. While this is not the place to review the vast literature addressing symbolism,[16] it is clear that the accumulated reservoir of symbols and meaning systems comprising all cultures provides numerous opportunities for the creative appropriation of those symbols to suit both traditional and novel purposes.

Modern modes of rationalization and control penetrate the lifeworld through the use of legal, educational, medical psychiatric, and media technologies (Offe, 1985). The hypostatized rationale for increasing domination stems from postindustrial competition and the belief that there are systemic needs for economic, political, and cultural predictability. Hence, unpredictable, irregular, or "deviant" modes of behavior in civil society must be minimized without producing crises of legitimacy.[17]

The relationship of domination continues when subjects seek validation of their sense of self through the exchange relationship, realizing their role as consumer, and through the sign value represented by those purchases. For Baudrillard, sign values must be considered as relevant as use value and exchange value in articulating a Marxist theory of commodity fetishism. This is due to the hegemonizing effect of hierarchizing sign values, that is, attributing social status, prestige, and position to the acquisition of certain commodities through their identification with their owners. Baudrillard argues further that insight into the meaning and interpretation of sign values provides us with a more precise mechanism for understanding precisely the ways in which dominant cultural capital permeate contemporary symbol systems, leading ultimately to the colonization of the lifeworld.

In a related way, Sassoon (1984), in his work on symbol systems, argues that the waning significance of totalizing ideology or meta-narratives as guiding revolutionary blueprints is primarily the result of the "derealization of social life and its resurrection in the universe of signs" (1984: 863). Sassoon initiates his discussion of ideology by arguing, along with Lucaks, that ideology is a system of ideas based on certain values (862). He concludes, however, that, "in our advanced societies, 'values' are more and more irrecoverable" (862). He suggests that the rapid circulation of values, a product of a postindustrial society, distorts their historicity, their traditional grounding, producing a vacuous facade represented solely through media-reproduced images as *signs*.[18] Sassoon then suggests that "an ideology is a reference model which orients an action aiming at affecting reality" (1984: 862). But, he argues following in the path of Baudrillard (1976), there is no sense today of how reality is being transformed. Experiences within the lifeworld are mediated by sign values that simulate tradition, beauty, love, and so forth. Finally, Sassoon argues that the loss of sedimented values has precluded the sanctioning strength of ideology. He carries his critique further to suggest that NSMs lack ideological passion.

Sassoon's articulation of the passing significance of ideology is relevant to the evolution of both NSMs and ICs. First, he recognizes the distinction between classical social movements, with their allegiance to revolutionary ideology, and NSMs, where ideological belief plays a minor role and where "self-limiting" revolution has emerged as a dominant "strategy." Next, following Bourdieu (1984), he successfully identifies the contemporary counter-hegemonic struggle surrounding the ownership of signs—nomination. Nomination is the practice of naming the world around us, of claiming what is real and what is true.[19] It is this struggle to rearticulate the meaning of norms, values, and beliefs, a struggle taking place at the level of the lifeworld, that distinguishes NSMs from previous social movements, and in particular ICs as a NSM. NSMs have strategically refrained from totalizing revolutionary strategy to focus on the foundations, to penetrate the root of domination in postindustrial society, to strive, as Sassoon concludes, to "take possession of representation opportunities, to impose the codes of relation with the world (with social life, with nature, with one's own body)" (1984: 864). NSM actors, like those in ICs, must engage adversaries at the level of symbolism, and to the extent that they offer alternative lifeworld experiences (imagination, play, love, nature, feminism, art, spirituality, and so forth) they represent a significant challenge to contemporary postindustrial society.

It is in this light that contemporary theorists, particularly those of the Critical Theory school, have addressed the issue of tradition.[20] And while this still may seem a broad deviation from our discussion of NSMs and ICs, it is rather precisely to the point. Recall that NSM actors have rearticulated political activity as aimed not at the state, but at the level of signification, of nomination within the lifeworld. In so doing, many NSM actors have adopted axiological orientations similar, if not identical, to those associated with premodernist institutions and social movements (anarchist, communal, spiritual) typically referred to as "utopian."[21] This label has been applied to attempts at creating intentional communities from their early presence in America as religious communities during the 1620s to their most recent incarnation in the 1990s. In short, ICs have largely been viewed as retreating from the mainstream, articulating a longing for a premodernist, typically agrarian past that would return them to a bygone age where presumably *Gemeinschaft* provided the context for social relations (a conclusion submitted by Zablocki). For this reason, it is worth reiterating, much of the NSM literature precludes recognition of ICs as a possible social movement.

Following what has been said, it is conceivable that a rearticulation of the associations between ICs and their references and analogies to traditional values and behaviors (e.g., play, valued work, love of nature) be viewed as a self-limiting revolutionary praxis. What is required is theoretical and political acceptance of the radical potential in the juxtaposition of tradition with postindustrial malaise. Among the early Critical Theorists, Walter Benjamin (1969) argued that a "utopian reflection" or "nostalgic utopianism" was potentially revolutionary in that it broke with reification and it engaged in the praxis of nomination, to pursue the essence of desire in daily life.[22] To accentuate his point Benjamin compared the experience of reading newspapers with the premodern act of telling tales. Newspapers exist, for Benjamin, as a way to reify the spectacular, the novel. The tale, however, exists as "a mode of contact with a vanished form of social and historical existence" (Jameson, 1972: 80) where the novel and spectacular are celebrated.

Recently, in a debate surrounding the topic of tradition, theorists in the Critical Theory tradition renewed Benjamin's belief in the revolutionary potential of "nostalgic utopianism."[23] Critical of the work of Adorno for its narrow view of tradition, Paul Piccone suggests that it is "impossible" to consider the reconstitution of communities, modes of governance, or individuality without recognition of the role played by tradition in constituting individuals (1993: 102). Jack Zipes (1992–93) contends that what drove Benjamin, Bloch, and Brecht to their reverence for storytelling and theater beginning in the 1920s was their fear that the Nazis would effectively appropriate their traditions. Folklore, tales, and popular culture represented ways people could digest and compare divergent worldviews. It allowed them the conceptual space to be momentarily removed from their involvement in current events. Here Zipes's interpretation of tradition comes closest to Marin's articulation of the function of myth discussed above. Recall that for Marin, mythic transposition of cultural history was a crucial vehicle for "deconstructing" dominant cultural capital. For Marin, myth "explains and clarifies what normally, in lived experience, would remain opaque, dangerous, and full of anxiety" (1984: 36). Here, myth and tradition serve as counter-hegemonic filters through which pass cultural codes, ideology, and the like. Dominant cultural codes are then subjected to interpretation and differentiation based on their juxtaposition with tradition, myth, folklore, and tales. America has formalized its own storytelling tradition with the initiation in 1975 of the National Association for the Preservation and Perpetuation of Storytelling (NAPPS). Again in agreement with Benjamin, Zipes concludes that "there is a strong tendency to reflect critically upon the past as the lore they recover, which is being used to mark out a future that can lead to a new sense of community" (1992–93: 29). While not writing in the Critical Theory tradition, Alain Touraine seems to intimate many of the same points when, while referring to communal efforts, he states: "Marginality, considered for so long considered a failure of integration, becomes a hallmark of opposition, a laboratory in which a new culture and a social counterproject are being elaborated" (1988: 106).[24]

Welch (1985) draws attention to a similar phenomenon in her work on liberation theology. She contends that at the core of liberation theology is the "fact of insurrection." That in order to fracture consciousness among the oppressed, liberation theologists rely on what Metz (1980) has referred to as "dangerous memory" to invoke recognition of repressive apparatuses in society. Welch argues that liberation theologists manipulate dangerous memory in one of two ways, either to expose the roots of suffering, or to encourage the hope found in resistance. In many ways parallel to Scott's (1990) hidden transcript (discussed below), liberation theologists recount the misery of the suffering masses, the "marginal, the vanquished, and the oppressed" to locate it within the broader political, economic, and cultural machinations of society. Suffering is not addressed in the abstract but rather by drawing on the direct histories of the oppressed. Welch contends that Latin American liberation theology, by virtue of its political allignment with peasants and Indians, is an expression of dangerous memory, since it challenges the organization of the state and the distribution of resources.

That dimension of dangerous memory emphasizing hope suggests a "contingency of resistance." This Welch has in common with Scott since each are cognizant of the disadvantaged position of the subaltern in struggles with the more powerful elite in any society. Recognition of the paucity of resistance by the subaltern does not mean, as I have argued here and as Scott reiterates in the following extract that there is no resistance. Rather, it is recognition of the inherent power of inequity defining relations between the powerful and the powerless which forces the subaltern to be more creative in their resistance efforts. In applying dangerous memory to matters of hope and resistance, liberation theology turns to actual historical accounts of each. Here, Welch (1985: 41) contends:

These accounts are a declaration of the possibility of freedom and justice, and they may be examined in an attempt to understand what enables resistance in specific, historical situations. Such memories are an affirmation of human dignity.

Dangerous memory, like nostalgic utopia, offers the subaltern interpretations of historical memory which can be used to understand the political, economic, and cultural forces acting upon them, and to articulate modes of resistance to those forces when circumstances required it.

It is worth noting that Laclau's (1990) articulation of Husserl's concept of "reactivation" closely parallels much of our emphasis on nostalgic utopia. Husserl (1960) argued that over time, those historical struggles, the product of which now are contemporary power inequities, are forgotten. All that remains are the "sedimented" remnants of ideology, symbolism, and constraint, revealing perceptions of social relations matter-of-factly as "objective." To confront sedimented or entrenched power, argues Husserl, we must "reactivate" reminiscences of what Laclau has interpreted as "the original dimension of power," not necessarily returning to the "original situation" but recognizing the contingency of contemporary power inequities. In a related manner, de Certeau (1984) documents peasant articulations of myth and folklore to divert, distort, and engage the scientism of the contemporary age. The association between him and Husserl is clearest when he states:

Where should we look for them [the logic of actions] in the West, since our scientific method, by substituting its "own" places for the complex geography of social ruses and its artificial language for ordinary language, has allowed and even required reason to adopt a logic of mastery and transparency? (1984: 22)

For de Certeau, as will become more apparent, scientific rationalism is subverted in numerous ways through the creative manipulation of folktales and legends, each prodding historical memory in the direction of "origins."

Laclau seemingly travels a path similar to our own. In addressing Husserl's concern with reactivation, recognition of the historically contingent nature of contemporary power relations, Laclau contextualizes his later analysis of the distinction between myth and dominant structural discourse. For Laclau, myth comprises "the space of representation which bears no relation of continuity with dominant 'structural objectivity' " (1991: 61). In his closest association with Hobsbawm and Ranger, Laclau suggests that "myth is essentially hegemonic: it involves forming a new objectivity by means of the rearticulation of the dislocated elements [tradition, cultural by-products]" (61). Here Laclau infuses our working definition of myth with the hopeful aspirations present in Bloch's articulation of not-yet-consciousness, where mythic reminiscences inspire structural transformations. But his nearest approximation to the position we are establishing here—that is, the creative appropriation of myth, folklore, and tradition by the disempowered—is his proclamation that

[M]ythical space constituted by the subject does not have the same "logical form" as the structure whose principle of reading the subject becomes. On the contrary, it is the critique and substitution of this "form" which characterizes the mythical operation. (1990: 62)

More important, what follows is the critical association between Laclau's conceptualization of myth and the emphasis I am attempting to establish between critical appropriation and opposition to dominant cultural capital. Laclau begins his articulation of "mythical space" by contending: "The mythical space is presented as an *alternative* to the logical form of the dominant structural discourse" emphasis added (1990: 62).

Moreover, and with specific reference to a "promised land" (one would be hard pressed to find a more obvious reference to ICs, yet Laclau avoids mentioning them), Laclau completes his recognition of the hopeful nature of mythical representations when he suggests: "The fascination accompanying the vision of a promised land or an ideal society stems directly from this perception or intuition of a fullness that cannot be granted by the reality of the present" (1990: 63).

A more precise articulation of the significance granted alternative constructions of cultural codes would be hard to find. And yet, for all its affinity with the position I put forth in this book, Laclau's description of myth is confusing. And, since this confusion is correlated with a similar proposition made by Hobsbawm and Ranger, I will combine my critique here.

Wholesale application of the theoretical innovations offered by Laclau, and Hobsbawm and Ranger can proceed only with all relevant caveats in order. Hobsbawm and Ranger contend that invented traditions emerge primarily during historically unstable periods characterized by "rapid transformations of society," when antiquated cultural codes are replaced by new ones. Laclau, again following Husserl, makes a similar yet different point. Laclau contends that mythic representations can appear only when sedimented power has been destabilized enough to produce in the minds of the oppressed a constitutive discernment of that power. That is, if the pole representative of the administration of power is so strong that it effectively precludes reactivation, there will be little opportunity for the counter-hegemonic articulation of mythical space. In this way, despite different theoretical emphases, Laclau, and Hobsbawm and Ranger view the emergence of the mythical space as a product of structural dislocation. As such, their analyses approach the problematic assertions of the classical and resource mobilization paradigms in social movement theory, which, as I have discussed, perceive the emergence of ICs within the historical context of structural transformation and dislocation. Moreover, Laclau presents an apparent confusion over the process of articulating mythical space, its timing and product. Laclau makes a point with which I firmly agree: "myth functions as a surface on which dislocations and social demands can be inscribed. The main feature of a surface of inscription is its *incomplete* nature" (1990: 63, emphasis added). That is, there exists in human beings the capacity to resist modes of domination. That resistance can have as one of its many incarnations the appropriation of myth. And, most important, this process persists wherever humans perceive their fate as one of restricted freedom, subhuman living conditions, and so forth. In general, mythical representations are and have always been (more or less detailed, given levels of symbolic sophistication) a component of human existence. This is a position with which I firmly agree and will address in greater detail below. However, in making this point Laclau seems to contradict his earlier statement that mythical representations are in some ways dependent upon destabilized power structures. He cannot, in my view, have it both ways; his own theoretical explication does not allow for it. The inspiration behind the analysis I offer here is recognition of the persistence of resistance. It exists on a plane much like that recognized by Laclau as a "surface of inscription," which is by definition incomplete, sempiternal. Contrary to Laclau, and Hobsbawm and Ranger, it does not require spectacular structural transformations for it to exist. That there have been historically significant representations of peasant rebellion accompanying cultural transformations is not to be doubted; the literature of these events is comprehensive.[25] But it is also the case that mythic representations of alternate ways of living persist throughout historical periods of ideological and/or authoritarian repression, and this must be recognized in order for us to perceive the vast constellation of counter-hegemonic articulations expressed as a component of day-to-day peasant and working-class existence.

Bond and Gilliam (1994) are among theorists arguing for recognition of the radical potential inscribed in the scripts of subaltern modes of resistance through acknowlegement of their "social constructions of the past." Much like Nietzsche and the new historicists, Bond and Gilliam contend that their is no one, true version of historical events, but rather a multiplicity of interpretations. Moreover, and much like de Certeau, Bond and Gilliam argue that the business of liberating the past for subaltern appropriation must begin by "confronting the language of paternalistic domination that resides in the tradition of Western Liberal thought and manifests itself in the common sense terms of spatial, temporal, and geographical subordinations" (12). In his work on Indian resistance, Ashis Nandy (1987) argues for the conceptualization of a theory of culture to oppose dominant theoretical models of resistance. For him, "a stress on culture is a repudiation of the post-Renaissance European faith that only dissent is true which is rational, sane, scientific, adult and expert" (113). Much like Scott's attention to " hidden transcripts," Nandy articulates culture as those "categories used by victims" to resist oppression. Nandy points out that at the cornerstone of resistance efforts stands "critical traditionality," the appropriation of elements from Indian folk history that provide a critical base. For him this includes not only symbolic, folk, and mythic imagery, but also a theory of oppression which produces a radical juxtaposition of tradition with contemporary modes of oppression.

What seems consistent in the articulation of the appropriation of cultural imagery for use in subaltern modes of resistance is the insistence that to truly recognize the value of subaltern perceptions of reality, we must free ourselves of the weight of dominant cultural theorizing on social movements. For it is the "cultural screens" emerging from occidentalism, orientalism, and africanism, which serve to "reduce complex and intricate historical and social diversities to a few prominent cultural images" (16). Bernal (1994) makes a similar point when he draws attention to the social construction in Europe and later the United States of an association between the intellectual capital of Plato and Aristotle, and our own moral, ethical, and intellectual foundations. The process, initiated in Germany as an academic discipline called *Altertumswissenschaft*, served to legitimate imperialism and neo-colonialism based on the rationale that Europe was the origin of civilization.

If the imposition of dominant essentialistic interpretations of historical reality can be "opened up," where the fields of political, economic, and cultural life are viewed as encompassing smooth rather than striated space (refer to Chapter 4), then we can clearly see that the subaltern "have the power to evoke the past, apprehend the present, and establish the basis of imagined communities" (Nandy, 1994: 17). This is accomplished through the critical appropriation of symbols "evoking a past that might have been." Rao's (1994) explication of postcolonial India's efforts to (re)construct Indian identity through the appropriation of Indian tradition provides yet another example. In an effort to remove the vestiges of colonization, the

Indian state has reached back in Indian history (primarily Hindu) and lore to recall Indian customs and culture. Rao makes the point that a similar experience can be found in Korea, where efforts have been underway to remove virtually any visible reference to Japanese occupation. Rao suggests that historical references to symbolism and tradition each conjure powerful images where "the past itself is sanctuary," that is, where the past appears as a reliable, comfortable, and predictable guide in rapidly changing times.

Other analyses of postcolonial efforts to procure in tradition a powerful symbolic and manifest counterweight to contemporary authority structures and modes of oppression appear in Gyani's (1993) recognition of a "return to history" by the Hungarian Socialist Worker's Party, and in Vautier's (1994) compelling poststuctural analysis of postcolonial Canadian literature. Gyani's analysis addresses an emerging discourse within postcommunist Hungary which draws upon tradition to "resurrect the more distant past for the purpose of shaping new historical mythologies" (1993: 898). That is, in the aftermath of the collapse of communism in the 1980s, Hungarians faced the overwhelming task of reinventing its economy, polity, and in many ways its culture, by establishing a market economy and instituting a constitutional democracy protecting civil and political liberties (1993: 907). The fist step in accomplishing this task was inventing a tradition of "a one time historically conceived nation state" (1993: 907). Ironically, for most postcommunist Europe, there is no "unbroken continuity of statehood" to refer to. Despite this, argues Gyani, "the identification of a certain past national interest with tradition seems to be a general practice in the Eastern European postcommunist states" (1993: 908).

Unlike the Indian and Korean search for identity discussed by Rao, Vautier contends that post-European Canadians have so internalized their experience with colonization that it has become a "vital part of themselves." Recognition of the assimilation of eurocentric "scripts" into the Canadian consciousness has led post-European Canadian author's Francois Barcelo, George Bowering, and Jacques Poulin, among others, to engage in "rewriting myths" which, as Vautier, here paraphrasing Habermas, contends is "a self-conscious effort to decolonize the mind" (1994: 17). If it is true that myths serve to center us, to provide us with our own historical sense of place and purpose, then post-European myth has as its purpose the destruction of eurocentric Mythology. Here, much like Nandy and Bernal, the primary effort of post-European novelists is to "challenge the teleological and ahistorical qualities of traditional myth" through juxtaposition of Eurocentric and mythic-universal exposition of the European explorer with the Amerindian. In these novels at least, Amerindians and Innuits are presented as symbols of cultural purity to indicate to post-European Canadians just how "impure" their traditions have become as a result of the colonial experience.

To sum, my point here is to suggest, within the present context of ritual, symbolism, signs, and references to tradition, that contemporary ICs, like the numerous examples presented here, engage the lifeworld in the praxis of nomination often by rearticulating traditional values appropriated from pre-modern efforts to create community. That this practice, where it occurs, and this is by no means the case with all ICs, be viewed not as a "utopian" transgression, but rather as a radical recognition of the inherent power of juxtaposition. And furthermore, that radical reflection as practiced by ICs be witnessed as an efficacious component of NSMs rather than, as is currently the case, an impediment to social movement status.

I will draw this section on hidden transcripts to a close with a discussion of Scott's (1990) rebuke of contemporary political and sociological theory for its neglect of subaltern resistance. The predominant hypothesis held by Scott is that members of classes in positions of political and economic vulnerability actively select modes of resistance which serve their dual interests in self-preservation and counter-hegemony. By virtue of their legitimate aversion to overt expressions of resistance, oppressed people must demonstrate cunning and deception when careening webs of power. To frame and define social movement activity as overt and confrontational, a characteristic of both classical and NSM theory, is to ignore the multifarious modes of resistance persisting between the poles of direct action and acquiescence. In his work on peasant resistance in Mexico, Esteva (1987) chides conventional wisdom for "inevitably reducing the peasant world to a mechanical structure and, in the process, losing the keys to understanding that world" (131). Bond and Gilliam concur by arguing that a new postcolonial discourse is attempting to shatter previously dominant disciplinary explanations of the past. Postcolonial theorists focus more intensively on common people, their interpretations of reality, and the ways in which they "make their own histories" when it comes to articulating a renewed sense of identity, violence, political, and economic arrangements, and the like. Applying a postcolonial frame to subaltern activities produces an entirely new kaleidoscope from which to view and interpret them. Following Parajuli:

The identity and autonomy of subalterns are becoming an assertive element rather than appendage in the nationalist discourse. The emerging consciousness expresses the subalterns' desire to conquer not only political and economic autonomy but also the power to redefine themselves, their aspirations, and the development process. (1991: 183)

The frame for this discussion follows the compelling articulation of peasant and working-class resistance offered by Scott. With a style and luminescence reminiscent of Goffman, Scott hypothesizes two significantly different modes of interaction between the subaltern and the powerful. He contends that when engaged in interaction with representatives of power, the oppressed "perform" by in various ways invoking a "public transcript." The public transcript is imbued with complicated role responsibilities that demand specific activities and responses in daily interaction. For example, deference to authority by those in powerless positions becomes inscripted in symbolic gestures which attain a taken-for-grantedness over time. This form of symbolic gesturing, however, conceals as much as it reveals. Scott suggests that each party engages in a charade of sorts, each conspiring to misrepresent the actual interpretations of relations of subordination. The quintessential example is the complicated array of negotiated modes of discourse constituting American slavery. Following folk wisdom, the oppressed engage in a careful process of assembling messages of the dominant classes, filtering them through complicated screens of historical experience, materialist and metaphysical, to discern their meaning. The folk belief in "playing fool, to catch wise." So it is that on the surface of human interaction between the subaltern and the powerful there exists the impression of peasant and working-class compliance with dominant hegemonic significaiton. It is of course true that the dominant classes, through the vehicle of mass education, mass media, and the like, endeavor to procure a picture of the world consistent with their own. However, to assume that there is an automatic linear correspondence between images and their interpretation by targeted audiences seems inaccurate. Indeed, it could be argued that a subaltern confirmation of dominant cultural hegemony may rather be a trick, a visible genuflection on the terrain of public discourse, all the while retaining folk wisdom through the vehicle of the hidden transcript.

In truly dialectical fashion and with direct reference to Goffman's theatrical metaphor, Scott argues that what takes place off-stage in the concealed milieu of the subaltern comprises the realm of the hidden transcript. It is here that the cauldron of counter-hegemonic discourse is given free expression. In general, there are three significant components of the hidden transcript: 1) They are limited to a particular social site and net of actors; 2) hidden transcripts contain a full range of public expressions from speech to "poaching, pilfering, tax evasion, [and] intentionally shabby work"; and 3) the "frontier between public and hidden transcripts is a zone of constant struggle between dominant and subordinant" (Scott, 1990: 14). Interesting parallels exist between point 3 above and the discussion of the preservation of the lifeworld in Chapter 3. Preservation and cultivation of the "frontier" allowing for free expression, assembly, and community discourse is a seminal component of the preservation of the hidden transcript. Without it, the hidden transcript becomes more difficult, although not impossible, to maintain. Scott confirms this point by suggesting: "The social spaces where the hidden transcript grows are themselves an achievement of resistance; they are won and defended in the teeth of power" (1990: 119). Like the Polish Solidarity Movement discussed in Chapter 3, which struggled to develop civil society, a "subordinate group must carve out for itself social spaces insulated from control and surveillance from above" (Scott, 1990: 118). It is my contention that ICs serve to construct alternative spaces relatively free from penetration by dominant cultural capital. The subaltern, in my case members of ICs, not only create the dialogical space for resistance, but also initiate counter-hegemony by offering alternative modes of living. Within the lifeworld, within the hidden transcript, emerges agentic voices capable of articulating counter-hegemonic interpretations of dominant cultural symbols.

To my knowledge, Parajuli (1991) is among the few social theorists recognizing the confluence of NSM theory and a sensitivity to the voices of the subaltern. For Parajuli, subalterns construct free spaces through critical reminiscences of the past by "referring to sybolic and ritual values." Like women in Jamaica, who draw upon an endless reservoir of cultural references through tale-telling to counter racism and sexism, Parajuli agues that women in Nepal have appropriated "socially sanctioned ritual spaces such as *teej* to criticize injustice in patriarchal society" (184). Perhaps most interesting in Parajuli's analysis is his suggestion that the knowledge of the subaltern is situated knowledge. Following Foucault, situated knowledge is wedged firmly in time and space, sensously experienced by the knower. Extrapolations from unique historical experiences to broader populations will explain little in the way of universal truth. However, as Parajuli explains, it is the immediacy of this experiential knowledge which marks it as inherently political. For, much like Scott has argued, situated knowledge "echoes the yearning for identity and survival of those who are the victims of exploitation and subordination" (Parajuli, 1991: 185).

How do subaltern people resist? The modes of resistance recognized by Scott and the others discussed in this section require an expanded view of it. For his part, Scott is quite clear that to penetrate the hidden transcript to locate subaltern modes of resistance means embarking on an analysis of an ensemble of resistance techniques alien to most social scientists. These techniques would include, but not be limited to: "rumor, gossip, disguises, linguistic tricks, metaphors, euphemisms, folk tales, ritual gestures, and anonymity" (137). Other forms of resistance could include spirit possession, (predominantly used by women and some marginal male groups where grievances typically left unspoken could be uttered without retribution), drunkenness, hysteria, and festivals.

For Scott, the most familiar and elementary form of resistance is gossip. Referring to the Malay's interpretation of gossip as "news on the wind," Scott contends that gossip is experienced as the rudimentary vehicle for subaltern solidarity, directed as it is against the powerful. A close relative of gossip is embellishment and exaggeration each of which are taken quite seriously in subaltern studies since they express the interests of the story-teller. Euphemism offers subordinated people the opportunity to code resistance in disguises ranging from folk tales to dance. Here is where Scott's analysis is most lucid. When discussing the range of opportunities and creative uses for folk culture to code resistance, Scott (158) contends: "by the subtle use of codes one can insinuate into a ritual, a pattern of dress, a song, a story, meanings that are accessible to one intended audience and opaque to another" (158).

By way of example, Scott refers to American slaves and their (re)presentations of coded Old Testament references to Joshua and Moses who were viewed as liberators. Other examples include the Filipino use of Christianity to convey their guarded yet passionate "dissent from elite culture," as well as the application of liberation theology to matters of oppression in Latin America (Welch).

Perhaps the most familiar folk-based resistance genre is that of folk tales. Folk or trickster tales are part of an oral folk culture which includes story-telling, songs, and jokes. While written transcripts of these tales do exist (e.g., Grimm Fairy Tales, Mother Goose Nursery Rhymes, Brer Rabbit Tales), efforts to discern their origins have been next to impossible. Consistent in each of these collections of folk tales, songs, jokes, and dances is the struggle of the weak against the powerful. The genre of subaltern tales reveals a fascinating acknowledgement on the part of the oppressed that resistance must take the form of calculation and cunning in opposition to direct confrontation. Cross-cultural analyses reveal similar themes of often violent revenge inflicted by the oppressed against the powerful. The "typical" frame of folk tales is recognition of the superior strength of the enemy, calling forth a strategy that plays to the strengths of the weaker opposition's interests. What unfolds is a characterization of competition which imparts to the subaltern the qualities of wit, speed, agility, intellect, deception, cunning, and awareness of the weaknesses of the more powerful opponent. In a similar way, particularly in Europe beginning in the sixteenth century, artistic sketches began to appear in which "mice ate cats and children spanked parents." These and other inverted expressions of culturally embedded power relations were referred to as the "world-upside-down." World-upside-down portraits played a radicalizing role in the sixteenth-century English Civil War, the Reformation and Peasant's War. For example, Thomas Munzer's portrayal of "peasants disputing with learned theologians, ramming the scriptures down the throat of priests, and pulling down the tyrants castle" (Scott, 1990: 171), and the French Revolution where world-upside-down prints expressed the coded anger of, and revenge sought by the subaltern. These, along with often bawdy carnivals, provided a radical fissure for a subaltern expression of defiance with calculated levels of risk.

The field of sociology is indebted to Scott's work for drawing scholarly attention to the expansion of the barriers of resistance. It is in the closing pages of his book where Scott strikes the most resounding blow to classical and contemporary social movement theory, and in so doing, comes closest to the position I articulate here. Returning to his mantra "resistance below the line," Scott (198–199) concludes with the following:

one sees that the luxury of relatively safe, open political opposition is both rare and recent. The vast majority of people continue to be not citizens but subjects. So long as we continue our conception of the political to activity that is openly declared we are driven to conclude that subordinate groups essentially lack a political life or that what political life they do have is restricted to those exceptional moments of popular explosion.

And in a final direct attack on the current theoretical shortcomings of contemporary sociological theorizing on social movements, Scott argues: "to [ignore subaltern resistance] is to miss the immense politcal terrain that lies between quiescence and revolt and that, for better or worse, is the political environment of subject classes"(199). Intentional communities are among prevailing modes of subaltern resistance that avoid direct confrontation with sources of power

To summarize, my endeavor has been to establish, within the present context of ritual, symbolism, signs, and tradition, that contemporary ICs engage the lifeworld in the praxis of nomination often by rearticulating traditional values appropriated from premodern efforts to create community. This practice, where it occurs (and this is by no means the case with all ICs), should be seen not as a "utopian" transgression, but rather as a radical recognition of the inherent power of juxtaposition. Furthermore, radical reflection as practiced by ICs should be understood as an efficacious component of NSMs rather than, as is currently the case, an impediment to social movement status.

Notes

1. Approximately 99 percent of human history has been spent hunting and gathering. Hunters and gatherers are believed to have dwelled in local bands of between twenty-five and fifty men, women, and children. Each local band was more or less politically and economically self-sufficient.

2. "Cockaigne" has been translated from the Germanic *kakan* to mean "cake."

3. I will pursue this tension in greater detail below with references to Mannheim and Ricoeur. For now, suffice it to say that Mannheim perceives the emergence of utopian juxtapositions as constituting historically recognizable forces for social change—that is, the realizability of utopian consciousness.

4. This is significant since Mannheim's account of utopia refrains from referencing its origins in the literary genre.

5. This is immediately apparent in More's selection of the name "Hythloday" which, according to Kumar (1991: 2), translates into "a distributor of nonsense."

6. The prolific literature addressing the constitution of communes and collectives, particularly in efforts prior to the twentieth century, has been documented by R. Fogerty (1990) in *All Things New*.

7. See K. Kumar (1991), especially Chapter 4.

8. A contemporary communitarian effort closely approximating the monastic model can be found in Grosseto, Italy. There, the Nomadelfia community, founded by Father Zeno Saltini in 1948, is composed of 320 people on four square kilometers. All land is held in common, all goods are shared, and there is no money. Moreover, upon joining the community, a prospective candidate must abide by the following constitutional provisions:

The candidate must be 21 years of age and must be a practicing Catholic who lives according to the teachings and discipline of Apostolic Catholic Church. He must live only on what is given him by the Association. He must accept poverty, although he will have whatever necessary for a decent life. He must be generous in his manners and he may not work for a third party. . . . Nomadelfians are not allowed to argue among themselves. If a conflict arises between two or more Nomadelfians or postulators, they are sent to a Judge who is appointed by the college to act as conciliator. If a member does not accept the Judge's decision, he must leave the community or else undergo a trial.

Rigid and hierarchical authority, combined with religious instruction, provides a community structure similar to the monastic models of medieval Europe.

9. See R. Levitas. 1990. *The Concept of Utopia*. (New York: Syracuse University Press: 67–82); and P. Ricoeur. 1986. *Lectures on Ideology and Utopia*. (New York: Columbia University Press: 159–180).

10. This critique of Mannheim, in my estimation, must not be carried too far. What appears in the initial pages of Chapter 4 as an overdetermined observable "reality" is later in the same chapter given a relational exposition. For example, in his discussion of the oppositional character of utopia, Mannheim stresses: "It [utopia] strives to take account of the dynamic character of reality, inasmuch as it assumes not a 'reality as such' as its point of departure, but rather a concrete historically and socially determined reality which is in a constant process of change" (1936: 198). While criticisms of Mannheim's inattention to symbolic interpretations at the level of the lifeworld do enable us to construct a rearticulated version of the correlation of ideology with utopia, particularly along the lines advocated by Geertz (1973) and Ricoeur (1986), it must also be recognized that Mannheim seems to have embedded within this study a relational and historically dependent criteria for the recognition of utopian acts, as well as determining their specific form.

11. Biting criticism of Mannheim's suggestion that utopian ideas spawn revolutionary activity can be found in Levitas (1990). In her analysis of Mannheim, Levitas argues that there is no causal relationship between utopian ideas and discontent, actual change, and the role played by utopian ideas and discontent in the constellation of change. As she puts it, "Bellamy's invention of credit cards in *Looking Backward* was not remotely connected with their introduction in reality" (1990: 76).

I suggest that Levitas pushes her point too far. Mannheim does seek to establish the relevant correspondence between ideas and actions in his socio-historical discussion of the Anabaptists (1936: 211–219). For example, anticipating the critique offered by Levitas, Mannheim proposes the linkage between ideas and action when he argues that "the only true, perhaps the only direct, identifying characteristic of Chiliastic experience is absolute presentness" (1936: 215). He contends, "The Chiliast expects a union with the immediate present. Hence he is not preoccupied in his daily life with optimistic hopes for the future or romantic reminiscences" (1936: 216). Chiliastic perceptions of "living the moment" mobilized a belief in revolution for revolution's sake, "the only creative principle of the immediate present."

12. For an explication of myth as it relates solely to the construction of utopia, in particular Thomas More's *Utopia*, refer to Louis Marin's (1994) publication of *Utopics: Spatial Play*. In general, Marin reproduces the dominant expression of myth in his initial articulation, deviating only slightly by drawing attention to the reflexivity and reciprocity of the interaction between story-teller and receiver. This seemingly minor deviation has radical implications for conceptualizing utopic storytelling as a process imbued with multiple interpretations, "fractured

consciousness," and the like. Indeed, for Marin, "[N]arrative is always more or less an expectation of the unexpected."

13. Barthes (1957) contends that myth is analogous to *doxa*, commonly held perceptions of cultural, political, and economic activities. This parallels Bourdieu's efforts to conceptualize the *Habitus*, and in some ways, Habermas's efforts to distinguish the lifeworld from system. Each endeavors to emphasize the relevance of an accumulated stock of knowledge serving metaphorically as a foundation upon which day-to-day activity rests, or as a complex weave of interactions providing actors with the necessary context to respond in culturally appropriate ways to situations.

14. In his 1994 article "Myth, History, and Theory," Heehs establishes his critique of logocentric analyses of historical phenomena by contending that over time, our "faith" in the legitimacy of scientific explanations of historical events (his reasoning could be expanded to include all scientific explanation) takes on mythic qualities in that we tend to accept uncritically the "scientific culture" that cultivates information. As a consequence, generations of occidental peoples (although this phenomenon also permeates the East) have witnessed the continued, formerly slow, now explosive dispersion of sedimented layers of scientific knowledge and consequent rationalism and the expansion to mythic proportions, as indicated by our extended levels of trust, legitimacy, and taken-for-grantedness. In this way, logos becomes *doxa*.

15. This is particularly the case where tradition has been appropriated by the market, repackaged, and "sold" to consumers as a vehicle for identification and remembrance. One of my favorite examples is the re-creation of nineteenth and early twentieth-century village facades in strip malls and shopping centers to serve as a counterweight to the cold, soulless architectural prisons they embody. Manipulation of tradition in this case serves market interests by creating an environment more conducive to appropriation.

16. With specific reference to new social movements and the significance of symbolism, see Joseph Sassoon (1984). "Ideology, Symbolic Action and Rituality in Social Movements: The Effects On Organizational Forms," *Social Science Information*, 23 (4/5): 861–873. For analyses of the correlation between symbolism and capitalism see Baudrillard (1981).

17. Habermas draws attention to the presence of a similar theme in Durkheim's work in his *Theory of Communicative Action*, Vol. 2 (Boston: Beacon Press, 1989): 153–197.

18. Sassoon's and Baudrillard's articulation of signs is not unlike Benjamin's (1969) use of the concept *symbolism*. First appearing in his *Elective Affinities*, Benjamin suggests that people succumb to the seduction of symbols when their autonomy as human beings has been eliminated.

19. My adaptation of the sociological criteria of the true stems from the work of Agnes Heller (1989: 313). Heller contends:

If a particular kind of knowledge provided by social science *impacts upon the very existence* of a person or a human group, if this person or group recognizes something in this "true knowledge" that has an essential bearing on their lives, prospects, hopes, fears, experiences, daily practices, choices, and the like, if a work of social science opens up new horizons, new expectations, if it illuminates depths hitherto unknown, unexplored, and obscure, if it makes men and women perceive something they have not yet perceived so far, if it elevates them or humiliates them, if it changes their lives—then, and only then, will it reveal *Truth* for them (original emphasis).

20. Critical theory emerged as a loosely organized body of researchers during the early 1920s in Frankfurt, Germany. Key figures included Max Horkheimer, Theodor Adorno, Friedrich Pollock, Erich Fromm, Herbert Marcuse, Franz Neumann, Otto Kirchheimer, Henryk Grossmann, Arkadij Gurland, Walter Benjamin, Ernst Bloch, and later Jurgen Habermas. Influenced by German idealist philosophy, critical theorists directed their research interests toward unraveling the complex web of institutions and social conditions "giving rise to the reproduction and transformation of society, the meaning of culture, and the relation between the individual, society, and nature" (Held, 1980: 16).

21. Consider, for example, Kanter's (1973) *Commitment and Community*. The first part of this book is dedicated to explication of the "utopian faith" which apparently inspires attempts at communal living.

22. Readers may find a similar theme developed by Gilles Deleuze and Felix Guattari (1983) in *Anti-Oedipus*. See especially pp. 322–339.

23. See Piccone, "The Actuality of Traditions." *Telos*, 94 (Winter): 889.

24. Touraine's juxtaposition is indicative of Derridean dualism and the significance of the marginalizations of the "other."

25. Refer, for example, to Ernst Bloch's (1995) elaboration on the not-yet consciousness in the first volume of *The Principle of Hope*. In it Bloch perceives the awakening of youth during times of revolution and tumult as a significant moment of wish fulfillment, in which the manifestation of day-dreams appears suddenly realizable. See especially pp. 114–178.

6

CONCLUSION:
EMBRACING HETEROGENEITY

> Your power symbol is a blade of grass. If you shoot at a blade of grass,
> it is so supple it will bend with the force of the arrow and come right
> back up.
>
> Bear Heart

In this book I have proposed that students of social movements expand their
current conceptualization to include one that captures the sempiternal
dynamism of resistances permeating civil society through the application
of chaos theory or nonlinear dynamics, and poststructuralism. To make this
case I have argued that ICs be considered as the penultimate resistance
movement, given their definitive penchant for cultural experimentation.
That they have not been so considered is evidence of a disciplinary bias that
privileges "classical" resistance movements, particularly class-based movements, given their state-directed rhetorical mandates and valuation of overt
conflict. Through the examination of multiple philosophical and pragmatic
innovations in daily life experiences, interpersonal conflict negotiation,
child care, work sharing, alternative economies, organic food harvesting,
ritual reproduction of community commitment, environmentally friendly
living, sex and relationship experimentation, reinvigorated sense of fun and
leisure, and the like, I have endeavored to establish the significance of ICs
and their members as more than mere "seeds for social change," arguing
that as subjects capable of producing their own historicity they are, in and

of themselves, social movement actors. Similarly, references were drawn from the work of poststructuralists Deleuze and Guattari, who view cultural innovations, like those cultivated by ICs, as "afterimages," a cultural watermark that may recede, producing relatively minor reverberations, only to be resurrected by generations to come in unforeseen configurations. Hobsbawm and Ranger's explication of invented traditions, and numerous references to literatures addressing mythistory serve to historically validate Deleuze and Guattari's claim.

While ICs have traditionally been ignored in the classical social movement literature, largely for their "utopian" constitution, it is precisely this utopian component that I argue is crucial to a successful social movement. Simultaneously granting the persistence of resistance within civil society, and recognition of a utopian vision for the future, make ICs the ideal social movement entity. Recalling Mannheim, Bloch, Adorno, and Ricoeur, a culture without a utopian vision would be dead because it would have no vision for the future. If it can be imagined, it is possible. In this sense, ICs are not demonstrating "regressive utopia" but rather a positive transcendental valuation of human potentiality. This characteristic reaffirms their link to preceding generations, each sharing a belief in the possible. Absent imagination there is only the dreary cloak of alienating postindustrial social relations predicted by Marx, Weber, and their many followers. Aside from his luminous critique of capitalism as a mode of production, perhaps Marx's greatest contribution to the liberation of humanity—from the constraints imposed by instrumentalist reason and unabashed capitalist exploitation—was to follow in the path of so many who had written before him to articulate a vision for a better place. While Marx never produced detailed architectural designs and illuminated paths to this place, in contrast to Owen, Fourier, and Saint Simon, he did nevertheless render the likelihood of its occurrence with all the might his persuasive pen and charismatic personality could muster. Given his evolutionary interpretation of history and the movement of modes of production throughout, there was no reason to suspect that capitalism would be the irrevocable realization of human economic, political, and cultural relations. Agentic and aware, human beings, although constrained by cultural imbalances of class, race/ethnicity, gender, and power, could aid in determining their historical course. Paraphrasing Marx, while human beings do make history, they do not make it as they please. The gift of Marx was at once his lucid account of capitalism and his promise of the future.

But for complex and contradictory reasons alluded to in Chapters 2 and 3, postindustrial societies display a limited array of culturally progressive means with which to address the concerns of NSM actors and those within ICs. Rather, contemporary culture continues to be ravaged by 1) increasing domination through state and local efforts to enhance measures of control (e.g., school, work, department stores, neighborhoods, welfare agencies); 2) rationalization; 3) atavism, largely promoted by an Enlightenment-inspired phantasmagoria to control, manipulate, and transform nature and to manufacture workers in the mold of highly predictable, largely unthinking automatons to meet the demands of a growing industrial capitalism; and 4) socialization to the bureaucratic mode of corporate control characteristic of primary-sector labor markets through the late 1970s and early 1980s. Capitalist social relations offered happiness and enjoyment only typically during those hours spent away from the workplace, where leisure, too, came to be commodified. Clearly Marx's four modes of alienation seem to have been realized by the end of the 20th century.[1] Social systems, however, are not closed. And while the negative effects of capitalist social relations have produced a considerable degree of postindustrial malaise, it is also true that global actors continue to struggle for recognition, realization, peace, and insight. That, indeed, has been the primary theme of this book.

Members of ICs actively embrace alternate associations and conventions in the construction of their immediate living conditions. And while their mode of transpraxis makes no pretensions to perfection (indeed, it is self-criticism that makes contemporary ICs so much more flexible than their predecessors), they offer a radical juxtaposition to life in dominant culture. Like the *brujo* of the Southwest, ICs are at once of, but not of. It is precisely this juxtaposition that produces a fractured consciousness, instability within the social system, small perturbations at the level of the lifeworld leading to the possibility of social change in the direction of more humane and compassionate sociocultural relations. It is this instability that is best addressed, and celebrated, by chaos theory and poststructuralism because these two paradigmatic schools of thought offer the most sophisticated theoretical tools with which to conceptualize and privilege heterogeneity and difference.

This analysis is thoroughly at odds with the recent work of philosophers writing in the "communitarian" literature. I raise the communitarian literature here, in the closing pages of this book, because I believe these writers will command the most significant voice in matters of policy and culture over the coming years. While this is not the time for a thorough analysis of the communitarian agenda and philosophy (such that one can be clearly identified), I believe it is important for us to consider the broad distinctions raised between their analysis of social problems and subsequent solutions, and those I have raised relative to chaos and postmodernism. To accomplish this I would like to briefly comment on recent publications by Charles Taylor, one of the early and consistent contributors to the communitarian literature, as well as David Hollenbach and Todd Gitlin. While Gitlin would probably object to being framed within the communitarian political and philosophical milieu, his (1995) *The Twilight of Common Dreams* suggests numerous lines of intersection between himself and this growing communitarian literature. I will conclude with a brief discussion of a recent work by Michael Walzer, who shares many of the communitarian concerns but who designates numerous points of distinction between he and the communitarian literature as a whole.

It is not until the last chapter of Charles Taylor's (1991) *The Ethics of Authenticity* that revealing contrasts surface between a chaos theoretic and his communitarian rendering. As a consequence, my critique begins where Taylor ends, with his concluding remarks concerning the possibility of mass democratic political movements.

In the chapter "Against Fragmentation," Taylor articulates what could be seen as a quite "progressive" cultural criticism of the extremes of laissez-faire capitalism, instrumentalist reason, and, following Tocqueville, the "soft" despotism characteristic of large bureaucratic states, which, rather than enhancing democratic liberties, serves to limit them. And, much like Cohen and Arato (1993) but lacking, at least in this book, the sophistication of their lucid analysis, he recognizes the futility of revolution to transform oppressive social structures while simultaneously invoking the perpetual nature of social movements and resistance "[T]hese [bureaucratic] institutions can never be simply abolished. [T]hat we have to live with them forever, has a lot to do with the unending, unresolvable nature of our cultural struggle" (1991: 111).

But having said this, Taylor continues, "Although there is no definitive victory, there is winning or losing ground" (1991: 111). Taylor sets out in this concluding chapter to attack two interrelated and significant components of the ecumenical communitarian thesis: 1) the continuing fragmentation of American (and Canadian) culture brought on by atavistic social relations producing ever more disparate and singular efforts to articulate group needs and interests; and relatedly; 2) an insatiable articulation of grievances through the courts expressed by Taylor as "politics-as-judicial-review." While never venturing too close to any actual prescriptions for promoting social change, Taylor's hope for the salvation of humane social and environmental relations is firmly ensconced in the principle of democratic freedom. Here he suggests that "the force that can roll back the galloping hegemony of instrumental reason is (the right kind of) democratic initiative" (1991: 112). It seems that his only endeavor in this final chapter is to suggest that there really is no "iron cage" that controls and manipulates our every thought and desire and that we can discover and actively promote alternative visions, a point that should come as no surprise to sociologists and historians who have documented subaltern modes of resistance.[2] But while Taylor offers no insight into what it is we *should* do to bring about humane changes in political, economic, cultural, and environmental relations, he is quite adamant about what we *should not* do.

I have argued throughout that NSMs represent an entirely unique expression of social movement actors living in a postindustrial time and space. Moreover, ICs, as an expression of subaltern resistance, seldom if ever turn their cultural animus toward state-based expressions of "legitimate" power since there are sound reasons for avoiding confrontations with the state and its enforcers (e.g., police, National Guard). And finally, juxtapositions of cultural alternatives with contempory social conditions produce the possibility of a fractured consciousness leading to unpredictable ends at the level of social structure. I made these arguments within the confines of chaos and postmodern theory, each privileging heterogeneity, unpredictability, and flux.

By way of contrast, Taylor reserves his most ardent critique for "fragmentation." He goes so far as to argue that the greatest threat to democracy is not despotism, but rather fragmentation. Fragmentation arises, to be sure, from atavistic social relations and the kind of instrumentalism that produced volumes of condemnation from Marx, Durkheim, and Weber. The product for Taylor is a degeneration into "partial groupings" rather than "common projects" and "allegiances."

They [fellow citizens] may indeed feel linked in common projects with some others, but these come more to be partial groupings rather than the whole society: for instance, a local community, an ethnic minority, the adherents of some religion or ideology, the promoters of some special interest. (1991: 113)

From here, Taylor moves to speculation concerning a general cultural malaise. As he puts it, "A sense grows that the electorate as a whole is defenseless against the leviathan state" (113). While he concedes that localized political activities may "make a dent" (he never goes beyond speaking in these kinds of generalities), Taylor laments that this kind of fragmentation will never produce national political movements.

Hovering as he does at such an abstract level of analysis makes Taylor's condemnation of localized political activity ring a bit hollow. NSMs have demonstrated the capacity of localized democratic organizing and the implementation of political, economic, and cultural innovations at the local level to transform regional and national relations. Rather than feeling "defenseless against the leviathan state," or perhaps because they feel little can or has been accomplished at that level, actors in NSMs, including members of ICs, have turned to the transformation of regional living experiences. Taylor has attempted, much like those theories of social movements discussed in Chapter 3, to portray NSMs as "regressive" and in some way a "negative" response to social conditions. They are portrayed as having relinquished the real struggle for political, economic, and cultural transformation, leaving democratic culture all the worse for it. Critical of "advocacy politics" (as he should be where there is no willingness to negotiate positions toward consensus), and the pursuit of redress of grievances through the courts, Taylor regards the current political spectrum in America as "abysmal." He cannot, however, address social movements that do not seek confirmation and acknowledgment through the courts (like ICs) and that have professed a concern with dialogical recognition of difference. But Taylor reserves his trump card for the few remaining pages of his book. Having conceded that American culture is permeated with atavistic social relations, the only way he sees to counter fragmentation is to cultivate "an effective common purpose through democratic action" (117). Says Taylor, "To lose the capacity to build politically effective majorities is to lose your paddle in mid-river. You are carried ineluctably down stream, which here means further and further into a culture enframed by atomism and instrumentalism" (118). Finally, just when Taylor poses the most significant question for himself and his communitarian brethren—that is, how do you fight fragmentation?—his answer is "It's not easy."

It is unfortunate that following Taylor's fine critique of the alienating consequences of contemporary bureaucratic modes of domination and its companion instrumentalism as experienced through postindustrial capitalist social relations, his only conclusion is that we must reaffirm our national sense of political identity. Rather than recognizing the inherent instability of natural and social systems recalled by chaos theory and postmodernism, Taylor reaches for a mode of political expression that characterized only a few significant movement actors (perhaps the labor movement of the mid-1800s and early 1900s, and the civil rights movement of the 1950s and 1960s), and even then with considerable heterogeneity within its ranks. But in my estimation, and that of NSM and chaos and postmodern theorists, a national political movement constituted by uniformity of agenda appears virtually impossible in a postindustrial, highly differentiated, heterogeneous society. In sum, what Charles Taylor proposes is cultivation of a mythological, politically homogenous confederation capable of returning us moderns to a mechanical state of mutual self-interest. His rhetorical reliance on the democratic pursuit of humane global relations never ventures far from jingoistic references. For example, Taylor never articulates historical expressions of democracy as practiced externally through the imperialism of occidental powers, or internally through the colonization of indigenous and slave populations. Had he recognized the persistence of resistance within the lifeworld that characterizes indigenous populations the world over, he would perhaps have recognized that there is a crucial distinction between the philosophical orations of democracy, and the actual conditions experienced by those living within democratic societies.

This point can, of course, be made more fervently with regard to authoritarian and dictatorial societies. And while my emphasis in my critique of the communitarian literature, and of Charles Taylor specifically, differs from those of say, Rondald Dwarkin, it is significant that the American Constitution's Bill of Rights enables, among other things, the expression of certain kinds of speech and assembly.[3] This is the point I made in Chapter 3 with references to civil society and the preservation of components of contemporary democratic culture that encourage the articulation of difference. Charles Taylor and the communitarians have a difficult time addressing issues of difference. Rather, I should say, they address matters of difference by urging adoption of the Durkheimian reliance upon moral/ethical consensus. This all seems to be reminiscent of the proverbial "closing the barn door after the horses are loose." It seems to me impossible to establish in such a heterogeneous culture a moral/ethical consensus on almost anything. How would communitarians do it? School prayer? English as the only language used to teach students? Other modes of ideological introctrination? Cultivation of the national populace was recognized by Gramsci, among many others, who argued that even then, with the full weight of myth-making ideological technology bearing down on a people, there would remain modes of resistance within civil society. Accepting flux, heterogeneity, and change as perpetual components of natural and social systems at least moves us in the direction of cultivating methods for managing difference. This would represent a far more beneficial line of theoretical and practical work than continuing a futile search for the torchbearers of democratic reform.

Echoing a similar theme is David Hollenbach (1995) of Boston College. Hollenbach shares the communitarian concern over the excessive promotion of individuation and self in contemporary culture. His criticism, like most within this literature, is focused on Rawls's suggestion that matters of values, tastes, moral correctness, and virtue be left out of the public discourse, due to the fear of an autocratic imposition of a defining cultural morality. Hollenbach argues that leaving these issues unaddressed has moved us further away from democracy by intensifying introspection in search of identity. Citing Bellah et al. (1985), Hollenbach argues against "fragmentation," where "the world comes to us in pieces, in fragments, lacking any overall pattern" (1995: 146). And like Bellah et al., he concludes that "this fragmentation can undermine the sense of overall purpose in the lives of individual persons, leading to a seemingly endless quest for one's own identity." Perhaps even more apropos given my emphasis on striated as opposed to smooth spaces he says: "Because [of] the complexity and high degree of differentiation characteristic of modern social existence, individuals lack a readily intelligible map by which they can locate themselves and chart their course through life" (1995: 146).

Hollenbach's evaluation of contemporary conditions exquisitely portrays the kind of modernist thinking pervasive in the social sciences. Obviously aware of the criticism leveled against communitarianism for its apparent effort to encourage universal moral-ethical-virtue consensus, Hollenbach provides a disclaimer in the first sentence of the second paragraph of his essay, which says, in effect, "We know you are skeptical, but we are not trying to impose *our* beliefs on you." Returning to the those references to fragmentation identified above, it is clear that historically there have been relatively few but always devastating authoritarian ways to demonstrate to "the people" the appropriate "chart" with which to master their life courses. Whether one refers to the power of the church, the state, charismatic authority, or some other mode of manipulation, the fear of popular subaltern compositions of cultural activity permeates modern human history. What chart is there for us to follow? Whose chart is it? To these questions Hollenbach performs a masterful and pragmatic flip. The second half of the essay describes the value inherent in the maintenance of an active civil society, and perhaps more important, invokes the possibility of local modes of communication to reach consensus on issues of popular concern. So is it conceivable, according to Hollenbach, that communities (left undefined in his essay) may simultaneously entertain multiple expressions of reality, leaving only the details to be communicatively negotiated? An approach somewhat like the one I have articulated here? As with much of the communitarian literature, Hollenbach's explication of this component of communitarian theory seems confused and at times contradictory. While he and the others in this growing tradition rail against fragmentation, his apparent unwillingness to go "too far" in the direction of a transcendent national morality provides confusion on issues of mulitiplicitous identity construction and the like.

Unlike Hollenbach, and ther are others articulating differing perspectives on communitarianism, Todd Gitlin's (1995) *The Twilight of Common Dreams* offers a much more incisive critique of identity politics. Gitlin's target, however, is what remains of the political left. In drawing to a close this invective against those claiming identity politics, I will turn to an overview of Gitlin's critique. I find it a compelling and fitting end since Gitlin, writing from within the political left, offers a critique of NSMs that parallels much of the admonition from within the communitarian literature and the political right.

The juxtaposition of Chapters 2 and 3 of Gitlin's book tells the story best. Chapter 2, "A Prodigious Amalgam," tells of an organic America histori- cally cemented by a shared sense of national pride and identity. Gitlin cites numerous authors and historical events to document a collective American psyche cultivating commonality and shared national purpose. Those virtues and subsequent behaviors cited by Gitlin as constituting the American conscious collective are progress, freedom, equality, constitutional faith, justice, a belief in leveling status for criticism, mastering the frontier, consumerism, dedication to work, suburbia, and family (1995: 39–66). Perceptions of homogeneity of purpose, and consensual political and civil responsibility begin to change, however, with the emergence in the 1960s of numerous lines of rhizomatic dissent demanding recognition within the predominant social movements. To establish this point, Chapter 2 closes with the "fragmentation of the left," according to Gitlin, a phenomenon largely initiated by factions within the anti-Vietnam War, civil rights, and feminist movements. These movements and their contingents fomented the minutiae of identity politics when they initiated their expression of values and identities as distinctly *anti*-American.

In the third chapter, "The Fragmentation of the Idea of the Left," Gitlin establishes his criticism of NSMs and what he, like so many others, contends is the denigration of left politics through the proliferation of "identity politics." His introduction to this topic is an uncharacteristically flippant reference to postmodernism: "What proliferates in the West is the 'post' mood. Universalism has a bad name. Reason seems frail—or worse, its claim to progress through understanding is billed as the instrument of white,

Western, male domination, and hence of the pollution and destruction of the earth" (1995: 85). Gitlin also directs his critique to communitarians who preserve as their Archimedean point of departure—the liberal reliance on individual rights. But like Taylor, Gitlin laments the perception of a lost "sense of common citizenship," particularly as it passes in contemporary politics as "the left." For him, the left historically stood for the representation of the ideal—a remnant of Enlightenment philosophical entreaties on the perfectability of the human.

Consider the following comment:

Defenders of some Platonic ideal of a Left have only a tattered flag to wave, and are today, like their counterparts on the Right, more adept at vituperation against their enemies than reflecting upon, let alone practicing, human arrangements that would make life more supportable and dignified for humanity at large. But it will not do to raise the trumpet for a restoration of the grand old unities. An abiding faith in the human future is not summoned up by an act of will. (1995: 87)

I cite this passage in full because it closely approximates to much of the communitarian lamentation over fragmentation. But perhaps more important, in my estimation Gitlin does a great disservice to the idea of the left by ignoring the multiple and untold ways that those inspired by left-wing ideals continue, possibly in more effective ways than did their predecessors,[4] to address local and regional issues (remember "think globally, act locally"?) of humane concern. I have considered the numerous rationales offered by NSM activists to explain their less than enthusiastic commitment to national politics (they, of course, do engage politics at that level but with great skepticism). But in this chapter in particular, Gitlin's superficial evaluation of left-wing activities as they are directed at local and regional issues seems to me inexplicable for a social historian, and probably ideological at its core. For example, Gitlin evokes the genius of Marx as his lucid ability to see the seeds of the future liberation of humankind in the conditions of the present. But in a curious approving reference to the work of University of Illinois English Professor Michael Berube, Gitlin genuflects to classical Marxist theory that: 1) that the base determines the superstructure; 2) class is the primary construct for social change; 3) there exists a historical inevitability leading us to communism; 4) class struggle is inevitable; and 5) ideology is merely false consciousness (1995: 95). Only the Marxist-derived belief that the ruling ideas in any epoch tend to be those of the ruling class can today be established with any assurance of social scientific validity.

Further, Gitlin contends that "Marxism without a revolutionary proletariat has all the pathos of a theology without God" (1995: 95–96). And finally,

Even at its best, this shapeless "Marxism," lacking a labor theory of value, lacking the transcendent homogenization of a universal class, lacking a univeralizing agency, shrinks into a set of analytic tools with which to grasp the globalization of capital and offer a moral critique of exploitation—a valuable angle from which to criticize some social arrangements, but hardly a mission or a politics, let alone the invocation of a universal spirit. (1995: 96)

Affirmative references to the universalist claims made by the Students for a Democratic Society (SDS) and Che Guevara are juxtaposed with the emergence during the late 1960s of a firm belief within the left that cultural transformation at the level of the state is inconceivable. Gitlin recognizes, rightly I think, that the trend toward movement activities that were less universalistic was the product of both intellectual and experiential catalysts. Recognizing that difference was emerging as the defining characteristic of American and European culture, this transformation articulated the dread of contemporary modes of discourse (both linguistic and physical), gender, power, economic dislocation, and the like. What emerges, according to Gitlin, is the exaggeration of group and status differences to the point that academics and politicians came to see them in the form of "essentialisms."[5] Being gay, female, physically impaired, or a member of a race or ethnic minority meant that one was in some way unique from people not possessing those qualities. From here, Gitlin spins into a well-rehearsed trashing of poststructuralism, naming Foucault as the primary agent of inconspicuous skullduggery.[6] Later, in Chapter 7, Gitlin acknowledges the American, German, and French history of postmodern thinking, but still offers nothing in the way of a thorough—dare I say it?—deconstruction of this literature. I find it interesting and politically flawed that one so committed to forging lines of discourse within the "commons" should issue a blanket condemnation of ideas contrary to his own, rather than offering a thorough critique of these ideas.

Multiple readings are possible in this chapter alone. What I find most disturbing in this work, however, is the superficiality of Gitlin's "analysis." His references to classical Marxism, the labor movement, and the civil rights movement are glossed over with the confidence and ease of a storyteller seemingly uncomfortable with the messy details inherent in social movements. Doing so allows him, I suppose, to avoid the struggles with identity emerging from within each of these movements in the course of its existence.[7]

In the final two chapters of Gitlin's book, it becomes clear that there is great tension permeating his thought. While in Chapter 7 Gitlin criticizes postmodernism by chiding the postmodern belief that there is no one singular truth, further into the chapter he confirms, with postmodernism, the multiple lines of intersection serving to constitute subjects in any culture. For example:

Anyway, just how firm is "women's" or "the Latino" or "the African American" or "the Jewish" perspective? Not only are there class, regional, age, political, and plain individual differences but people of every description change their perspectives. (1995: 206)

Gitlin continues by claiming that it is part of the self-definition of America to destroy tradition, to renew. But as is characteristic of his heuristic juxtaposition of polarities, Gitlin draws distinctions between those he accuses of identity politics, and the value of commonality in nearly cartoon-ish caricatures.

Gitlin contends that the "exponents of identity politics" (as though this were a "movement" in and of itself) have as their sole purpose the appropriation of the new, the ephemeral. Two points can be directed to these concerns. First, as I mentioned in discussions of nostalgic utopia, movement actors from around the globe partake in the construction, symbolic interpretation, and reconceptualization of their history, often through the practice of mythistory. By creatively appropriating images, historical personages, events, and places, actors find in history the material foundation for cultivating modes of resistance to contemporary forms of oppression. This is what Hobsbawm and Ranger (1983) referred to as the storehouse of cultural artifacts. The second point, and one I am surprised to see Gitlin confuse, is the way in which he seems to homogenize all forms of cultural dissonance indicative of postmodern modes of expression (e.g., blurring of temporal and spatial media present in the symbolic expression of clothing, hair styles, music, art, architecture). Gitlin speaks too casually about modes of cultural expression. In the categorization of identity politics, he lumps together all modes of cultural expression that seem to appropriate the lexicon and feel of postmodernism. Where would he locate those, particularly young people, who tempt the purveyors of taste with the often mixed and purposefully confused identity expressions found in tatoos, shaved heads, body scarification, multicolored hair, and "retro" clothing? How do they differ from activists working to transform political, economic, and cultural expressions of reality? Do they? In short, Gitlin's caricature is too neat. Those working for social change from within NSMs, including members of ICs, are not the isolated, self-seeking, multicultural individual[s] that Gitlin portrays. Again, in attempting to argue for a left-wing version of a return to the commons, Gitlin assembles a straw man, the group afflicted with the ephemeral search for identity. He does so in vague generalities, never looking too deeply into those social movements or "identity-based" groups toward which he directs his invective. Furthermore, in an awkward opening sentence to the final chapter, Gitlin contends: "[I]dentity politics confronts a world in flux and commands it to stop" (223). I thought it was the flux that gave rise to identity politics! Now it appears as though having "located" our lost identity,[8] actors in NSMs are compelled by "fundamentalist" fervor to retreat from dialogical interaction with our cultural adversaries, interested, we are told, solely in purification of self-sameness. Is it truly the case that NSMs have articulated an "identity, love it or leave it" (208) manifesto? It could be argued, and it would not be novel, that among the most orthodox of the left have been those adhering to an unwavering interpretation or interpretations of Marx. Even without returning to the 1930s, but remaining within Gitlin's own historical memory of 1960s social movements, he surely must concur with critics that organizational hierarchy, unequal distributions of power, and gender and race inequity each constituted many of the more noteworthy of the 1960s organizations (including SDS), ultimately inhibiting political effectiveness.

NSMs, like all movements before them, are multidimensional. Gitlin's typology, as much as he constructs one, simplistically characterizes those articulating the relevance of identity construction as purely self-seeking. Identity construction and the cultivation of social movement activity exist on a continuum. As I argued in Chapters 3 and 4, while we must recognize the heterogeneity and unpredictability of social systems and the actors that constitute them, we must not lose sight of their coexistence within broader social structures. It is civil society and a constitutional democracy that preserves the rights of dissident actors and organizations to gather, speak, and distribute information. This was explained as a consistent property of chaos theory in that flux persists at the level of the lifeworld, the micro, whereas order begins to emerge at the macro-structural level, or for us, at the level of the state. Gitlin turns to the insights of Michael Walzer to address difference with an interest toward the preservation of the whole. I too would like to address the recent work of Michael Walzer since among communitarians, he appears to approximate most closely some of the ideas I have raised.

My discussion of Walzer's work will focus on his 1994 publication of *Thick and Thin: Moral Argument at Home and Abroad*. In it, Walzer addresses what I perceive to be the most pressing matter of human intercourse to confront the late twentieth century: the simultaneous construction, recognition and celebration of difference, and the resolution of domestic and international conflicts that this privileging of difference inevitably gives rise to. Walzer proceeds by constructing what I find to be a useful heuristic distinction between minimal and maximal morality. This duality, he contends, is a permanent feature of every morality (1994: 4).[9] If I have accurately interpreted Walzer, minimal morality very closely resembles what I alluded to in Chapter 3 as civil society. Walzer contends that it is the minimal recognition of the other. Minimal morality is perceived to be the rules for engaging one another within the realm of a shared cultural discourse, which enables us to debate the details of our cultural existence.

[I]t consists in principles and rules that are reiterated in different times and places, and that are seen to be similar even though they are expressed in different idioms and reflect different histories and different versions of the world. Minimalism depends on the fact that we have moral expectations about the behavior not only of our fellows but of strangers too. (1994: 17)

So it is that the preservation of rights that ostensibly affords us the possibility of engaging in the transmission of ideas without fear of repression. Our culture maintains, through the Bill of Rights, a set of prescriptions designating the path over which individuals may travel to arrive at decisions certain to affect public perceptions of pending cultural issues. We have, as it were, a skeletal frame from which to pursue redress of conscience. Left undefined by this minimal morality is the actual content of our moral discourse. For that, Walzer contends, we must focus on moral maximalism.

There is a strong affiliation between Walzer's articulation of moral maximalism and my emphasis in chapter four on chaos theory. That is not to say that Walzer refers to his own work in the light of chaos, but that there are manifest similarities in his insistence that at the level of the micro—for him, the cultural and subcultural levels—the details of life must be viewed as the culmination of indigenous thought and action. Walzer's concern is with distributive justice, identifying the most efficacious way to assure equitable distributions of political, economic and cultural resources. Moral maximalism requires that any reference to distributive justice be framed within the context of the needs unique to specific cultures and subcultures. To speak in real terms of the need for equity with respect to justice means social scientists must recognize the primacy of cultural capital, including:

unique language skills, perceptions of life chances, tastes in music, literature and film, and differences in educational experiences, especially as they
effect the perpetuation of marginalization.[10] In his critique of Descartes, for
example, Walzer argues against articulation of a singular expression of "the
good," asserting instead that "the good" is prioritized as such by those who
hold it dear. For those who do not, it is not. But in what is perhaps his closest
approximation to the theme I have been drumming here, Walzer pushes the
envelope by making a full defense of difference. Again while resting his
logic within the realm of distributive justice, he explains that in order to
effectively administer justice we must adopt a maximalist recognition of
the vast and often varying needs of the people. Doing so requires recognition
of the multiple ways in which people engage their surroundings, interepre-
tations mediated by religion, historical memory, tradition, external social-
structural factors, and so on.

Later in the book, in the chapter addressing "Justice and Tribalism,"
Walzer makes direct reference to mythmaking, storytelling, fables, and tales
as a historically transcendent characteristic of those Eastern European
regimes emancipated from Soviet rule. The tribalism, explains Walzer,
persists where repression is most severe. But his is not an effort to naively
privilege tribalism, especially those expressions of mythistory and storytelling that instill hatred of perceived enemies in the minds of children. Rather,
Walzer contends, that while we in the West may wish for the eradication of
hate through the global adoption of Enlightenment principles privileging
human emancipation, we can and should recognize that hopes of achieving
such lofty and noble results are doomed by maximal definitions of reality,
and that moral minimalism has no "imperial tendencies"—that is, "it
doesn't aspire to global rule" (1994: 64). In the end, Walzer calls for not
only recognition of difference but an approach to difference that respects
the unique composition of subcultural historicity. Moral maximalism requires that tribes will and must persist, but a minimal morality based on a
universal commitment to justice and self-determination is what binds
humanity. Defining precisely what justice means is a maximalist function
that can take place only within the political and cultural realms generated
by free expression, assembly, and the like. Walzer draws his chapter on
tribalism to a close with comments closely approxiamting my own. He says,
"[T]he crucial commonality of the human race is particularism: we participate, all of us, in thick cultures that are our own" (1994: 83).

Our culture, certainly not alone in this regard, comprises multiple perceptions of the real, the good. Through the recognition and privileging of
difference, our culture is better positioned to continue our longstanding

encounter with modes of managing conflict. Moreover, sociologists studying social movements must reconsider their continued reliance on conventional theoretical models to initiate recognition of the persistence of
resistance, an ongoing struggle to manage, rationalize, and sometimes
confront perceived modes of oppression.

Notes

1. Marx explained that the capitalist mode of production left workers alienated from: 1) their product; 2) the means of production; 3) their co-workers; and 4)
themselves. Harry Braverman's (1974) account of deskilling provided the most
poignant restatement of the Marxist thesis on alienation. For Braverman, like
Marx, skilled craftwork had largely been deskilled by the time merchant capitalism was exhausted. What remained of craft specialization was exposed to rigorous
attack from so-called "scientific managers" at the turn of the 20th century. The
most notorious advocates of scientific management were Frederick Taylor and
Frank and Lillian Gillbreth. Later, "Fordism" intensified point-of-production control through various technological and managerial efforts designed to remove
thought work from workers, placing it in the hands of industrial planners and
technicians, while simultaneously exposing workers to a deskilling and disciplinary process that required their adaptation to stationary assembly-line production.
Since workers no longer participated in the entire production process, relegated as
they were to manipulating but one meager component, they had been alienated
from the fruits of their labor. For Marx this was the crux of being human. Humans
are different from the rest of the animal world in that we can imagine a product in
our minds before setting about to produce it, possibly transforming the product.
This productive activity is what satisfies our human nature; we must make things
in order to satisfy what Marx referred to as our species-being. One level of
alienation emerged as soon as we were separated from the product. Moreover,
workers were no longer involved in the planning, design, and marketing of
products. This amounted to what Braverman referred to as the separation of
conception from execution.

With merchant capitalism came the initial efforts to transfer control over the
means of production from the workers to the capitalist employer. Spinning wheels
and looms often had to be rented or purchased from the merchant under the first
appearance of the putting-out system. Later, when workers were first organized to
work under one roof, they were supplied by the merchant with the goal of
enhancing control over the pace and quality of production. Workers were beginning to lose control over the means of production. Next, Marx was convinced that
increased emphasis on instrumental social relations, following John Lock and
Adam Smith, would intensify competition among workers, driving a wedge between their natural affinity to work together to procure social change. Other
factors leading to a separation among workers included piece-rate pay, the devas-

tating ramifications of not being able to find work in a capitalist society (e.g., imprisonment, punishment including flogging and the loss of an ear, hunger, disease), the design of work and relationships to technology, and the enclosure movement, which forced workers off the land and into the cities to work *for* another. Finally, since workers were no longer able to satisfy their species-being through the totalizing experience of producing a product that had use-value to the community, workers became alienated from themselves.

2. As an aside, I found Taylor's apparent elation at the idea that the "iron cage" was really quite porous to be extremely naive. For nearly 150 years, sociologists and historians have produced credible accounts of the numerous ways people navigate oppressive social conditions. That there is often great disparity between what official decree requires and what people do should come as no surprise to any student of labor, or of social movements, for that matter. In this regard, I find Taylor's call to mass social movements to be antithetical to contemporary postindustrial social relations and perhaps more at home in a pre-1980s effort to discern the most credible bearer of social movement status. This was, of course, a component of my critique in Chapter 3. In addition to those references cited in Chapter 5, readers should review the numerous works documenting modes of worker resistance (e.g., Armstrong et al., 1981; Burawoy, 1985; Roy, 1954, 1957).

3. To his credit, Amitai Etzioni (1995b) has made a similar point in his *New Communitarian Thinking*. In the chapter "Old Chestnuts and New Spurs," Etzioni responds to criticisms such as the one I direct at Taylor through references to the value of the Bill of Rights. Arguing that America is not a "simple democracy" but rather a "constitutional" one, Etzioni makes the case that America does make provisions for "differentiation," which protects minority rights, the rights of the individual. The problem with Etzioni's argument as I see it is his polarization of community interests and rights. That is, he fails to see that contemporary actors continue to participate in their local affiliations, their voluntary associations, and the like, generating, filtering, and negotiating new meanings for cultural stimuli. We are not, as he would have it, thoroughly isolated due to an obsessive reliance on rights and individuation. That there exists cultural angst over oppressive working conditions, decreasing monetary valuation, psychological and psychosexual repression, destruction to the earth, and so on is clear. Political and corporate scandals too numerous to name here characterize what many view as a crucial stimulus for the violation of the national trust (e.g., Simon, 1996; Mokhiber, 1989). While they periodically appear as a component of communitarian rhetoric, this emphasis is typically marginalized for the more appealing directives aimed at the life experiences of the poor and working classes.

4. Friends of mine who attended the national student organizing effort held at Rutgers University during the late 1980s, returned to the West Lafayette, Indiana, campus where we were graduate students at Purdue University to complain about the inability to fuse a national platform agenda. There were simply too many

political interests, each wanting its agenda to be *the* agenda. When frustrations peaked, students turned to one of the many veteran 1960s radicals in attendance for advice. While refusing to intervene to resolve disputes among the conference participants, Abby Hoffman did make the well-received and, I believe, accurate point that student and community organizers are much better prepared to implement significant structural changes in our local communities than was ever the case in the 1960s. This is due in large part to the fact that activists from the 1960s are now living and working in these communities and have honed their organizing and canvassing skills. I relate this story here because I believe that Gitlin, like many in the communitarian literature (which does not formally include him), views the past with glowing reminiscences of a "better" time.

5. This represents an interesting lexical play. In the literature addressing postmodernism, the construct of essentialism is reserved for dominant ideological belief systems. Essentialisms construct images of the world as closed and centered totalities. Life is provided a certain order whereby explanation stems from ancillary conceptualizations of life events, always in keeping with the dominant system of ideas. Marxism, capitalism, socialism, anarchism, most organized religions were and continue to be the predominant modes of ordering reality. They are essentialisms. To my knowledge, the construct of essentialism has not been used to evoke any sense of individual or group identity.

6. I say "well-rehearsed" because Gitlin's criticism of Foucault, like most of his book, never goes far beyond superficiality. Foucault is seen by Gitlin as an "essentialist" himself, as he proposed that power was the determining characteristic of contemporary polititcal, economic, and cultural relations. What is astonishing to me is that for one so astutely aware of the interstices of American culture, his own references to Foucault (they were hardly analyses) are limited by Foucault's writings through the 1970s. Gitlin never bothers to cite specific references to or discuss specific insights stemming from any of Foucault's works. If Gitlin were only arguing that it was this particular historical moment that initiated the swing to "identity," after which Foucault and identity politics died out, his interpretation would be little cause for notice. However, since this book specifically addresses contemporary issues of political fragmentation with Foucault playing a seminal role, and since Foucault's publications continued into the 1980s with often considerable revision of his earlier emphases on power and political closure, not to address these works seems at best academically delinquent, a distortion of Foucault's ideas. This is important since it is part of Gitlin's overall intention to capture the contradictions inherent in identity politics. Marking a seminal figure in the poststructural and postmodern theoretical traditions as contradictory is an obvious frame to discredit the work of NSMs and all who claim to have benefited from the resonance of his work.

7. The very existence of the CIO should indicate a certain level of craft-based identity consciousness. Or perhaps the fact that the American Federation of Labor refused to recruit black workers or women?

8. Because for Gitlin truth is conspicuous, tangible, existing somewhere "out there" for all to see, it must be the case that those afflicted with the ephemeral need for identity confirmation will, in searching for it, find the truth, which then confirms their uniqueness and possibly their unwillingness to budge when confronted with differences where, to use his words, "the impulse is to purge impurities" (1995: 223).

Gitlin cannot have it both ways. To argue as he does in this book snares him in a logical trap. To avoid the phenomenon he refers to above, he would benefit from a reconceptualized notion of truth, where truth is relative, ambulant, negotiated. Only then would we find ourselves in a situation where we as citizens begin to view *our* convictions as fluid, and diaphanous. Perhaps then we can attain the level of tolerance I perceive to be Gitlin's primary objective.

9. Walzer acknowledges his dedication to Clifford Geertz's (1973) book *The Interpretation of Cultures*. Walzer's appropriation of Geertz refers not to the methodlogical emphasis on thick and thin description, but rather on ways to perceive experiences with morality as being thick or thin.

10. Walzer does not use the concept of cultural capital. That he does not raises a minor criticism of this book. Much of what he articulates here has been addressed in other works using the terminology of other disciplines. Perhaps his point could have been more forcefully delivered had he ventured into these literatures, especially those addressing moral maximalism from within the cultural capital "milieu" (e.g., Bourdieu, Giroux, Freire).

SELECTED BIBLIOGRAPHY

Ackerman, Bruce. 1980. *Social Justice in a Liberal State*. New Haven, Conn.: Yale University Press.

Aglietta, Michael. 1976. *A Theory of Capitalist Regulation*. London: NLB.

Alberoni, F. 1984. *Movement and Institution*. New York: Columbia University Press.

Altman, D. 1971. *Homosexual: Oppression and Liberation*. New York: Outerbridge and Dienstfrey.

Anders, Jentri. 1990. *Beyond Counterculture: The Community of Mateel*. Pullman: Washington State University Press.

Anderson, Benedict. 1991. *Imagined Communities*. London: Verso.

Arendt, Hannah. 1977. *On Revolution*. New York: Penguin.

————.1969. *On Violence*. New York: Harcourt Brace Jovanovich.

————.1958a. *The Origins of Totalitarianism*. New York: Meridian Books.

————.1958b. *The Human Condition*. Chicago: University of Chicago Press.

Armstrong, P. J., J.F.B. Goodman, and J. D. Hyman. 1981. *Ideology and Shop-Floor Industrial Relations*. London: Croom Helm.

Bagguley, P. 1992. "Social Change, the Middle Class and the Emergence of 'New Social Movements': A Critical Analysis." *The Sociological Review*, 92: 26–48.

Baker, P. 1993. "Chaos, Order, and Sociological Theory." *Sociological Inquiry*, 63 (2): 123–49.

Barnes, S. H. June 1982. "Parties, Mobilization, and the New Citizen." Unpublished paper presented to the "Future of Party Government" project in Florence, European University Institute.

Barthes, Roland. 1974. *S/Z*. New York: Hill & Wang.

Baudrillard, Jean. 1981. *For a Critique of the Political Economy of the Sign*. St. Louis: Telos Press.

————. 1975. *The Mirror of Production*. Translated by M. Poster. St. Louis: Telos Press.

Bell, Daniel. 1989. "American Exceptionalism Revisited: The Role of Civil Society." *The Public Interest*, 95: 38–56.

Bellah, Robert, Richard Madsen, William Sullivan, Ann Swidler, and Steven Tipton. 1985. *Habits of the Heart*. New York: Harper and Row.

Bellamy, Edward. [1888] 1996. *Looking Backward*. New York: Signet Classic.

Benedict, Ruth. 1934. *Patterns of Culture*. New York: Houghton Mifflin.

Benhabib, Syla. 1992. *Situating the Self: Gender, Community and Postmodernism in Contemporary Ethics*. New York: Routledge.

Benjamin, Walter. 1969. *Illuminations*. Edited by Hannah Arendt, translated by Harry Zohn. New York: Schocken Books.

Bennett, William. 1984. "To Reclaim a Legacy: Text of Report on Humanities in Education." *The Chronicle of Higher Education*, 29 (14): 16–21.

Berger, Bennett. 1981. *The Survival of Counterculture*. Berkeley: University of California Press.

Berger, John. 1979. *Pig Earth*. New York: Vintage Books.

Bernal, Martin. 1994. "The Image of Ancient Greece as a Tool of Colonialism and European Hegemony." In G. C. Bond and A. Gilliam (eds.), *Social Construction of the Past*. New York: Routledge, pp. 119–28.

Bester, A. E. 1950. *Backwoods Utopias: The Sectarian and Owenite Phases of Communitarian Socialism in America, 1663–1829*. Philadelphia: University of Pennsylvania Press.

Bloch, Ernst. 1995. *The Principle of Hope*. Vols. I and II. Cambridge, Mass.: MIT Press.

————. 1988. "Something's Missing: A Discussion Between Ernst Bloch and Theodor Adorno on the Contradictions of Utopian Longing." In J. Zipes (ed. and trans.), *The Utopian Function of Art and Literature*. Cambridge, Mass.: Cambridge University Press, pp. 2–17, 19.

Blumer, Herbert. 1955. "Social Movements." In A. M. Lee, (ed.) *Principles of Sociology*. New York: Barnes and Noble.

Boggs, Carl. 1985. *Social Movements and Political Power*. Philadelphia: Temple University Press.

Bond, G. C., and A. Gilliam. 1994. Introduction. In G. C. Bond and A. Gilliam (eds.), *Social Construction of the Past*. New York: Routledge, pp. 1–22.

Bourdieu, Pierre. 1984. *Distinction: A Social Critique of the Judgement of Taste*. Translated by Richard Nice. Cambridge, Mass.: Harvard University Press.

Brand, Karl-Werner. 1990. "Cyclical Aspects of New Social Movements." In R. Dalton and M. Kuechler (eds.), *Challenging the Political Order: New*

Social and Political Movements in Western Democracies. Cambridge, England: Polity.

Braverman, Harry. 1974. *Labor and Monopoly Capital.* New York: Monthly Review Press.

Brion, D. 1991. "The Chaotic Law of Tort: Legal Formalism and the Problem of Indeterminacy." In R. Kevelson (ed.), *Peirce and Law.* New York: Peter Lang Publishing.

Burawoy, Michael. 1985. *The Politics of Production.* London: Verso.

Burchlen, Wilhelm. 1982. "Die Gruenen und Die 'Neue Politik.' " *Politisch Vierteljahresschrift*, 22: 360–75.

Butler, J. 1990. *Gender Trouble: Feminism and the Subversion of Identity.* New York: Routledge.

Calhoun, Craig. 1982. *The Question of Class Struggle: Social Foundations of Popular Radicalism During the Industrial Revolution.* Chicago: University of Chicago Press.

Castells, Manuel. 1983. *The City and the Grassroots: A Cross-Cultural Theory of Urban Movements.* Berkeley: University of California Press.

Cohen, Jean. 1985. "Strategy or Identity: New Theoretical Paradigms and Contemporary Social Movements." *Social Research*, 52 (4): 664–716.

Cohen, Jean, and Andrew Arato. 1992. *Civil Society and Political Theory.* Cambridge, Mass.: MIT Press.

Cohen, Norman. 1957. *Pursuit of the Millennium.* New York: Essential Books.

Conover, Patrick. 1978. "Communes and Intentional Communities." *Journal of Voluntary Action Research*, 5 (34): 5–17.

———. 1975. "An Analysis of Communes and Intentional Communities with Particular Attention to Sexual and Genderal Relations." *The Family Coordinator*, 24 (4): 453–64.

Conrad, Peter, and Joseph Schneider. 1980. *Deviance and Medicalization: From Badness to Sickness.* St. Louis: Mosby Co.

Cotgrove, S., and A. Duff. 1981. "Environmentalism, Values and Social Change." *British Journal of Sociology*, 32 (1): 92–110.

———. 1980. "Environmentalism, Middle Class Radicalism and Politics." *The Sociological Review*, 28 (2): 333–51.

Crawford, Robert. 1978. "You Are Dangerous To Your Health: The Ideology and Politics of Victim Blaming." *Social Policy*, 8: 10–20.

Danto, Arthur. 1985. *Narration and Knowledge.* New York: Columbia University Press.

Davis, Mike. 1986. *Prisoner of the American Dream.* London: Verso.

de Certeau, Michel. 1984. *The Practice of Everyday Life.* Berkeley: University of California Press.

Deleuze, Gilles, and Felix Guattari. 1987. *A Thousand Plateaus: Capitalism and Schizophrenia.* Minneapolis: University of Minnesota Press.

———. 1983. *Anti-Oedipus*. Translated by Robert Hurley, Mark Seem, and Helen R. Lane. Minneapolis: University of Minnesota Press.

della Porta, Donatella. 1988. "Recruitment Processes in Clandestine Political Organizations." *International Social Movement Research*, 1: 155–69.

Derrida, Jacques. 1976. *Of Grammatology*. Baltimore: Johns Hopkins University Press.

Durkheim, Emile. [1893] 1984. *The Division of Labor in Society*. London: Macmillan.

———. [1895] 1982. *The Rules of Sociological Method*. London: Macmillan.

Eisenstein, Zillah. 1988. *The Female Body and the Law*. Berkeley: University of California Press.

Etzioni, Amitai. 1995a. "The Responsive Communitarian Platform: Rights and Responsibilities." In A. Etzioni (ed.), *Rights and the Common Good*. New York: St. Martin's Press, pp. 1–24.

———. 1995b. *New Communitarian Thinking: Persons, Virtues, Institutions, and Communities*. Charlotte: University Press of Virginia.

Evans, Sara, and Harry Boyte. 1986. *Free Spaces*. New York: Harper and Row.

Fantasia, Rick, and Eric Hirsch. 1995. "Culture in Rebellion: The Appropriation and Transformation of the Veil in the Algerian Revolution." In Hank Johnston and Bert Klandermans (eds.), *Social Movements and Culture*. Minneapolis: University of Minnesota Press, pp. 144–62.

Feigenbaum, Mitchell. 1980. "Universal Behavior in Nonlinear Systems." *Los Alamos Science*, 1: 4–27.

Feitkau, Hans-Joackim. 1982. *Umwelt im Spiegel der Offenlichen Meinung*. Frankfurt, Germany: Campus.

Flacks, Richard. 1988. *Making History*. New York: Columbia University Press.

Fogerty, Robert. 1990. *All Things New*. Chicago: University of Chicago Press.

Foucault, Michel. 1980. *History of Sexuality*. New York: Vintage Books.

———. 1979. *Discipline and Punish: The Birth of the Prison*. New York: Vintage Books.

———. 1976. *The Archeology of Knowledge*. New York: Harper and Row.

Freidman, Jonathan. 1993. "Order and Disorder in Global Systems: A Sketch." *Social Research*, 60 (2): 205–34.

Freire, Paulo. 1973. *Pedagogy of the Oppressed*. New York: Seabury Press.

Fromm, Eric. 1941. *Escape From Freedom*. New York: Holt, Rhinehart and Winston.

Gampson, William. 1975. *The Strategy of Social Protest*. Homewood, Ill.: Dorsey.

Geertz, Clifford. 1973. *The Interpretation of Cultures*. New York: Basic Books.

Giddens, Anthony. 1991. *Modernity and Self-Identity: Self and Society in the Late Modern Age*. Stanford, Ca.: Stanford University Press.

Gilmore, David. 1987. *Aggression and Community: Paradoxes of Andalusian Culture*. New Haven, Conn.: Yale University Press.

Giroux, Henri. 1988. "Antonio Gramsci: Schooling for Radical Politics." In H. Giroux (ed.), *Teachers as Intellectuals: Toward a Critical Pedagogy.* Boston, Mass.: Bergin and Garvey: 196–221.

Gitlin, Todd. 1995. *Twilight of Common Dreams.* New York: Metropolitan Books.

Gleick, James. 1987. *Chaos: Making a New Science.* New York: Viking.

Godel, K. 1962. "On Formally Undecidable Propositions in 'Principia Mathematica' and Related Systems." In R. B. Braitewaite (ed.), title: New York: Basic Books, pp. 173–98.

Gordon, David, Richard Edwards, and Michael Reich. 1982. *Segmented Work, Divided Workers: The Historical Transformations of Labor in the United States.* New York: Cambridge University Press.

Gowan, Susanne, G. Lakey, W. Moyer, and R. Taylor. 1983. "Living the Revolution," *Small Groups and Interaction,* 2: 307–16.

Gross, David. 1992–93. "Rethinking Traditions." *Telos,* 94 (Winter): 5–10.

———. 1992. *The Past in Ruins: Tradition and the Critique of Modernity.* Amherst: University of Massachusetts Press.

Gundelach, Peter. 1984. "Social Transformation and New Forms of Voluntary Associations." *Social Science Information,* 23 (6): 1049–81.

Gusfield, Joseph. 1994. "The Reflexivity of Social Movements: Collective Behavior and Mass Society Theory Revisited." In E. Larana, H. Johnston, and J. Gusfield (eds.), *New Social Movements.* Philadelphia: Temple University Press, pp. 58–78.

Gyani, Gabor. 1993. "Political Uses of Tradition in Postcommunist East Central Europe." *Social Research,* 60 (4): 893–913.

Habermas, Jurgen. 1989. *The Theory of Communicative Action.* Vol. 2. Translated by Thomas McCarthy. Boston: Beacon Press.

———. 1987. *The Theory of Communicative Action.* Vol. 1. Translated by Thomas McCarthy. Boston: Beacon Press.

Hayles, N. Katherine. 1990. *Chaos Bound.* Ithaca: Cornell University Press.

Head, Simon. 1996. "The New Ruthless Economy." *New York Review of Books,* XLIII (4): 42–52.

Heberle, Rudolf. 1951. *Social Movements.* New York: Meredith Corporation.

Heehs, Peter. 1994. "Myth, History, and Theory." *History and Theory,* 33 (1): 1–19.

Heller, Agnes. 1989. "From Hermeneutics in Social Science Toward a Hermeneutics of Social Science." *Theory and Society,* 18: 291–322.

Hemple, Carl. 1965. "The Function of General Laws in History." (eds.) In *Aspects of Scientific Explanation and Other Essays.* New York: Free Press, pp. 231–43.

Hirsch, Eric. 1990. *Urban Revolt: Ethnic Politics in the Nineteenth Century Chicago Labor Movement.* Berkeley: University of California Press.

Hobsbawm, Eric. 1982. *History of Marxism.* Bloomington: Indiana University Press.

Hobsbawm, Eric, and Terence Ranger. 1983. *The Invention of Tradition*. London: Cambridge University Press.

Hollenbach, David. 1995. "Virtue, the Common Good, and Democracy." In A. Etzioni (ed.), *New Communitarian Thinking*. Charlotte: University Press of Virginia, pp. 143–53.

Holloway, Mark. 1966. *Heavens on Earth*. New York: Dover.

Hunt, G. 1987. "The Development of the Concept of Civil Society in Marx." *History and Politcal Thought*, 8 (2): 263–76.

Husserl, Edmund. 1960. *Cartesian Meditations: An Introduction to Phenomenology*. Translated by Dorion Cairns. The Hague: Nijhoff.

Ingelhart, Ronald. 1990. *Culture Shift in Advanced Industrial Society*. Princeton, N.J.: Princeton University Press.

————. 1977. *The Silent Revolution: Changing Values and Political Styles Among Western Publics*. Princeton, N.J.: Princeton University Press.

Jameson, Fredrick. 1972. *Marxism and Form*. Princeton, N.J.: Princeton University Press.

Jamison, Andrew, and Ron Eyerman. 1991. *Social Movements: A Cognitive Approach*. University Park: Pennsylvania State University Press.

Jenkins, Craig. 1989. *States and Social Movements: Recent Theory and Research*. Social Science Research Council Newsletter.

Jenson, Jane. 1995. "What's in a Name? Nationalist Movements and Public Discourse." In Hank Johnston and Bert Klandermans (eds.), *Social Movements and Culture*. Minneapolis: University of Minnesota Press, pp. 107–26.

Johnston, Hank, and Bert Klandermans. 1995. "The Cultural Analysis of Social Movements." In Hank Johnston and Bert Klandermans (eds.), *Social Movements and Culture*. Minneapolis: University of Minnesota Press, pp. 3–24.

Kamminga, Harmke. 1990. "What is This Thing Called Chaos?" *New Left Review*, 181: 49–59.

Kanter, Rosabeth Moss. 1972. *Commitment and Community*. Cambridge, Mass.: Harvard University Press.

Kinkade, Kat. 1995. "Benevolent Dictators in Community?" *Communities* (Fall): 28–30.

Klandermans, Bert. 1990. "New Social Movements and Resource Mobilization: The European and the American Approach Revisited." Unpublished manuscript. Department of Social Psychology, Vrije Universiteit, Amersterdam.

————. 1988. "The Formation and Mobilization of Consensus." In B. Klandermans, H. Kriesi, and S. Tarrow (eds.), *International Social Movement Research, Vol. 1, From Structure to Action: Comparing Movement Participation Across Cultures*. Greenwich, Conn.: JAI Press.

Klandermans, Bert, and Sydney Tarrow. 1988. "Mobilization in Social Movements: Synthesizing European and American Approaches." *International Social Movement Research*, 1: 1–38.

Klandermans, Bert, Hanspeter Kriesi, and Sydney Tarrow (eds.). 1988. International Social Movement Research, *Vol. 1: From Structure to Action*. Greenwich, Conn.: JAI Press.

Knights, David. 1990. "Subjectivity, Power, and the Labour Process." D. Knights and H. Willmott (eds.), *Labour Process Theory*. London: Macmillan Press, pp. 297–335.

Kriesi, Hanspeter. 1989. "New Social Movements and the New Class in the Netherlands." *American Journal of Sociology*, 94 (5) (March): 1078–1116.

Kriesi, Hanspeter, and Philip Von Praag Jr. 1987. "Old and New Politics: The Dutch Peace Movement and Traditional Political Organizations." *European Journal for Political Science*, 15: 319–46.

Kozeny, Geoff. 1995. "Constructive Criticism." *Communities*, (Fall): 6–7.

Kumar, Krishnan. 1993. *Utopias and the Millennium*. London: Reaktion.

————. 1991. *Utopianism*. Minneapolis: University of Minnesota Press.

Kuron, Jacek. 1981. "Not to Lure the Wolves out of the Woods: An Interview With Jacek Kuron." *Telos*, 47 (Spring): 93–97.

Lacan, Jacques. 1977. *Écrits*. Translated by A. Sheridan. New York: Norton.

Laclau, Ernesto. 1990. *New Reflections on the Revolution of Our Time*. London: Verso.

————. 1988. "Metaphor and Social Antagonisms." In C. Nelson and L. Grossberg (eds.), *Marxism and the Interpretation of Culture*. Chicago and Urbana: University of Illinois Press, pp. 249–257.

Laclau, Ernesto, and Chantal Mouffe 1985. *Hegemony and Socialist Strategy*. London: Verso.

Laidler, Harry. 1968. *History of Socialism*. New York: Thomas Y. Crowell.

Larana, Enrique, Hank Johnston, and Joseph Gusfield 1994. *New Social Movements: From Ideology to Identity*. Philadelphia: Temple University Press.

Lasch, Christopher. 1995. "Communitarianism or Populism?" In A. Etzioni (ed.), *Rights and the Common Good*. New York: St. Martin's Press, pp. 59–66.

Lazlo, Ervin. 1987. *Evolution: The Grand Synthesis*. Boston: Shambhala.

LeBon, G. 1960. *The Crowd*. New York: Viking.

Lefort, C. 1986. *The Political Forms of Modern Society: Bureaucracy, Democracy, Totalitarianism*. Translated by John Thompson. Cambridge, Mass.: MIT Press.

Levitas, R. 1990. *The Concept of Utopia*. New York: Syracuse University Press.

Lipset, S. M. 1983. *The Confidence Gap: Business, Labor and Government in the Public Mind*. New York: Free Press.

————. 1977. "American Exceptionalism in the North American Perspective: Why the United States Has Withstood the World Socialist Movement."

In G. Adams (ed.) *The Idea of America*. Cambridge, Mass.: Harvard University Press.

Lofland, John. 1995. "Charting Degrees of Movement Culture: Tasks of the Cultural Cartographer." In H. Johnston and B. Klandermans (eds.), *Social Movement and Culture*. Minneapolis: University of Minnesota Press, pp. 188–216.

Lorenz, Edward. 1963. "Problem of Deducing the Climate from the Governing Equations." *Tellus* 16: 1–11.

Luke, Timothy. 1992–93. "Neo-Populism: Fabricating the Future by Rehabbing the Past?" *Telos*, 94: 11–18.

———. 1991. "Touring Hyperreality: Critical Theory Confronts Informational Society." In Philip Wexler (ed.), *Critical Theory Now*. New York: Falmer Press: 1–26.

Lyotard, Jean-Francois. 1984. *The Postmodern Condition: A Report on Knowledge*. Translated by Geoff Bennington and Brian Massumi. Minneapolis: University of Minnesota Press.

MacIntyre, Alasdaire. 1990. *Three Rival Versions of Moral Enquiry*. London: Duckworth.

Mandelbaum, Maurice. 1961. "Historical Explanation: The Problem of 'Covering Laws.'" *History and Theory*, 1: 233–38.

Mandelbrot, Benoit. 1983. *The Fractal Geometry of Nature*. New York: W. H. Freeman.

Mannheim, Karl. 1936. *Ideology and Utopia*. New York: Harcourt, Brace and World.

Marcuse, Herbert. 1964. *One Dimensional Man*. Boston: Beacon Press.

Marin, Louis. 1984. *Utopics: Spatial Play*. Translated by Robert A. Vollrath. Atlantic Highlands, N.J.: Humanities Press.

Marx, Karl, and Frederick Engels. [1975] 1984. *The German Ideology*. New York: International Publishers.

McAam, Doug. 1988. "Micromobilization Contexts and Recruitment to Activism." *International Social Movement Research*, 1: 124–54.

McCarthy, John, and Mayer Zald. 1977. "Resource Mobilization and Social Movements: A Partial Theory." *American Journal of Sociology*, 82 (6): 1212–41.

McLaughlin, Corinne, and Gordon Davidson. 1990. *Builders of the Dawn: Community Lifestyles in a Changing World*. Salisbury: Sirius Publishing.

Melucci, Alberto. 1995. "The Process of Collective Identity." In Hank Johnston and Bert Klandermans (eds.), *Social Movements and Culture*. Minneapolis: University of Minnesota Press, pp. 41–63.

———. 1994. "A Strange Kind of Newness: What's "New" in New Social Movements." In E. Larana, H. Johnston, and J. Gusfield (eds.), *New Social Movements: From Ideology to Identity*. Philadelphia: Temple University Press, pp. 101–30.

————. 1990. *Nomads of the Present: Social Movements and Individual Needs Contemporary Society*. Philadelphia: Temple University Press.

————. 1988. "Getting Involved: Identity and Mobilization in Social Movements." *International Social Movement Research*, 1: 329–48.

————. 1985. "Symbolic Challenge of Contemporary Movements." *Social Research*, 52 (4, Winter): 790–816.

————. 1980. "The New Social Movements: A Theoretical Approach." *Social Science Information*, 19 (2): 199–226.

Michels, Roberto. 1959. *Political Parties*. New York: Dover.

Michnik, Adam. 1985. *Letters From Prison and Other Essays*. Berkeley: University of California Press.

Miller, James. 1978. "Some Implications of Nietzsche's Thought for Marxism." *Telos*, 37: 22–41.

Milovanovic, Dragon. 1997. *Chaos, Criminology and Social Justice: The New (Dis)order*. Westport, Conn.: Greenwood Press.

————. 1995. "Dueling Paradigms: Modernist versus Postmodernist Thought." *Humanity and Society*, 19 (1): 19–44.

————. 1994. "The DeCentered Subject in Law: Contributions of Topology, Psychoanalytic Semiotics, and Chaos Theory." *Studies in Psychoanalytic Theory*, 3 (1): 93–127.

————. 1993a. "Borromean Knots and the Constitution of Sense in Juridico-Discursive Production." *Legal Studies Forum*, 17 (2): 171–92.

————. 1993b. "Lacan's Four Discourses, Chaos and Cultural Criticism in Law." *Studies in Psychoanalytic Theory*, 2 (1): 3–23.

Mokhiber, Russell. 1989. *Corporate Crime and Culture: Big Business Power and the Abuse of the Public Trust*. San Francisco: Sierra Books.

More, Thomas. 1969. *Utopia*. Edited by Edward Surtz. New Haven, Conn.: Yale University Press.

Muller-Rommel, Ferdinand. 1985. "New Social Movements and Smaller Parties: A Comparative Perspective." *Western European Politics*, 8: 41–54.

Nandy, Ashis. 1987. "Cultural Frames for Social Transformation: A Credo." *Alternatives*, 12: 113–23.

Nedelmann, Birgitta. 1984. "New Political Movements and Changes in Processes of Intermediation." *Social Science Information*, 23 (6): 1029–48.

Neville-Sington, Pamela, and David Sington. 1993. *Paradise Dreamed*. London: Bloomsbury.

O'Donnell, Guillermo, Philippe Schmitter, and Laurence Whitehead. 1986. *Transitions From Authoritarian Rule: Prospects for Democracy*. Baltimore: Johns Hopkins University Press.

Offe, Claus. 1985. "New Social Movements: Challenging the Boundaries of Institutional Politics." *Social Research*, 52, (4, Winter): 817–68.

————. 1984. *Contradictions of the Welfare State*. Cambridge, Mass.: MIT Press.

Olson, Mancur. 1965. *The Logic of Collective Action*. Cambridge, Mass.: Harvard University Press.

Owen, Robert. 1836. *Book of the New Moral World, Part IV*. London.

Owens, Craig. 1983. "The Discourse of Others: Feminists and Postmodernism." In H. Foster (ed.), *The Anti-Aesthetic: Essays on Postmodern Culture*. Port Townsend, Wash.: Bay Press, pp. 57–82.

Parsons, Talcott. 1971. *The System of Modern Societies*. Englewood Cliffs, N.J.: Prentice Hall.

————. 1937. *The Structure of Social Action*. New York: Free Press.

Piccone, Paul. 1993. "The Actuality of Traditions." *Telos*, 94 (Winter): 889–1102.

Pirsig, Robert. 1991. *Lila: An Inquiry Into Morals*. New York: Bantam Books.

Pollard, Sydney. 1969. *The Development of the British Economy*. New York: St. Martin's Press.

Porush, David. 1991. Fictions as Dissipative Structures: Prigogine's Theory and Postmodernism's Roadshow." In N.K. Hayles (ed.), *Chaos and Order*. Chicago: University of Chicago Press, pp. 54–84.

Prigogine, Ilya, and Isabelle Stengers. 1984. *Order Out of Chaos: Man's New Dialogue With Nature*. Toronto: Bantam.

Rao, Nandini. 1994. "Interpreting Silences: Symbol and History in the Case of Ram Janmabhoomi/Babri Masjid." In G. C. Bond and A. Gilliam (eds.), *Social Construction of the Past*. New York: Routledge, pp. 154–64.

Raschke, Joachim. 1985. *Soziale Bewegungen. Ein Historisch-Systematischer Grundriss*. Frankfurt, Germany: Campus.

Rawls, John. 1971. *A Theory of Justice*. Cambridge, Mass.: Harvard University Press.

Reisch, George. 1991. "Chaos, History, and Narrative." *History and Theory*, 30 (1): 1–20.

Ricoeur, Paul. 1986. *Lectures on Ideology and Utopia*. Edited by G. H. Taylor. New York: Columbia University Press.

Robinson, P. 1969. *The Freudian Left: Wilhelm Reich, Geza Roheim, Herbert Marcuse*. New York: Harper and Row.

Rosanvallon, Pierre. 1981. *La crise de l'État-providence*. Paris: Seuill.

Rosenberg, Justin. 1996. "Isaac Deutscher and the Lost History of International Relations." *New Left Review*, 215: 3–15.

Roth, Paul. 1988. "Narrative Explanations: The Case of History." *History and Theory*, 27 (3): 8–12.

Roy, Donald. 1957. "Quota Restrictions and Goldbricking in a Machine Shop." *American Sociological Review*, 57 (5): 427–42.

————. 1954. "Efficiency and 'the Fix': Informal Intergroup Relations in a Piece-work Machine Shop." *American Journal of Sociology*, 60: 255–66.

Rundell, J. 1987. *Origins of Modernity*. Madison: University of Wisconsin Press.

Ryan, Michael. 1982. *Marxism and Deconstruction: A Critical Articulation*. Baltimore: Johns Hopkins University Press.

Sahlins, Marshall David. 1972. *Stone Age Economics*. New York: Aldine.

Sassoon, Joseph. 1984. "Ideology, Symbolic Action and Rituality in Social Movements: The Effects on Organizational Forms." *Social Science Information*, 23 (4/5): 861–73.

Schehr, Robert. 1995. "Divarications of Employee Drug Testing Through Deconstruction and Discourse Analysis." *Humanity and Society*, 19 (1): 45–64.

Scott, James. 1990. *Domination and the Arts of Resistance*. New Haven, Conn.: Yale University Press.

Seligman, A. 1992. *The Idea of Civil Society*. New York: Free Press.

Serres, Michel. 1982. *The Parasite*. Translated by L. Schehr. Baltimore: Johns Hopkins University Press.

————. 1977. *La Naissance de la physique dans le texte de Lucrece*. Paris: Minuit.

Shaw, Robert. 1981. "Strange Attractors, Chaotic Behavior, and Information Flow." *Zeitschrift fur Naturforschung,* 36A: 79–112.

Shell, S. M. 1980. *Rights of Reason*. Toronto: University of Toronto Press.

Shils, Edward. 1991. "The Virtue of Civil Society." *Government and Opposition*, 26 (2): 3–20.

Simon, David. 1996. *Elite Deviance*. Boston: Allyn and Bacon.

Smelser, Neil. 1962. *Theory of Collective Behavior*. New York: Free Press.

Snow, David, and Robert Benford. 1992. "Master Frames and Cycles of Protest." In A. Morris and C. McClurg Mueller (eds.), *Frontiers in Social Movement Theory*. New Haven, Conn.: Yale University Press, pp. 133–55.

————. 1988. "Ideology, Frame Resonance, and Participant Mobilization." *International Social Movement Research*, 1: 197–217.

Snow, David, E. Burke Rochford, Steven Worden, and Robert Benford. 1986. Frame Alignment Processes, Micromobilization, and Movement Participation." *American Sociological Review*, 51: 464–81.

Sombert, Werner. 1975. *Why There Is No Socialism In the USA*. London: Macmillan.

Sorel, G. 1925. *Reflections on Violence*. London: Allen and Unwin.

Tarrow, Sydney. 1994. *Power in Movement: Social Movements, Collective Action, and Mass Politics in the Modern State*. New York: Cambridge University Press.

————. 1989. *Democracy and Disorder: Protest and Politics in Italy, 1965–1975*. Oxford, England: Clarendon Press.

————. 1983. "Struggling to Reform: Social Movements and Policy Change During Cycles of Protest." *Western Societies Paper*, 15, Cornell University, Ithaca, N.Y.

Taylor, Charles. 1991. *The Ethics of Authenticity*. Cambridge, Mass.: Harvard University Press.

————. 1990. "Modes of Civil Society." *Public Culture*, 3 (1): 95–118.

Taylor, Verta, and Nancy Whittier. 1995. "Analytical Approaches to Social Move-
    ment Culture: The Culture of the Women's Movement." In H. Johnston
    and B. Klandermans (eds.), *Social Movements and Culture*. Minneapolis:
    University of Minnesota Press, pp. 163–87.

Thompson, E. P. 1963. *The Making of the English Working Class*. London: V.
    Gollancz.

Tilly, Charles. 1985. "Models and Realities of Popular Collective Action." *Social
    Research*, 52 (4, Winter): 717–47.

————. 1978. *From Mobilization to Revolution*. Reading, Mass.: Addison-
    Wesley.

Tilly, C., L. Tilly, and R. Tilly. 1975. *The Rebellious Century*. Cambridge, Mass.:
    Harvard University Press.

Tokar, Brian. 1992. *The Green Alternative: Creating an Ecological Future*. San
    Pedro: R.& E. Miles.

Tonnies, Ferdinand. [1887] 1957. *Gemeinschaft und Gesellschaft*. Translated and
    edited by Charles Loomis. East Lansing: Michigan State University.

Touraine, Alain. 1988. *The Return of the Actor*. Minneapolis: University of Min-
    nesota Press.

————. 1985. "An Introduction to the Study of Social Movements." *Social
    Research*, 52 (4, Winter): 750–87.

————. 1981. *The Voice and the Eye*. New York: Cambridge University Press.

————. 1971. *The May Movement*. New York: Random House.

Turner, Ralph. 1994. "Ideology and Utopia After Socialism." In E. Larana, H.
    Johnston, and J. Gusfield (eds.), *New Social Movements: From Ideology
    to Identity*. Philadelphia: Temple University Press, pp. 79–100.

Turner, Ralph, and Louis Killian. 1972. *Collective Behavior*. Englewood Cliffs,
    N.J.: Prentice Hall.

Vautier, Marie. 1994. "Postmodern Myth, Post-European History, and the Figure
    of the Amerindian: Francois Barcelo, Goerge Bowering, and Jacques
    Poulin." *Canadian Literature*, 141: 15–37.

Walzer, Michael. 1994. *Thick and Thin: Moral Argument at Home and Abroad*.
    Notre Dame, Ind.: University of Notre Dame Press.

————. 1991. "The Idea of Civil Society," *Dissent* (Spring): 293–304.

Waters, M. C. 1990. *Ethnic Options*. Berkeley: University of California Press.

Weber, Max. 1975. *Roscher and Knies: The Logical Problem of Historical Eco-
    nomics*. Translated by Guy Oaks. New York: Free Press.

————. 1968. *Economy and Society*. Translated by Ephraim Fischoff, Edited by
    G. Roth and C. Wittich. New York: Bedminster Press.

Welch, Sharon. 1985. *Communities of Resistance and Solidarity: A Feminist
    Theology of Liberation*. New York: Orbis Books.

West, Cornel. 1993. *Keeping the Faith: Philosophy and Race in America*. New
    York: Routledge.

White, Eric Charles. 1991. "Negentropy, Noise, and Emancipatory Thought." In N. K. Hayles (ed.), *Chaos and Order*. Chicago: University of Chicago Press, pp. 263–77.

Wilson, Kenneth. 1983. "The Renormalization Group and Critical Phenomena." Review of Modern Physics, 55: 583–600.

Wimmer, Ernst. 1985. "Ideology of New Social Movements." *World Marxist Review*, 28, (July): 36–44.

Wirth, Louis. 1938. *Local Community Fact Book*: *Chicago Metropolitan Area*. Chicago: Chicago Review Press.

Young, T. R. 1992. "Chaos Theory and Human Agency: Humanist Sociology in a Postmodern Era." *Humanity and Society*, 16 (4): 441–60.

————. 1990. "Chaos and the Drama of Social Change: A Metaphysic for Postmodern Science." Red Feather Institute. Weidman, Michigan.

Zablocki, Benjamin. 1980. *Alienation and Charisma*. New York: Free Press.

Zipes, Jack. 1992–93. "The Utopian Function of Tradition." in *Telos*, 94 (Winter): 25–29.

INDEX

afterimage, 126–27, 174
alienation, 2, 45, 106
Alpha Farm, 47, 48
alternative energy devices, 48
alternative farming cooperatives, 46
alternative logics, 116
alternative money, 2, 33, 46
Amana, 27
American Cooperative Union, 42–43
American Indian spiritualism, 153
American labor movement, 38–39
American Railroad Union, 38
Amish, 27
Anabaptists, 141, 145
anomie, 2, 8, 106
anti-movements, 13
appropriate technology, 46, 149
Aristotle, 110, 138, 161
Asia Minor, 26
attractors, 111–13, 122–24
autonomy, 2, 7, 8, 13, 41, 46, 115, 130, 155, 164, 178

The Bear Tribe, 47

Benjamin, Walter, 119, 134, 142, 148, 152, 156
Bellamy, Edward, 28, 141
The Big Rock Candy Mountains, 136
Blumer, Herbert, 54, 55, 56
Bourdieu, Pierre, 18, 107
Brook Farm, 27, 36
brujo, 116–17, 140, 175
Buddhism, 153
butterfly attractor, 112–13

capitalist social relations, 3, 29, 182, 186
Carlyle, Thomas, 28, 33
chaos theory, 3, 9, 10, 14–22, 108, 109, 110–15, 117, 118, 119, 121–26, 129, 130, 186
Christianity, 155, 167
Christian monasteries, 26
Christians, 26, 39, 49
City Upon a Hill, 27
civil society, 3, 4, 5, 7, 8, 9, 22, 48, 71, 91, 95–99, 107, 108, 123, 154, 165, 179, 180, 181, 185

class, 4, 7, 9, 12, 29, 30, 31, 34, 37–38, 43, 47, 147, 160, 164, 182, 183
clinamen, 113
collective behavior, 4, 13, 14, 54, 55, 56, 57, 58, 59, 105, 106, 107
colonization, 7, 11, 40, 41, 42, 43, 155, 162, 163
Coming Nation, 42
Common Place, 50
communal living, 11, 13, 22, 26, 30, 38, 128, 178, 188
commune belt, 26
communicative action, 93, 97
Communist League, 31
Communist Manifesto, 31, 34
Communities Directory, 50
community activism, 13
Community Evolving, 48
constitutive analysis, 17
consumer cooperatives, 49
cooperative colonizers, 29
counter-hegemony, 150, 164, 165
covering-law history, 118
critical memory, 18, 120, 123, 127, 128, 134
cultural capital, 2, 11, 16, 18, 21, 45, 108, 116, 124, 147, 155, 157, 158, 161, 167

dangerous memory, 119, 157, 158
daydreams, 139, 149, 150
decolonization, 1, 47, 97, 98, 155
Deleuze, Gilles, 19, 127, 128, 174
Derrida, Jacques, 15, 17

East Wind, 48
Esperanza Community, 40
Euclidean geometry, 111, 113
eugenics, 138, 140

fairy tales, 140, 150, 166
The Farm, 13, 45, 47
Farralones Community, 47

Federation of Egalitarian Communities, 48
Feigenbaum, Mitchell, 15, 111
festivals, 136, 153, 167
folklore, 17, 18, 107, 108, 119, 123, 127, 135, 140, 148
food circles, 2, 46
fractal geometry, 113
Free Socialist Union of Chicago, 41
Freire, Paulo, 6

Ganas, 48, 49
The *German Ideology*, 30, 34, 36
Gitlin, Todd, 181–85

habitus, 107, 151, 177
Halcyon, 28
Harmony Society, 33
Hiawatha Colony, 41
hidden transcript, 150, 161, 165–67
Hinduism, 155
historical memory, 120, 128, 146, 156–58, 160, 161
Hobsbawm, Eric, 151, 152
Holloway, Mark, 28
Hutterian Brethren, 27

inventing tradition, 151
Islam, 155

Judaism, 155

Kanter, Rosabeth Moss, 11
Kaweah, 42
King Henry VIII, 140
Kinkade, Kat, 49
Knights of Labor, 40, 41, 43
Krotona, 28
Kuron, Jacek, 81, 83

labor credits, 33
labor exchanges, 31, 32
Laclau, Ernesto, 73–80, 106

Locofocos, 39
Lucretius, 113, 114

Mannheim, Karl, 145, 146, 147, 148
Mardi Gras, 136
Marginalization, 6, 157
Marin, Louis, 151
Marxism, 17, 30, 31, 33, 34, 35, 36,
    37, 42, 62, 88, 89, 90, 115, 119,
    148, 174, 175, 182, 183
Massachusetts Bay Colony, 27
master narrative, 6, 8
Melucci, Alberto, 9, 10, 12, 13, 64,
    65, 66, 69, 70
Monasteries, 26, 141
Mondragon, 48
Moral maximalism, 186, 187
Morovian colony, 27
Movement for a New Society in
    Philadelphia, 13, 45
multiplicity, 19, 123–25, 127–29, 130
mythistory, 17, 134, 148, 150

near-equilibrium conditions, 2
New Age spiritualism, 155
new citizen, 67
new historicism, 120
New Testament, 139
Newtonian physics, 18, 19, 20, 110,
    111
nomination, 155, 156, 167
nostalgic utopia, 119, 124, 125, 128,
    148, 152, 153
nuclear proliferation, 7

Offe, Claus, 64, 69, 70
outcome basins, 123
overproduction and underconsump-
    tion, 32
Owen, Robert, 31, 32, 33

Parallelograms, 33
paralogism, 16

paraprimitive community, 149
Parsons, Talcott, 54, 55, 56, 91, 92
participatory government, 48
Peirce, C. S., 20
phalanx, 35
phase space, 17, 111
Pirsig, Robert, 115, 116, 117
planetary consciousness, 13, 49, 123
plateaus, 19, 126–28
PLENTY, 47
Plymouth Pilgrims, 27
Poincaré sections, 122
Point Loma, 28
principle of attraction, 35
promised land, 159

quantum mechanics, 16

radical democracy, 22, 72, 73, 76, 77
Rainbow Construction Company, 48
Rappist community, 33
reactivation, 158, 159
regressive utopia, 12, 17, 134, 143
Renaissance, 140, 141, 161
rhizome, 127, 128, 130
Roman Saturnalia, 136
Rosenberg, Justin, 19
Ryan, Michael, 16, 17, 18

Saint-Simon, 34–36, 42–44, 173, 175
Sassoon, Joseph, 154–55, 188–90
scientific management, 143
Scott, James, 163, 164, 165, 166, 167
service-credit systems, 33
Shakers, 27
Sirius, 47, 48
Smelser, Neil, 56, 57, 58
Socialists, 27–43
species being, 109
spirituality, 5, 45, 123, 155
state-directed conflict, 12, 107
state regulation, 9
steering mechanisms, 7

Stelle Community, 47
strange attractors, 111–13, 122–24
Students for a Democratic Society,
    183
symbolic violence, 18
syndicalist movement, 142

Taylor, Charles, 176–79
Taylorism, 143, 175
Tilly, Charles, 59, 60, 61
Tonnies, 10, 27
torus attractors, 123
Touraine, Alain, 12, 13, 14, 59
transpraxis, 2, 5, 21

twelve passions, 35

Walzer, Michael, 185, 186, 187
Welch, Sharon, 157, 158
welfare agencies, 7
Wicca, 153
wish imagery, 137

Year of Indigenous Peoples, 120
Young, T. R., 19, 20

Zablocki, Benjamin, 10, 11, 26, 57
Zoar, 27

About the Author

ROBERT C. SCHEHR is Assistant Professor of Sociology at the University of Illinois at Springfield.